Research Ethics
and Integrity for
Social Scientists

Research Ethics and Integrity for Social Scientists

Beyond Regulatory Compliance

Mark Israel

2nd Edition

Los Angeles | London | New Delhi
Singapore | Washington DC

Los Angeles | London | New Delhi
Singapore | Washington DC

SAGE Publications Ltd
1 Oliver's Yard
55 City Road
London EC1Y 1SP

SAGE Publications Inc.
2455 Teller Road
Thousand Oaks, California 91320

SAGE Publications India Pvt Ltd
B 1/I 1 Mohan Cooperative Industrial Area
Mathura Road
New Delhi 110 044

SAGE Publications Asia-Pacific Pte Ltd
3 Church Street
#10-04 Samsung Hub
Singapore 049483

Editor: Katie Metzler
Production editor: Sushant Nailwal
Copyeditor: Andy Baxter
Proofreader: Dick Davis
Indexer: Caroline Eley
Marketing manager: Sally Ransom
Cover design: Shaun Mercier
Typeset by C&M Digitals (P) Ltd, Chennai, India
Printed and bound by CPI Group (UK) Ltd,
Croydon, CR0 4YY [for Antony Rowe]

This second edition first published 2015

First published 2006, reprinted in 2008, twice in 2009,
2010, 2011, 2012 and 2013

Library of Congress Control Number: 2014938160

British Library Cataloguing in Publication data

A catalogue record for this book is available from
the British Library

ISBN 978-1-4462-0748-2
ISBN 978-1-4462-0749-9 (pbk)

Contents

List of Tables

About the Author

Mark Israel is Winthrop Professor of Law and Criminology in the Faculty of Law at the University of Western Australia. He has a degree in law and postgraduate qualifications in sociology, criminology and education. He has published on research ethics and integrity, higher education and research policy, political exile and migration, criminology and socio-legal studies. His books include *South African Political Exiles in the United Kingdom* (Palgrave Macmillan, 1999), *Crime and Justice* (Thomson Reuters, 2006, eds with Goldsmith and Daly), and *Research Ethics for Social Scientists: Between Ethical Conduct and Regulatory Compliance* (Sage, 2006, with Hay).

He has won teaching and research prizes in Australia, the United Kingdom and the United States, including the Prime Minister's Award for Australian University Teacher of the Year in 2004. Mark has undertaken consultancy for, among others, the National Health and Medical Research Council, the Commonwealth Scientific and Industrial Research Organisation, Federal and State governments in Australia, as well as the European Research Council, and a range of higher education institutions and professional associations in Australia, Hong Kong, New Zealand and the United Kingdom.

Acknowledgements

Like most books, this would not have been completed had it not been for the kind assistance of family, friends and colleagues. For allowing me time, I am grateful to Deborah Hersh and the boys, and to my colleagues in the Faculty of Law at the University of Western Australia. For their valuable comments, I would like to thank Antje Deckert, Iara Guerriero, Linda Hantrais, David Hunter, Cathy Pitkin, Barry Poata Smith, Martin Tolich, Will van den Hoonaard and Lisa Wynn.

Since 2007, I have worked, as part of the Australasian Human Research Ethics Consultancy Services (AHRECS) with Gary Allen and Colin Thomson on a fascinating variety of projects on ethical conduct, research integrity and regulatory compliance. Gary and Colin have challenged and sharpened my understanding of ethical guidelines and regulations and have gently but persistently encouraged me to think more creatively and constructively.

Research Ethics for Social Scientists was the result in 2006 of a long-standing collaboration with Iain Hay at Flinders University. When Iain decided not to revisit this book, he agreed that I could continue alone. While I take responsibility for all changes to the first edition, this volume owes much to that book and, obviously, to Iain. The first book contained a range of elements no longer appreciated in research monographs by assessors of research excellence. In Australia, their evaluations are likely to shape university funding. I was particularly sad to cut the Appendix which I thought encouraged multiple perspectives to enter learning and teaching in research ethics. I have replicated that material at www.ahrecs.com and will add further case studies there as they flow from other projects.

Finally, I would like to express my appreciation to Katie Metzler of Sage Publications, for her encouragement, and willingness to share my sense of humour. Paddling across a lake may encourage serenity and reflection. All too often, it also yields a cliché. One I could not resist.

Mark Israel
Perth, Australia

Abbreviations

AAA	American Anthropological Association
AAAS	American Association for the Advancement of Science
AARE	Australian Association for Research in Education
AAU	Association of American Universities
AAUP	American Association of University Professors
AEA	American Economic Association
AERA	American Educational Research Association
AHEC	Australian Health Ethics Committee
AIATSIS	Australian Institute of Aboriginal and Torres Strait Islander Studies
ALLEA	ALL European Academies
APA	American Psychological Association
ARC	Australian Research Council
ASA	American Sociological Association
AV-CC	Australian Vice-Chancellors' Committee
BERA	British Educational Research Association
BPS	British Psychological Society
BSA	British Sociological Association
CAIRE	Committee on Assessing Integrity in Research Environments (United States)
CCA	Corrections Corporation of America
CEHAT	Centre for Enquiry into Health and Allied Themes (India)
CIOMS	Council for International Organizations of Medical Science
CITI	Collaborative Institute Training Initiative (United States)
CONEP	National Commission for Ethics in Research (Brazil)
COPE	Committee on Publication Ethics
CPC	Correctional Privatization Commission (United States)
CSAA	Canadian Sociology and Anthropology Association
CTCWG	Canadian Tri-Council Working Group
DHEW	Department of Health, Education and Welfare (United States)
DHHS	Department of Health and Human Services (United States)
ESRC	Economic and Social Research Council (United Kingdom)
EUREC	European Network of Research Ethics Committees
FERCIT	Forum for Ethical Review Committees in Thailand

FRE	Framework for Research Ethics (United Kingdom)
FUNAI	National Indian Foundation (Brazil)
GERAIS	Guidelines for Ethical Research in Australian Indigenous Studies
HREC	Human Research Ethics Committee (Australia)
HSFR	Swedish Council for Research in the Humanities and the Social Sciences
HSRCSA	Human Sciences Research Council of South Africa
ICMJE	International Committee of Medical Journal Editors
ICMR	Indian Council of Medical Research
IRB	Institutional Review Board (United States)
IRENSA	International Research Ethics Network for Southern Africa
MHC	Māori Health Committee (New Zealand)
MRCSA	Medical Research Council of South Africa
NCESSRH	National Committee for Ethics in Social Science Research in Health (India)
NCPHSBBR	National Commission for the Protection of Human Subjects of Biomedical and Behavioral Research (United States)
NESH	National Committee for Research Ethics in the Social Sciences and Humanities (Norway)
NHMRC	National Health and Medical Research Council (Australia)
NHRPAC	National Human Research Protections Advisory Committee (United States)
NIH	National Institutes of Health (United States)
NSERC	Natural Sciences and Engineering Research Council (Canada)
OHRP	Office for Human Research Protections (United States)
OHSR	Office of Human Subjects Research, NIH (United States)
OPRR	Office for Protection from Research Risks (United States)
ORIUS	Office of Research Integrity (United States)
OSTP	Office of Science and Technology Policy (United States)
PRE	Panel on Research Ethics (Canada)
RCUK	Research Councils United Kingdom
REB	Research Ethics Board (Canada)
REC	Research Ethics Committee (Denmark)
REF	Research Ethics Framework (United Kingdom)
SARETI	South African Research Training Initiative
SRA	Social Research Association (United Kingdom)
SRC	Swedish Research Council
SSHRC	Social Sciences and Humanities Research Council (Canada)
SSHWC	Social Sciences and Humanities Research Ethics Special Working Committee (Canada)
TCPS	Tri-Council Policy Statement (Canada)
TENK	The Finnish National Advisory Board on Research Integrity
TRREE	Training and Resources in Research Ethics Evaluation

UNESCO	United Nations Educational, Scientific and Cultural Organization
USPHS	United States Public Health Service
WAME	World Association of Medical Editors
WHO	World Health Organization
WMA	World Medical Association

ONE

Why Care About Ethics?

Social scientists are angry and frustrated. Still. They believe their work is being constrained and distorted by regulators of ethical practice who neither understand social science research nor the social, political, economic and cultural contexts within which researchers work. In many countries, including Australia, Brazil, Canada, India, New Zealand, the United Kingdom and the United States, researchers have argued regulators are imposing, and acting on the basis of, biomedically driven arrangements that make little or no sense to social scientists. How did we reach this point? How is it that social scientists find themselves caught between their clear commitment to ethical conduct and unsympathetic regulatory regimes with which they are expected to comply? Why is there such antagonism between researchers who believe they are behaving ethically and regulators who appear to suggest they are not? How can this happen when regulators are often also researchers? Finally, how do we move beyond merely assuaging the concerns of regulators and focus on thinking creatively and intelligently about ethical conduct?

In this book, I set out to do four things. The first is to demonstrate the practical value of serious and systematic consideration of ethical conduct in social science research. Second, I identify how and why current national and international regulatory regimes have emerged. Third, I seek to reveal those practices that have contributed to adversarial relationships between researchers and regulators. Finally, I hope to encourage all parties to develop shared solutions to ethical and regulatory problems.

It is disturbing and not a little ironic that regulators and social scientists find themselves in this situation of division, mistrust and antagonism. After all, we each start from the same point: that is, that ethics matter. Indeed, we share a view that ethics is about what is right, good and virtuous. None of us sets out to hurt people. None of us seeks to draw research into disrepute. In this chapter, I outline why social scientists do, and should, take ethics seriously. I return later to describe the structure of this book.

1

Protecting others, minimizing harm and increasing the sum of good

Ethical behaviour helps protect individuals, communities and environments, and offers the potential to increase the sum of good in the world. As social scientists trying to make the world a better place we should avoid (or at least minimize) doing long-term, systematic harm to those individuals, communities and environments. Sadly this has not always occurred. But, this is not a book of lists of research misconduct. This is also not a book that equates brutality, exploitation and indifference in the name of medical research with those physical, economic, social, financial and psychological harms that have flowed from social science research projects. However, there are examples in this book where social scientists have condemned the actions of their peers when: social scientists were coopted into American intelligence and military operations in Iraq and Afghanistan; political scientists involved in embedded experimentation may have enabled the use of repressive measures by state agencies; Harvard sociologists studying Facebook failed to protect the anonymity of their students; Australian experimental psychologists replicating Stanley Milgram's studies caused long-term distress to their participants; American historians and Dutch social psychologists engaged in fabrication and falsification; Chinese anthropologists at Beijing University were censured for plagiarism; and economists became mired in conflicts of interest following the Global Financial Crisis. Clearly, some research *is* antithetical to the emancipatory aspirations of social science, and undermines the legitimacy of our disciplines and our ability to work with the wider community.

Assuring trust

Social scientists do not have an inalienable right to conduct research involving other people. That we continue to have the freedom to conduct such work is, in large part, the product of individual and social goodwill and depends on us acting in ways that are not harmful and are just. Ethical behaviour may help assure the climate of trust in which we continue our socially useful labours. If we act honestly and honourably, people may rely on us to recognize their needs and sensitivities and consequently may be more willing to contribute openly and fully to the work we undertake. When we behave ethically as social scientists, we maintain the trust of the various 'publics' with and for whom we work. In some cases where prior trust might have been violated we may have to work very hard if people are once again to have faith in us.

Incautious practice and cultural insensitivity can lead to community withdrawal of support for social science research. The effects of ethically questionable research on an institution's or individual's capacity to work with affected communities can be profound and of long duration. Not only might communities withdraw their support, but so too might the organizations that back and oversee research. The Office for Human Research Protections has suspended research in a number of major United States institutions as a result of malpractice outside the social sciences. Suspension means the end of: federal government research funding; data analysis; travel to conferences; years of work; and, for some, the shredding of professional reputations.

So, it is important to avoid causing suspicion and fear, and thereby maintain the trust of sponsors and broader communities, for it is from a position of trust that we are able to continue the work that we – and hopefully others – value.

Ensuring research integrity

By caring about ethics and by acting on that concern we promote the integrity of research. Since much of what we do occurs without anyone else watching, there is ample scope to conduct ourselves in improper ways. For instance, researchers can fabricate quotations or data or gain information under false pretences. No one might ever know. In some forms of work, such as those involving covert methods where the anonymity of subjects and locations is protected, it is difficult – if not impossible – for other social scientists to validate the research. If we can assure ourselves and our colleagues that we are behaving ethically, we can be more confident that the results of work we read and hear about are accurate and original.

Our individual research endeavours form part of interconnected local, national and international networks of activity. We build incrementally on each other's advances. If any of these contributions are inaccurate, unethically acquired or otherwise questionable, we all bear the costs. Poor practices affect not only our individual and professional reputations but also the veracity and reliability of our individual and collective works.

However, the pressures on academic integrity are growing. The greater dependence of universities and their researchers on sponsorship and the linking of government grants and salary increments to research performance have heightened the prospects of unethical behaviour by researchers. Relationships of integrity and trust between colleagues draw, in part, from modelled good behaviour. Conversely, unethical researchers appear to model unethical behaviour for their colleagues. It is vital therefore that students, colleagues and other community members see us setting good examples by behaving ethically.

Satisfying organizational and professional demands

In the face of a mountain of popularly reported evidence of corruption, scientific misconduct and impropriety from around the world, there are now emerging public and institutional demands for individual accountability that form the basis of another reason to care about ethics. Schools, universities, funding agencies, employers and professional societies all seek to protect themselves from the unethical actions of an employee, member or representative. The prospect and reality of legal action is driving many universities to monitor research practices more closely as part of broader risk management strategies. As costs of failing to comply with institutional requirements rise, individual researchers may be inclined to reflect on their own practices, if only as a matter of self-preservation.

Coupled with institutional and individual self-preservation as reasons for social scientists to behave ethically is the role of ethics in professionalization. Historically, professionalization has played a role in sealing 'a bargain between members of the profession and the society in which its members work' (Marcuse, 1985, p. 20). As part of claims to professional status for their members, professional bodies adopt processes and procedures for self-regulation of members' moral conduct. In return, members of those organizations lay claim to professional status and receive special associated rights that might include the ability to conduct research with particular individuals and communities.

Research ethics governance sits within broader structures and power relations and is shaped by and may even shape a combination of macro and micro forces that include government policies, economic indicators, social trends, institutional politics and resources. Some stakeholders seek to extend the remit of ethics review by both intensifying its gaze and expanding the areas for which it claims oversight in an effort to support ethical research or, at least, to stop malpractice. Others oppose what they term 'ethics creep' (Haggerty, 2004) and 'ethical imperialism' (Schrag, 2010a). Adrian Guta and his colleagues argued that, in Canada at least, the result is a 'simultaneous growing and retreating of ethics review as it expands into new terrain while losing control of its traditional domain' (2013, p. 307).

Coping with new and more challenging problems

Social scientists commonly confront ethical problems. Not only are ethics an everyday matter of research practice but they may be becoming more complex. This reflects new methodological and technological patterns of working in social sciences as well as broader social, political and economic shifts in our societies. Codes, regulations and even training materials may offer little help if, subject to a cultural lag, they struggle to grapple with new conditions. Individually and collectively, researchers have little choice but to identify and work through the ethical issues, reflecting upon and justifying their decisions as best they can. Some issues are very familiar. Some have been addressed in some contexts, but are more difficult when encountered in new environments. Some issues are completely new to social scientists.

For instance, following renewed interest in videoethnography as a research tool (Heath et al., 2010), scholars need to: identify the potential uses to which the images may be put; minimize the possibility of causing distress to families of participating patients in health institutions; ensure the anonymity of participants; obtain consent from incidental people who enter the frame; negotiate access to those parts of the institution controlled by professional groups that are not participants in the study, maintain data security and control secondary use of data. Educational researchers are familiar with having to protect students from the effects of non-participation in research but not necessarily with the social and educational consequences of locating students who do not wish to be filmed in a 'blind spot' in a classroom.

Take another example. Mayer-Schönberger and Cukier (2013) claimed the emergence of predictive analytics and mining of petabyte-sized datasets containing billions of pieces of information, so called 'big data', will undercut the concept of informed consent in research. Political scientists studying everyday political communication in Scandinavia were able to gather over 100,000 'tweets' using just one election-related hashtag on Twitter covering a one-month period in the lead up to the Swedish national election in 2010 (Moe and Larsson, 2012). It was impractical to obtain consent from all the communicators and, even if it were possible, this might have introduced a bias into the sample. So, the researchers had to argue with a research ethics committee in Sweden and the privacy commissioner in Norway that publishing on Twitter constituted a public rather than a private act.

New disciplines are engaging in human research as they move beyond traditional boundaries. Empirical research is growing in computer sciences, particular in those parts of the discipline that investigate human-computer interaction (HCI), and the line between human and non-human data is blurred in data aggregation, transaction log analyses, and data mining and linking processes (Buchanan et al., 2011). In some cases, testing of HCI can even place human operators at physical risk. For example, testing mountain search-and-rescue drones may put human rescue teams in danger of triggering an avalanche. In the field of information and communication technologies for development (ICTD), researchers explore ways technologies might be used to promote social aims. Some research may be interventionist, with new technology being trialled in locations targeted for development aid. Discussions of research ethics are rare in ICTD, but Dearden (2013) pointed to the need to assess the socioeconomic, cultural and political factors in a disadvantaged community that might influence: how harms and benefits might be distributed; the line between coercive inducement and fair compensation; the connections between research, aid and development; and, who might be considered legitimate representatives of the collective group.

Many non-social scientists now need to understand the ethics of gathering and using social science data as a result of their interactions with stakeholder communities. However, social scientists working within multidisciplinary teams also need to be able to tackle the novel ethical issues that arise as a direct result of their collaborative approaches. At the Commonwealth Scientific and Industrial Research Organisation (CSIRO), Australia's national science agency, anthropologists, sociologists, psychologists and economists work with scientists in multidisciplinary teams to explore connections between natural, agricultural, industrial and urban ecosystems and social and economic processes inside and outside Australia. These teams also analyse community and agency perspectives on climate change and energy technologies, and study human-technology interactions in order to create new tools and platforms for information and communication technologies. Researchers need to reach ethically-defensible practice in situations rarely encountered in the research ethics literature. For example, teams of biophysical and social scientists working to improve farming yields in the Sahel or south-east Asia, energy efficiency in households, or seeking to understand the environmental impact of indigenous water use, fire management or fishing need to consider the patterned impact their findings may have on social justice in host communities.

Change bears not only on the character of ethical issues social scientists face, but also on the broader context within which researchers and their research are received in communities. In many settings, and on the basis of the heightened profile of various scientific, biomedical, social, political and environmental controversies, potential participants may be attuned to ethical issues. They know when they are not being consulted and are well aware of some of the harms caused by thoughtless researchers. Participants are less likely now to accept that researchers know best. Where a project is based on participant action research, professional researchers may therefore need to rethink their role in shaping responses to ethical questions.

At the same time as we are confronted by such new challenges, traditional religious and other sources of moral justification are, for many people, decreasing in authority. The blame for drifting moral anchors has been associated with all manner of social change and a variety of events, from liberalism to sexual scandals, and to increasing social fragmentation with corresponding declines in civic life and engagement. More broadly, but perhaps as part of the same cultural processes, the decline in moral authority has been linked to postmodernism. Some critics such as Zygmunt Bauman (1993) and Jean-François Lyotard

(1979) have gone so far as to suggest that, through its 'incredulity towards metanarratives', postmodernity has dashed notions of universal, solidly grounded ethical regulation.

Facing the collapse of metanarratives, Slavoj Žižek (2000) claimed we look to create a panoply of smaller entities (like research ethics committees) that might assert authority over a particular portion of our lives. These, he argued, were bound to fail because they reproduce and embed the cynicism associated with our times. More simply put, perhaps postmodernism – as one of the most profound influences on social scientific thought of the past three decades – has, together with Feminist, Critical and Indigenous perspectives, encouraged debate about authoritative definitions and singular narratives of events. As a result, it raises questions about the legitimacy of any individual or institution's claims to moral authority.

From concern to conduct

Social scientists are concerned about ethics. We behave in ways that are right and virtuous: for the sake of those who put trust in us and our work; for those who employ us, fund our research, and otherwise support our professional activities; and as a result of our own desires to do good. Less charitably, we may also be motivated to behave ethically by desires to avoid public censure.

Unfortunately, some find it is more difficult to act ethically than it should be. Why? In part, many of us do not possess the philosophical training that allows us to negotiate effectively with biomedical scientists and ethicists about appropriate means of regulating social science research. So, in the next chapter, I offer a short and accessible overview of ethical theory as a non-ethicist writing for non-ethicists.

I argue that researchers need to develop better understandings of the politics and contexts within which ethics are regulated. Chapter 3 focuses on the development of the major codes and principles that have underpinned institutional approaches to ethical regulation since 1945. Though all are statements on biomedical research, each has influenced the regulatory trajectories for social science. This impact has been felt across the world. I examine a broad range of jurisdictions in Chapter 4.

Researchers also need to be reflexive, holding up their activities to ethical scrutiny. Chapters 5 to 9 investigate how social scientists have developed and evaluated their practices around the concepts of informed consent, confidentiality, beneficence, non-maleficence, justice, research integrity and the problems relating to research relationships. These chapters reveal tensions within the research community as well as between researchers' beliefs about what is right and research ethics committees' ideas about what is correct.

This book does all that *Research Ethics for Social Scientists* did, and more. Each chapter has been extensively revised and the majority of the book is indeed new. It responds to limitations of the first volume – reviewers were overwhelmingly positive but there were several areas that deserved greater attention. It also looks forward to the future of the social sciences and considers how ethical conduct and research ethics governance might grapple with new research environments, technologies, interactions and methodologies. As a result, this book updates its coverage of regulation and guidelines, including an examination of the UNESCO Declaration (2005), Australia's National Statement (2007), Canada's revised Tri-Council Policy Statement (2010), the Singapore Statement on Research Integrity (2010), the United Kingdom's Framework for Research Ethics (2012), Brazil's Resolution 466/12 (2012), the New Brunswick Declaration (2013) and the Declaration of Helsinki (2013). It assesses those approaches such as virtue ethics, situated ethics, feminist, postmodernist and postcolonial approaches that challenge the orthodoxy that underlies most ethical codes and guidelines. It extends international coverage well beyond North America, Australasia, the United Kingdom, South Africa and the Nordic countries to include far more on Asia, Latin America and Africa. It explores new frontiers for social science research ethics: international, comparative and transnational research; new technologies and digital tools, including internet-mediated research; interdisciplinary research beyond the social sciences; research with Indigenous peoples; evaluation and commercial research. Finally, as the change in the title of this book implies, I explore the connections between research ethics and research integrity.

This book is even more ambitious than its predecessor, but it remains practical and realistic. It is ambitious because it deals with a broad array of topics: ethical theory, ethical regulation in different jurisdictions, and ways of resolving ethical dilemmas. It spans a far greater range of subject material than other recent works on social science research ethics. It is practical in that it is a book written in accessible language and informed by my experience communicating some of the ideas in this book to diverse audiences. Finally, the book is realistic. It is based on an appreciation of the practical dimensions to ethical conduct in social science research. In the final chapter I argue that, as social scientists engaging with non-social scientists, we need to increase both the perceived and actual legitimacy of our research investigations. As a result, we have to present and defend cogently the ethical nature of our activities both individually at the local level and collectively at local, national and international levels.

TWO

Ethical Approaches

Ethics, in the words of Tom Beauchamp and James Childress (1994, p. 4), is 'a generic term for various ways of understanding and examining the moral life'. It is concerned with perspectives on right and proper conduct. Not surprisingly, the disciplines that analyse ethics have their own discursive practices, many of which are opaque to outsiders. This makes it difficult for non-ethicists to find a language to discuss issues of ethics across disciplinary boundaries. This chapter is aimed at opening up the language of normative ethics to develop a common lexicon for social scientists.

Normative ethics offers the moral norms which guide or indicate what one should or should not do in particular situations. It provides frameworks – sometimes contradictory – that allow us to judge people's actions and decisions as 'right' or 'wrong', 'good' or 'bad'. The primary question in normative ethics is 'how may or should we decide or determine what is morally right for a certain agent ... to do, or what he [sic] morally ought to do, in a certain situation' (Frankena, 1973, p. 12). That is, on what grounds can we decide whether an act is right? This is a difficult question because the criteria employed for considering whether an act is 'right' or 'wrong' are variable, and, in some instances, quite contradictory.

Most studies of research ethics concentrate on a limited number of approaches. Consequentialism and non-consequentialism (deontological approaches) are both act-oriented approaches. These have been the dominant ways of assessing ethical behaviour in the West since the end of the nineteenth century. More often than not, books on research ethics work through these ethical theories but struggle to apply these approaches directly to the substantive issues that confront researchers. Ethical principles and codes, and the overall approach of principlism, represent attempts to provide an intermediate step between theory and practice, grounded in, justified by, but also guiding application of theory (Kitchener and Kitchener, 2009). However, the dominance of both consequentialism and non-consequentialism has been threatened by both longer-standing and newer ways of thinking. As I discuss later in the chapter, these approaches shift attention from abstract principles and universalist claims to either the ethical agent as decision-maker (virtue ethics), or the particular context or the relationship within which decisions are made (situational ethics, feminist, postmodernist and postcolonial approaches).

Consequentialist approaches to ethics

Consequentialist theories (sometimes also known as teleological approaches) draw from the works of Jeremy Bentham (1781/2000) and John Stuart Mill (1863). In its most common form, consequentialists maintain an action can be considered to be morally right or obligatory if it will produce the greatest possible balance of good over evil (Reynolds, 1979). That is, the moral status of an action is determined by evaluating the balance of its good and bad consequences. If the benefits that flow from a decision or action outweigh the risks of either not acting or of doing something else, then the action may be morally desirable or defensible. Consequentialist approaches to ethical decision-making mean, of course, that we must know what is good or bad. For instance, are pleasure, knowledge, power, self-realization and growth necessarily good? Are pain and ignorance necessarily bad?

In this approach, the consequences of an action determine its merit, not the intent or motivation that lie behind it. From a consequentialist position, an ill-intentioned act with beneficial outcomes may be understood to be more appropriate than a well-intentioned act with undesirable consequences. Breaking a promise or violating some other trust might be seen by some people as immoral, but that same action could be justified from the consequentialist approach on the grounds that it produced a greater benefit than the costs imposed or because it reduced the overall level of 'evil'. So, for example, one might argue that it would be appropriate to violate and make public the secret and sacred 'women's knowledge' of an Indigenous community to prevent the construction of a road through the sacred places associated with that knowledge. Or a social scientist might choose to avoid making public the results of research revealing that residents of undesirable parts of a city lie to prospective employers about their addresses to heighten their chances of securing employment.

Utilitarianism is the best-known form of consequentialism. It takes up Mill's (1863) principle of utility, summarized by Kimmel: 'an individual ought to do that act that promotes the greatest good, happiness, or satisfaction to most people' (1988, p. 45). Utilitarianism asks 'How does the action impinge on everyone affected by it?'. From a utilitarian perspective, no one person – including the decision-maker – is more important than other people in this determination. Utilitarian perspectives may be subdivided into *act-utilitarian* and *rule-utilitarian* approaches. In the former the act that is ethically correct is the one that, for the largest number of people yields the greatest level of happiness or the highest average for happiness (average utilitarianism). Alternatively, it might be the one that leaves the most people at a satisfactory level (satisficing utilitarian) or at the lowest level of suffering (negative utilitarianism). The rule-utilitarian perspective sees ethical determinations made on the basis of a higher level of abstraction, those consequences that would flow from a particular rule instituted (and generally applied) by the act, not from the act itself.

Critics of consequentialism have noted the difficulties – if not the impossibility – of evaluating the consequences of every act, for every person, for all time (Sinnott-Armstrong, 2003). They have also suggested the approach encounters difficulties in situations where, for instance, it might allow slavery or torture if the benefits to the majority outweigh the harms to those enslaved or tortured. Specific versions of consequentialism have addressed this problem with some success, including those developed by Bentham himself (see, for example, Kelly, 1989).

Non-consequentialist approaches to ethics

Non-consequentialist, or deontological, theories take considerations other than good and bad effects into account when deciding on an ethical course of action. They:

> deny what teleological theories affirm. They deny that the right, the obligatory, and the morally good are wholly ... a function of what is nonmorally good or of what promotes the greatest balance of good over evil for self. (Frankena, 1973, p. 14)

More colourful perhaps than Frankena's quote is a Latin proverb used as a deontological slogan: 'Let justice be done though the heavens fall'. In other words, non-consequentialist approaches reject the notion that what is 'right' can be determined by merely assessing consequences. Indeed, something may be regarded as morally right or ethically obligatory even if it does not promote the greatest balance of good over evil. Since, in this approach, the balance of good over evil for an individual or community provides insufficient grounds for determining whether behaviour is moral or ethical, then considerations other than harmful consequences need to be taken into account. Certain acts are good in themselves. They are morally right or obligatory because, for example, they keep a promise, show gratitude or demonstrate loyalty to an unconditional command. Returning to the example of the researcher given access to sacred Indigenous 'women's knowledge', a deontological view might require the researcher to maintain the confidence, even if non-disclosure meant construction of the road would destroy sacred places.

Like their consequentialist counterparts, deontological approaches to ethics can have an act- or rule-focus. *Act-deontological* (or *particularist*) approaches acknowledge that general rules may not be applicable in every situation and suggest principles or rules applied by individuals should recognize those unique circumstances. This approach has been summed up in the phrase 'do the right thing'. *Rule-deontological* approaches take a less contextually sensitive approach and give firm priority to rules.

Deontological theories are most closely associated with the work of Immanuel Kant (1785/2005). Kant's position was that obligations do not flow from consequences but instead from a core expectation that we should treat ourselves and others in ways consistent with human dignity and worth. An aim of Kantian thought is to make this somewhat vague exhortation more precise. How might we know, for example, what is the 'right thing' to do? The key to that refinement lies in the categorical imperative which has been translated from the original German as: 'I shall never act except in such a way that I can also will that the maxim of my action become a universal law'. That is, one should act only in ways that one would wish or recommend all other people to act. It is important to note this is not the same as the so-called Golden Rule – 'do unto others as you would have them do unto you' – for two reasons. First, the Golden Rule provides moral guidance on the basis of a previous moral judgement about how you believe others would treat you. Second, the Golden Rule does not allow a person to generate judgements about how to treat themselves. So, for example, the categorical imperative would suggest to an individual that he or she has a moral duty not to commit suicide. This same conclusion could not be reached through the Golden Rule.

In summary, consequentialist approaches see the judgement of acts as ethical or not on the basis of the consequences of those acts. Deontological approaches suggest that our evaluation of moral behaviour requires consideration of matters other than the ends produced by people's actions and behaviours. Deontological approaches emphasize duties, or doing what is right – irrespective of consequences. Consequentialism exhorts us to promote the good; the latter to exemplify it. Pettit (1993, p. 231) makes the point: for consequentialists,

> agents are required to produce whatever actions have the property of promoting a designated value, even actions that fail intuitively to honour it. Opponents of consequentialism see the relation between values and agents as a non-instrumental one: agents are required or at least allowed to let their actions exemplify a designated value, even if this makes for a lesser realization of the value overall.

Jim Thomas (1996) invited us to consider the fictional case of two researchers who had promised participants complete confidentiality in exchange for information. Having discovered from prison staff how particular prisoners were mistreated, the researchers are subpoenaed to testify against their research participants. Thomas located the research project in prison, but the example works in other situations where revealing information might place informants at risk, and Chapter 6 considers several such examples. Thomas uses the case to demonstrate how alternate decisions might be justified by drawing on various consequentialist and non-consequentialist approaches:

> One researcher broke his vow of confidentiality and testified, with unpleasant consequences for subjects. The other did not. Both appealed to the 'rules' of an ethical theory to justify their actions. The researcher who testified adhered to an act-deontological position in which the particular circumstances, abuse of authority and corresponding subversion of justice by those sworn to uphold it, compelled him in this situation to break his promise in order to fulfil a higher principle. The researcher who remained silent adhered to a rule-deontological position: He made a promise that he was duty-bound to keep, regardless of the consequences ...
>
> Consider again the researcher who broke his vow of confidentiality to testify against his informants. If, instead of appealing to a transcendent rule, he had argued that his testimony was necessary to end abuse of prisoners by staff and thereby promote justice as a social good, he could make his case from an act-utilitarian position. By contrast, a rule-utilitarian approach is not uncommon amongst journalists who argue that invasions of personal privacy are outweighed by the public's 'right to know', or amongst researchers who intentionally lie to gain access to 'deviant' research settings on the grounds that it is the only way to obtain information on an intellectually important topic. (1996, pp. 109–110)

While distinctions between deontological and consequentialist approaches form major separations in Western normative ethics, there are other ways of approaching moral deliberations.

Principlist approaches

Scottish philosopher W.D. Ross (1930) argued our ethical conduct should be based on widely accepted principles. These would include concepts such as fidelity, non-maleficence, justice, beneficence and self-improvement. Sometimes these principles might conflict with each other, however, in which case we ought to use our moral judgement and intuition to decide what we should do. Ross' approach avoids some of the controversial assumptions associated with consequentialism and non-consequentialism, offers a relatively simple way of doing ethics and has broad appeal because all the principles it adopted are commonly held. Based on Ross' argument, principlism was further developed in the 1970s by American bioethicists Beauchamp and Childress specifically for research ethics, and extended by Raanan Gillon (1994) in the United Kingdom. The approach is based on *prima facie* principles of respect for autonomy, beneficence, non-maleficence and justice. The term *prima facie* was introduced by Ross and implies a principle is binding unless it conflicts with another, in which case it is necessary to choose between principles (Gillon, 1994; Dancy, 1993). Principlism offers calculability and simplicity in ethical decision-making irrespective of 'deeper epistemological or theoretical commitments' (Evans, 2000, p. 33). Indeed, Evans observes that the foremost advocates of principlism, Beauchamp and Childress, were a professed rule-utilitarian and rule-deontologist respectively.

In a piece that looked at the historical emergence of principlism, Evans (2000) linked its development to needs for practical and 'objectively transparent' (p. 35) ways of dealing with ethical decisions when the state began to intervene in ethics. Principlism attracted particular interest in medicine after the United States Congress decided in 1974 to identify ethical principles and guidelines for biomedical research (see Chapter 3). According to Callahan, philosophers working on bioethics during the 1970s tried to apply arguments from utilitarianism and deontology to that field, but found them to be too broad and cumbersome for clinical decision-making and policy formulation:

> Principlism, as a middle level approach, seemed much more helpful and more attuned to different levels of ethical problems. It seemed to have a special appeal to physicians not too interested in ethical theory, but in need of a way of thinking through ethical dilemmas. (2003, p. 287)

Despite the claims of its advocates that principlism provides a straightforward framework for problem-solving that is 'neutral between competing religious, cultural, and philosophical theories, [and that] can be shared by everyone regardless of their background' (Gillon, 1994, p. 188), it has been criticized for a lack of foundational theory, its Western-dominated methodology, failure to capture common morality adequately, capacity to obstruct substantive ethical inquiry and contemplation, and its individualistic bias (Evans, 2000; Walker, 2009; Wolpe, 1998). More recently educational and social researcher, Martyn Hammersley (2013), argued that while principles might indeed offer a useful series of prompts, triggering consideration of particular issues, the institutionalization of those prompts in a set of regulatory principles is problematic, as a set of principles can be neither exhaustive nor can it operate as a coherent system as there is always the possibility of conflict between principles. In addition, principles might undercut attempts to tackle broader ethical issues and we always need to consider 'who is setting principles on behalf of whom, with what authority, and with what potential effects' (p. 3).

Not only has principlism been attacked from outside, but according to Ezekiel Emanuel's influential 1995 review of Beauchamp and Childress' fourth edition of *Principles of Biomedical Ethics*, even its two key advocates developed reservations about the coherence and justifications for their own approach. Callahan (2003) suggested principlism fell from favour during the 1990s in the face of a broad array of criticisms and the emergence of other more critical approaches to ethics, including feminist and postmodernist ethics, to which I return later in the chapter.

Virtue ethics

Taking inspiration from Aristotle's *Nicomachean Ethics* (358 BCE/2003), virtue theory emphasizes the moral character of ethical decision-makers and not the consequences of their actions or the rules or duties that led to those actions. For Aristotle, a good person was someone disposed to do the right thing and to determine what is right on the basis of rational thought. Asian bioethicists have noted similar traditions in Hindu, Buddhist and Confucian writings (Kishore, 2003; Tai, 2011). Whereas consequentialist and non-consequentialist approaches to ethics might be regarded as rule- or act-centred, virtue ethics is an agent-centred approach directed primarily at the character and moral quality of people involved (Peach, 1995). The fundamental assumption underpinning practical applications of virtue ethics is that morally upstanding individuals will, as a matter of course, act appropriately and in accordance with established rules and standards. Good acts flow from good people.

Until Kant, virtue ethics was the dominant form of ethical theory. However, Classical and Medieval explorations of virtue ethics were subsequently eclipsed by consequentialist and non-consequentialist approaches. Only in the Twentieth Century did virtue-based approaches experience a revival following publication of Elizabeth Anscombe's essay *Modern Moral Philosophy* in 1958, Philippa Foot's book *Virtues and Vices* in 1978 and Alasdair MacIntyre's *After Virtue* in 1984. Virtue ethics were applied to research ethics in 1966 in Henry Beecher's account of the failings of medical research. Beecher argued that virtue rather than regulation should provide the foundation for the education and training of researchers. In a more recent book, Bruce Macfarlane (2008) identified six important character traits for researchers: courage, respectfulness, resoluteness, sincerity, humility and reflexivity, and went on to criticize the damage caused to researchers' values by principle-based ethics review:

> Being ethical is about developing a deep, personal understanding of our own values rather than trying to substitute individual responsibility with the mantras of bioethics. Getting better at handling ethical issues comes only with

15

> practice, experience, and learning from the good or bad examples of others. Being an ethical researcher requires an authentic engagement with our own beliefs and the values of our disciplines. Ethics is a bit like jazz, in that it is about more than simply following the notes on the page. It demands an ability to improvise and to think for ourselves. (Macfarlane, 2010, p. A30)

Resnik (2012) suggested we might wish to add the further traits of: fairness, openness, resourcefulness, conscientiousness, flexibility and integrity.

Virtue ethics does offer some possibility for those keen to rethink current practices, and is probably most commonly considered in relation to the question of trust. When members of a community choose to trust a researcher with whom they have a long-standing relationship, they may well be doing so because they trust the researcher to do the right thing on the basis of an assessment of character, rather than a respect for his or her ability to apply an ethical code or a formal agreement. For example, Jonathan Stillo (2011), an American medical anthropology graduate student researching in a Romanian sanatorium, was introduced to patients by a fifty-year-old Roma man dying of tuberculosis: 'Jonathan is a good person. He wants to know about your lives and your families. You should talk to him'. Indeed, in calling for greater trust to be placed on the individual researcher, several critics of current research ethics review processes are effectively arguing for greater weight to be placed on virtue ethics (Iphofen, under review). Support for this proposition also comes from as unlikely a source as the architect of principlism, Tom Beauchamp, and his colleagues:

> A trusted person has an ingrained motivation and desire to do what is right and to care about whether it is done. Whenever the feelings, concerns and attitudes of others are the morally relevant matters, rules and principles are not as likely as human warmth and sensitivity to lead a person to notice what should be done. From this perspective, virtue ethics is at least as fundamental in the moral life as principles of basic obligation. (Beauchamp et al., 2008, pp. 18–19)

However, in its application to research ethics, there is some disagreement between those like Macfarlane who see virtue ethics as standing alone, and Resnik who advocates use of virtue ethics to augment principlism, on the basis that while a principle-based approach might be more effective than virtue ethics in policy development, it might not do so much for promoting ethical conduct through mentoring and leadership.

Virtue-based approaches have been criticized: for their relativism (for instance, it is unclear what constitutes a virtue); for their inability to handle conflicts between different virtues; for their failure to provide specific guidance on behaviour; on the basis that even virtuous people are less moral when placed in less rewarding or more stressful situations (Appiah, 2008); and because virtue theory is generally morally conservative, in that it focuses on and perhaps even entrenches established ways of being and doing (Annas, 2005).

Casuistry

Casuistry is a situation-based approach to normative ethics in which specific cases and challenges inform moral principles, not the converse. Cases and analogies help to define and clarify 'the inherently fuzzy ethical principles (e.g., "do not lie", "return what you borrow") that we use to guide our practice' (Thacher, 2004, p. 271). Researchers reach conclusions about ethical issues by drawing principles from similar, but less problematic, dilemmas and applying them to the complexities of the question at hand (Peach, 1995). Typically too, reasoning through casuistry is based on reference to paradigmatic cases on which (nearly) everyone agrees. For example, a case of informed consent might be illuminated through reference to sociologist Laud Humphrey's covert work on homosexuality (see Chapter 3). Decisions about ethical behaviour are generated by analogy rather than by appealing to consequence or principle.

> By using analogical reasoning to analyze hard cases – those in which the proper application of the principles is unclear – casuistry helps to clarify how the principles apply to unfamiliar contexts, and it helps to mark out the principles' boundaries by investigating situations in which they conflict with other considerations. (Thacher, 2004, p. 271)

Returning to the example of Indigenous secret knowledge and the road, the ethical social scientist adopting casuistry might consider, for example, the ways he or she would be inclined to act if a repressive government sought the names of dissidents who had agreed to be interviewed in confidence. That analogous situation might provide clues to appropriate ways of behaving in the new predicament.

Critical approaches to ethics

Enlightenment philosophies envisaged a world of autonomous individual decision-makers – invariably code for people who were white, European, adult and male. By contrast, critical approaches to ethics recognize that interactions between researchers and research participants are grounded in the broader structural relationships within society. So, a society stratified according to race, gender or class will replay these relationships of domination and subordination through research (Harding, 1991). While different groups of researchers have focused on various kinds of stratification, they often share an overall interest in challenging power relations as well as reflecting on their own place within hierarchies.

One distinct feminist approach to ethics draws on relational ethics. Relational ethics is not, in itself, a critical approach. Early elements can be found in the work of the Scottish Enlightenment philosopher, David Hume (1740/1967), who regarded moral sensibility as innate and based on feelings rather than simply on reason. Hume's work was adopted by feminist authors such as Carol Gilligan (1977, 1982) and Nel Noddings (2003). Interpreting Hume to argue that moral actions could be founded on emotion instead of abstract principle, they called for an ethics of care that focused on care, compassion and relationships. In her pioneering work, Gilligan (1977) questioned conventional emphases on rights and obligations in ethics, which she argued were founded on masculine understandings. She identified two ways of thinking ethically: one founded on an ethics of justice and rights; the other on an ethics of care. For Gilligan, whereas traditional approaches to normative ethics emphasize rights, autonomy and abstract reasoning (ethics of justice) and are used more commonly by men, an ethics of care is employed more consistently by women and stresses people's relationships with one another, the importance of context and nurturing relationships. Annette Baier (1994) marked the significance of Gilligan's break with Kant and its implications for some of the central assumptions of research ethics:

> The emphasis in Kantian theories on rational control of emotions, rather than on cultivating desirable forms of emotion, is challenged by Gilligan, along with the challenge to the assumption of the centrality of autonomy, or relations between equals, and of freely chosen relations. (p. 31)

So, an ethics of care requires researchers to understand how their positions in hierarchies of power might affect their perceptions and to challenge the possibility and value of maintaining neutral and distanced relationships with research participants (Brabeck and Brabeck, 2009).

While supporting greater emphasis on care, both Baier (1994) and Virginia Held (1995) questioned Gilligan's initial assertion that an ethics of care was irreconcilable with an ethics of justice. Baier went on to maintain: 'the best moral theory has to be a cooperative product of women and men, has to harmonize justice and care' (p. 31). Consequently, an ethics of care need not signal total rejection of other approaches to ethics. Instead, the search for just outcomes to ethical problems requires us to care about and act to promote the good of others and engage in reciprocal relationships with individuals and groups (Tronto, 1993).

The ethics of care approach has not been without its detractors (Allmark, 1995). However, Noddings (2003, p. xv) observes that, in practice:

empirical evidence suggests that individuals only rarely consult moral principles when making decisions that result in the prevention of harm. More often, people respond directly as carers (out of sympathy) or as faithful members of a community that espouses helping and not harming.

Kathryn Daley (2012), a former drug outreach worker, interviewed 63 young people in Australia about their experiences of problematic drug use. Daley described how and why in one case she steered an interviewee away from discussing a traumatic experience of sexual assault, while in another instance she enabled an interviewee to download 'all of his thoughts and feelings' about his girlfriend's suicide. She assessed the appropriateness of each response on the basis of the relationship she had formed with the interviewee and her understanding of cues offered by him or her, the setting within which the interview was taking place and the availability of professional support. In the first case, Daley explained to the research participant why she had not probed further, while in the second she returned to find out how the interviewee was coping with the consequences of the 'heavy experience' and to check residential facility staff were alert to his needs. Daley reflected on the different decisions that she had made and concluded that, although they were situationally specific, each was grounded in an ethics of care:

> One cannot prepare the solutions to all of the potential scenarios that may occur, but to care for one's participants, and to do as much as possible to enable them to be cared for, is the most ethical response, as it protects and respects the person whose life story has just been shared. (p. 33)

An ethics of care is often located within broader progressive feminist ethical commitments to illuminating women's experiences, understanding them within the context of oppressive power relations and intersections between different social identities, and acting to achieve greater social justice (Spelman, 1988). As a result, as feminist ethics has matured, it has joined with other post-positivist approaches to engage with forms of oppression and marginalization associated with race, ethnicity, poverty, development, and state and institutional power. As Daley's account illustrates, it also raises questions about the importance of the context within which a decision will be made.

Many social scientists question research ethics governance structures that require them to predict the methodological and ethical issues that they are likely to encounter in the field and then to respond only in premeditated ways. They have pointed to the messiness and complexities of field relations and argued that how they resolve ethical tensions must depend on the nature of the context, place, situation, technologies, methodologies and research participants. Few ethicists would claim that the context is irrelevant. The issue is the degree to which decisions made in context are anchored in a more formal ethical approach. In an early piece on situated ethics, Christina Allen (1996) drew on the work of Mikhail Bakhtin to reject 'absolutist' ethics, and instead suggested ethical wisdom grew from past experience and an awareness that what had been learned needed to be applied to new situations both flexibly and creatively:

> since the ethical researcher cannot a priori adjudicate what will be harmful, it is necessary to redevelop ethical research practices by engaging in creative 'ethical work' in situ ... (p. 177)

In education (Simons and Usher, 2000), and subsequently in sociology, geography and media studies, researchers have defended an ethics that can respond to the local and the specific. For example, British sociologist Dick Hobbs saw that:

> Ethnographic work is highly personal. Professional bodies who attempt to regulate the activities of researchers working in highly volatile environments come across as naive and pompous, spouting bland liberal platitudes rather than informing and supporting researchers. For most of us our everyday ethical decisions are not governed by formal codes. Decisions emerge situationally as part of the ongoing process of accruing cultural capital. It would be arrogant to expect academic labour to be any different. (personal communication, in Israel and Hay, 2006, p. 153)

This book contains numerous examples of how social scientists have sought to understand harm and benefit, and negotiate consent and degrees of anonymity within a particular research setting. Situated ethics has found favour with researchers operating in new environments. For example, researchers of online communities like Allen (1996) and Whiteman (2012), have been dissatisfied by clumsy attempts by scholars and regulators to extend existing codes and guidelines to or develop one-size-fits-all new codes for online domains.

> the 'ethical' researcher does not stumble into the online field and apply general principles in respect of how he/she will collect data ... Instead, researchers' decisions should be based upon an understanding of their research settings and consideration of the specificities of their research interests ... that enables them to make decisions that are context specific. (Whiteman, 2012, pp. 9–10)

Situated ethics may be attractive to social scientists seeking to assert their positions as professionals and experts in the face of bioethics-orientated regulatory regimes. However, it is not without its dangers. Advocates of situational ethics may not be claiming that anything goes, but as an explicit link with ethical theory has disappeared from much of their writing, it is not always clear on what basis decision-making is actually shaped to respond to a particular context, and how decisions might be justified. One of the more specific depictions is provided by Beach and Eriksson (2010) when they identified, on the basis of an empirical study of Scandinavian educational ethnographers,

> an ethical commitment that is process-framed and that requires both self-regulation and 'self-reflexivity' over the effects or implications of the researcher's presence within, and representation of, the communities they research ... (p. 134)

By linking the claims of situated ethics to a broader social theory, critical approaches may offer a more sophisticated position. Postmodernist theorists distrust the metanarrative. As a result, they resist authoritative definitions and all-encompassing, reductivist universal explanations. This, of course, makes it difficult to pin down postmodern ethics (Bauman, 1993). Instead, it may be easier to tease out some of the challenges postmodern ethics pose for researchers. Clegg and Slife (2009) identify the characteristics of postmodernist perspectives in terms of attention to the particular individual and context, the value-laden nature of all knowledge, and sensitivity – shared with many feminist positions – to power relations. Postmodernists eschew the abstract and the generalized in favour of uncovering the particular in context, which makes some of the arguments of researchers influenced by postmodernist approaches appear similar to those who advocate a situated approach. However, postmodernist researchers may do so with less certainty about knowledge, their interpretation and their own standpoint, coupled with a more clearly articulated concern for the impact of research on marginalized and oppressed groups (Cannella and Lincoln, 2011):

> ... ethical research has less to do with an attempt to reason about ethical research practices and more to do with an uncertain researcher perpetually struggling with the obligations and responsibilities of a particular situation to a particular community, and to a particular participant. (Clegg and Slife, 2009, p. 30)

Critical scholars have rejected the idea that individuals can be considered in isolation. Instead, we live within a web of shifting power relations. This has implications for the consent process, for an assessment of harm and benefits, and for an analysis of research ethics governance. Critical scholars have advocated research *for*, *with* and ultimately *by* (rather than *on*) disempowered groups (Ellis, 2007). Such research might contest patterns of domination and, by growing out of the perspective of the historically disadvantaged, might produce new knowledge (Fine, 2005; Halse and Honey, 2005). In the field of refugee studies, there is tension between positivists who use large-scale datasets and statistically representative samples, and critical scholars who engage in small-scale qualitative studies. Rodgers (2004) was dismissive of the former, who he maintained might serve a highly polarizing social agenda by silencing the voice of refugees and limiting the potential for researchers to speak out against the abuses of power. While refuting the suggestion that qualitative research might be inherently more ethical than quantitative, Mackenzie et al. (2007) argued:

> relational approaches to autonomy give rise to both negative and positive obligations on the part of researchers. The negative obligation is to ensure that participation in research does not compromise or further erode partici-pants' capacities for self-determination or their scope for exercising these capacities ... The positive obligation is that, wherever possible, social researchers should aim to develop research projects that not only identify the problems experienced by refugees and their causes, but that help to promote their autonomy and re-build capacity ... (p. 310)

Halse and Honey (2005) not only challenged research ethics committees to grapple with a postmodernist agenda but also to work with researchers in an 'ongoing collaborative process shaped by dialogue and responsive relation-ships' (p. 2158) that reflected an ethics of care.

A further challenge to the apparent neutrality of ethics and ethical review has come from postcolonial approaches. Postcolonial theorists have taken a critical agenda and combined it with a recognition that contemporary social relations occur in the presence or the aftermath of colonialism. This has triggered reflec-tions on the ethics of how we choose the questions for and how we create rela-tionships within research. Tikly and Bond (2013) drew on postcolonial theory to locate ethical discourses within power relations and point out that the practices of research ethics 'legitimise social practices that have material effects' (p. 423). In particular, research ethics governance renders as universal Eurocentric (or global North) forms of knowledge and ethics. And so, other contexts and experi-ences are excluded or, if incorporated, seen as offering only inflexible, historical points of reference. This is a theme repeatedly encountered in Chapter 4 when I review ethical regulation in different countries. Postcolonial theorists have not invested much time in writing specifically about research ethics, but the approach is likely to favour a cross-cultural dialogue that affirms the diversity of ethical approaches to research, critically reflects on the role of the researcher in the research process, and recognizes the broader and situated relationships within which research occurs. While relevant across the world, these insights have been developed furthest in relation to research involving indigenous peo-ples, a matter I return to throughout this book.

Conclusion

For social scientists looking for unequivocal ethical direction in their research practice, the range of normative ethical theories presents problems, as the discussion of the women's secret knowledge case and Thomas' prison example (1996) reveal. Different normative positions lead to different and sometimes irreconcilable positions. The fact that normative ethics have come under strong theoretical critique from various post-positivist positions should offer little comfort to those seeking short-cuts to defensible and reflective ethical practice. Given the presence of moral difference, we must enter into debate about whether we should base our ethical decisions on the consequences of our actions, on some other notions of 'justice' or 'care', or whether we reject any overarching approach. Do we make decisions based on the primacy of the individual (liberal) or on collective needs (communitarianism)? We need to consider the approaches on which we might vest our faith and future. Do we need to apply one approach consistently? Or can we put them together in some way to help us towards sound ethical decision-making? In the next part of the book, I review how approaches to ethical research behaviour have been institutionalized and formalized, particularly since the end of the Second World War, and identify key principles underpinning ethical decision-making in social science research.

THREE

Codes and Principles

Introduction

There is a conventional story told about the emergence of research ethics. After the Second World War, horrified by the medical experimentation undertaken by Germany, the West developed the Nuremberg Code (1947) which, coupled with the World Medical Association's Declaration of Helsinki in 1964, became the cornerstones of bioethics. Slowly, concepts developed in bioethics have been extended to research endeavours across the disciplinary spectrum, including social science and, more recently, humanities and the creative arts.

Of course, real life is rarely so simple (see Table 3.1). First, regulations governing medical experimentation existed before the war in, of all places, Prussia and then Germany (Vollmann and Winau, 1996). Second, the Nuremberg Doctors' Trial was largely an American initiative – Britain distanced itself from it publicly, though its agencies worked covertly both in the trial and in establishing the framework for the Code (Hazelgrove, 2002). Third, both American and British medical researchers engaged in highly questionable experimentation before and during the Second World War (Hazelgrove, 2002). Far from putting a stop to these activities, Nuremberg marked the beginning of a utilitarian approach to human experimentation on prisoners in the United States (Hornblum, 1998). Finally, the spread to social science of regulations based on bioethics has been neither uniform nor uncontested (Dingwall, 2012; Israel et al., under review; Schrag, 2010a; Sieber and Tolich, 2013) and an alternative set of stories should be told about the emergence of research ethics in those fields.

Table 3.1 Ethical codes and regulatory developments since 1945

Year	Event
1945	Nuremberg trials commence
1946	

Year	Event
1947	Nuremberg Code released
1948	United Nations Universal Declaration of Human Rights
1949	
1950	
1951	
1952	
1953	Wichita jury study
1954	
1955	
1956	Willowbrook hepatitis studies commence in New York and continue until 1972
1957	
1958	
1959	
1960	
1961	Milgram's 'obedience to authority' experiments commence Draft Declaration of Helsinki released
1962	Pappworth's paper on 'human guinea pigs' published in popular magazine *Twentieth Century*
1963	Jewish Chronic Disease Hospital study
1964	Declaration of Helsinki adopted by World Medical Association
1965	
1966	Beecher paper on unethical research published in *New England Journal of Medicine* First institutional research ethics committee in South Africa formed at University of Witwatersrand Australia's NHMRC publishes Statement on Human Experimentation and Supplementary Notes Cervical cancer experiments commence at New Zealand's National Women's Hospital
1967	Pappworth's book *Human Guinea Pigs: Experimentation on Man* published
1968	
1969	
1970	Laud Humphreys' book *Tearoom Trade* published
1971	San Antonio contraception study Zimbardo's mock prison experiments at Stanford University
1972	Tuskegee syphilis trials conclude, after running for 40 years Willowbrook hepatitis studies conclude
1973	
1974	US National Commission for the Protection of Human Subjects of Biomedical and Behavioral Research ('The National Commission') created as part of the National Research Act. Prepares the 1979 Belmont Report
1975	
1976	

(Continued)

Table 3.1 (Continued)

Year	Event
1977	Canada Council's Consultative Group on Ethics publishes report on ethical principles for researchers and review committees
	Medical Research Council of South Africa (MRCSA) publishes Guidelines on Ethics for Medical Research
1978	Medical Research Council of Canada publishes Ethics in Human Experimentation
1979	Belmont Report published
1980	Indian Council of Medical Research (ICMR) publishes Policy Statement on Ethical Considerations Involved in Research on Human Subjects
1981	Report of the US President's Commission for the Study of Ethical Problems in Medicine and Biomedical and Behavioral Research released, recommending a 'Common Rule' for all Federally funded research be developed
1982	Council for International Organizations of Medical Sciences with World Health Organization first proposes International Ethical Guidelines for Biomedical Research Involving Human Subjects
1983	
1984	
1985	
1986	
1987	South Africa's Human Sciences Research Council publishes Code of Research Ethics
1988	New Zealand's 'Cartwright Inquiry' reports on the treatment of cervical cancer at New Zealand's National Women's Hospital
1989	United Nations Convention on the Rights of the Child
1990	Norwegian Parliament approves establishment of three national committees for research ethics, including NESH
1991	'Common Rule' (CFR 46) adopted by 16 US Federal departments and agencies
	Interim Guidelines on Ethical Matters in Aboriginal and Torres Strait Islander Research released in Australia
1992	Australian Health Ethics Committee (AHEC) established
	Research ethics committees established in Denmark
1993	Vancouver Protocol published by International Committee of Medical Journal Editors
1994	US Advisory Committee on Human Radiation Experiments formed
	Canada's three key research Councils (MRC, NSERC and SSHRC) release Statement on Integrity in Research and Scholarship
	US Advisory Committee on Human Radiation Experiments reports. US President Clinton apologizes to the citizens who were subjected to these experiments, their families and communities
1995	Australian Commonwealth Government releases Report of the Review of the Role and Functioning of Institutional Review Committees
1996	President Clinton apologizes to Tuskegee experimental subjects
	National Health Council in Brazil adopts Guidelines and Norms Regulating Research Involving Human Subjects (Resolution 196/96)

Year	Event
1997	Joint NHRMC/AV-CC Statement and Guidelines on Research Practice released in Australia
	Canada's Tri-Council Policy Statement: Ethical Conduct for Research Involving Humans
1998	
1999	
2000	United States Federal Policy on Research Misconduct
	Canadian Interagency Advisory Panel on Research Ethics (PRE)
	National Committee for Ethics in Social Science Research in Health (NCESSRH) in India publishes Ethical Guidelines for Social Science Research in Health
2001	Values and Ethics: Guidelines for Ethical Conduct in Aboriginal and Torres Strait Islander Health Research published in Australia
2002	American Anthropology Association's El Dorado Task Force final report
	Council for International Organizations of Medical Sciences most recent revision of International Ethical Guidelines for Biomedical Research Involving Human Subjects
	Association of Internet Researchers' recommendations on ethical decision-making and internet research
2003	Canadian PRE's Working Party report *Giving Voice to the Spectrum*
2004	RESPECT Principles for Ethical Socio-Economic Research
	2004 Health Act in South Africa
2005	EUREC Declaration to establish a European Network of Research Ethics Committees
	OHRP sets out preliminary criteria for determining whether institutions outside the United States offer protections equivalent to their 'Common Rule'
	British ESRC's Research Ethics Framework
2006	Australian Code for the Responsible Conduct of Research and National Statement on Ethical Conduct in Human Research
	NESH publishes guidelines for cultural and social studies in Norway
2007	Swedish Research Council's *Good Research Practice* guide
	Forum for Ethical Review Committees in Thailand produces guidelines for research on human subjects
	South Korean Ministry of Science and Technology's *Guides for Securing Research Ethics*
2008	Canadian PRE's Working Party report on ethical issues in internet-based research
2009	British ESRC revises Framework for Research Ethics
	Finnish National Advisory Board on Research Integrity publishes principles for the social sciences and humanities
	Qatar's Guidelines, Regulations and Policies for Research Involving Human Subjects
2010	Second edition of Canada's Tri-Council Policy Statement: Ethical Conduct for Research Involving Humans (TCPS 2)
	Te Ara Tika drafted for Māori research ethics

(Continued)

Table 3.1 (Continued)

Year	Event
	Singapore Statement on Research Integrity adopted by the second World Conference on Research Integrity
	Saudi Arabia's System of Ethics of Research on Living Subjects
2011	Canada's Tri-Agency Framework: Responsible Conduct of Research
2012	AIATSIS Guidelines for Ethical Research in Australian Indigenous Studies
	National Health Council in Brazil adopts Resolution 466/12
2013	The New Brunswick Declaration: A Declaration on Research Ethics, Integrity and Governance
	International Committee of Medical Journal Editors (ICMJE) releases its Recommendations for the Conduct, Reporting, Editing, and Publication of Scholarly Work in Medical Journals
	Seventh revision of the Declaration of Helsinki

Nevertheless, broad changes have occurred in research ethics regulation since 1945 through the development of major and highly influential formal ethical statements: the Nuremberg Code (1947); the Declaration of Helsinki (1964); the Belmont Report (1979); the Council for International Organizations of Medical Sciences (CIOMS) Proposed Guidelines (1982); and the United Nations Educational, Scientific and Cultural Organization's (UNESCO) Universal Declaration on Bioethics and Human Rights (2005). These statements on biomedical research provide key, albeit contested, foundations for much current thinking and practice in research ethics and have an impact on the social sciences – either intellectually or through the dominance of the biomedical research model in shaping institutional ethical practice – and for this reason justify exploration of their development in this book.

The Nuremberg Code

Before the Second World War, most biomedical research was conducted on a small scale and, when patients agreed to participate in research, their consent was typically made on the basis of trust rather than informed consent: 'Patients trusted their physicians not to harm them, to do something positive for them (even if they could not cure them – and cure was not routinely expected in the 1940s), and to act in their best interests' (Kaufman, 1997, p. 179).

In this pre-War era, some medical and professional organizations took tentative steps to move from a relationship based on covenant to something slightly more contractual by formalizing ethical dimensions of the doctor–patient or researcher–subject relationship. For instance, in developments of relatively limited immediate significance, the American Psychological Association (APA) established an ethics committee in 1938 (Adams et al., 2001) and German and American doctors developed voluntary guidelines for ethical research (Adair, 2001).

Much greater and broader attention was directed to relationships between researchers and their subjects as a result of the Nuremberg trials after the Second World War. Revelations at the trials about Nazi 'science' threatened to undermine 'public faith in the "normal" science of the western liberal democracies' (Hazelgrove, 2002, p. 111), so high-level British officials, for example, endeavoured to ensure that research undertaken by the Allies not be tainted. These activities included development of a set of tenets upon which future research might be conducted.

The Nuremberg Code emerged in part from fear of the consequences for science of any public loss of trust in doctors and researchers as well as from straightforward public abhorrence of cruel wartime experimentation. The Code set out ten key principles for medical experiments on human beings. The preamble declared that 'certain basic principles must be observed in order to satisfy moral, ethical and legal concepts', renouncing a position taken by defendants in the Nuremberg trials that the community or species ought to have precedence over the individual (Bower and de Gasparis, 1978). Its drafters were concerned with experimental or non-therapeutic research involving healthy, adult, competent and fully informed subjects, and not with therapeutic research conducted during medical care. The Code gave considerable emphasis to the voluntary and informed consent of people competent to make decisions and placed personal responsibility on 'each individual who initiates, directs, or engages in the experiment' (Article 1) to ensure that appropriate consent is given.

Under the Code, subjects had the right to cancel experiments (Article 9). In turn, researchers were required to minimize harm (Articles 4, 7), justify any risk in relation to the humanitarian benefit of the study (Article 6) and to stop work if they were likely to cause injury or death to their subjects (Articles 5, 10). The Nuremberg Code became a central building block for subsequent codes of ethics, but its impact was not universal.

Public revelations about Nazi experimentation and the outcomes of the Nuremberg trials raised concerns about medical research in some parts of the world such as France (Weisz, 1990). However, Nuremberg had imperceptible significance in the United States (Oakes, 2002). The American public maintained their faith in the Hippocratic Oath and the integrity of doctors, faith and trust that would be tested repeatedly by a series of shocks and scandals. Nevertheless, before these incidents came to public attention some medical researchers began to develop their own codes of practice.

29

The Declaration of Helsinki

The World Medical Association's (WMA) Declaration of Helsinki (1964) drew from, but amended, some provisions of the Nuremberg Code (Bošnjak, 2001; Carlson et al., 2004). The Declaration has been described as 'the fundamental document in the field of ethics in biomedical research' and has done much to influence subsequent international, regional and national legislation and codes of conduct (Council for International Organizations of Medical Sciences, 2002).

The Declaration traces its beginnings to work of the WMA's Medical Ethics Committee in 1953. After several years of preliminary effort, a draft Declaration was tabled in 1961 and in 1964 was adopted at the WMA's 18th General Assembly in Helsinki, Finland.

> This document spells out in more detail, in medical language specific to the scientific understanding that has evolved since Nuremberg, the nature of the arguments that must be weighed before asking a patient (not a healthy, competent volunteer) to consent to participate in diagnostic or therapeutic research. It does not contain an absolute requirement that informed consent be obtained in the setting of therapeutic research and introduces the notion of guardianship as a means of obtaining consent from incompetent subjects. (Leaning, 1996, p. 1413)

Ten of the 12 original markers of ethical research that were identified in the Nuremberg Code were adopted in the Declaration of Helsinki while two were amended significantly (Carlson et al., 2004; Seidelman, 1996). First, where the Nuremberg Code had stated that 'the voluntary consent of the human subject is absolutely essential', the Helsinki Declaration allowed consent to be given by legal guardians in cases of 'legal incapacity'. Second, the requirement that 'During the course of the experiment the human subject should be at liberty to bring the experiment to an end if he has reached the physical or mental state where continuation of the experiment seems to him to be impossible' was removed. In its place, and over and above the subject's freedom to withdraw, was the paternalist recommendation that researchers should discontinue research if they believed it could prove harmful.

The 1964 Declaration set out 12 basic precepts which required that research conform to scientific principles, that it be conducted by an expert and that research procedures be considered, commented on and guided by specially appointed independent committees to ensure they were procedurally and legally acceptable (Levine, 1993). This recommendation has now been extended significantly. Research risks need to be justifiable in terms of likely outcomes, and respect for the subject is critical in terms of reporting (for example, issues of privacy) and ensuring free and informed consent – particularly with dependent populations.

Like the Nuremberg Code before it, the Declaration of Helsinki gave emphasis to autonomy. However, the Declaration made it quite clear that in all instances the researcher was responsible for research subjects: 'The responsibility for the human subject must always rest with a medically qualified person and never rest on the subject of the research, even though the subject has given his or her consent' (World Medical Association, 1964, I. 3).

Various revisions to the Declaration of Helsinki have been made since 1964, with the most recent changes being adopted in Fortaleza, Brazil in 2013. Revisions have occurred with increasing frequency since the early 1980s but the central tenets remain the same. However, one particularly interesting amendment to the Declaration set the document up as a guideline that superseded national regulations. Before 2000, the Declaration stated 'It must be stressed that the standards as drafted are only a guide to physicians all over the world. Physicians are not relieved from criminal, civil and ethical responsibilities under the laws of their own countries' (World Medical Association, 1996, Introduction, para. 8). This was amended eventually to read:

> No national or international ethical, legal or regulatory requirement should reduce or eliminate any of the protections for research subjects set forth in this Declaration. (World Medical Association, 2013, para. 10).

Consequently, while other 'applicable international norms or standards' should be considered, the Declaration was positioned as having universal ethical primacy and standing above diverse, culturally specific regulations. Unfortunately, parts of the Declaration were vague, internally inconsistent, tendentious, or excessively general, failing to elaborate those circumstances where exceptions might be appropriate (Millum et al., 2013). For example, paragraph 25 dealt with informed consent without allowing for the possibility of deceptive or covert research in any circumstances. Rid and Schmidt (2010) argued that such requirements were, 'if strictly interpreted, misguided and risk[ed] complicating or forestalling valuable research' (p. 144). In addition, the Declaration provided no guidance to researchers confronted with a clash between the ethical guidelines of the world's largest global grouping of doctors and local laws and standards. Singer and Benatar (2001) concluded the Declaration would achieve little in itself without efforts to build capacity to grapple with and implement its provisions.

The globally homogenizing thrust of the Declaration of Helsinki with its apparent resistance to local variation was taken up in the Council for International Organizations of Medical Sciences' International Ethical Guidelines for Biomedical Research Involving Humans (Council for International Organizations of Medical Sciences, 2002), discussed later in this chapter. A pattern was set, and by failing to confront the ethical concerns that real researchers face, the Declaration threatened either to curtail researchers seeking to tackle new ethical issues, or encourage the undercutting of its own moral authority. These concerns might not have troubled social scientists if we had avoided working with medical researchers and were satisfied guidelines and codes developed within bioethics had no influence on our disciplines. However, social scientists clearly do work in the area of health and we have discovered that research ethics policies have a habit of being exported from the medical field. For those of us concerned about mission creep in bioethics documents, the 2008 Declaration imperiously encouraged all scholars engaged in academic research to adopt its principles, and the 2013 version purports to impose some requirements on 'every research study involving human subjects' (para. 35) even though both documents clearly remained rooted in the context of physicians engaged in clinical trials.

The Belmont Report

The Declaration of Helsinki and the Nuremberg Code served as models for some professional organizations' approaches to ethical research conduct (Jones, 1994) but proved difficult to use in non-biomedical settings. Moreover, it became increasingly evident from revelations of medical and scientific misconduct in North America and Europe in the 1960s and 1970s that doctors and medical researchers were betraying the trust members of the public placed in them.

First, in the United Kingdom in the 1960s, Maurice Pappworth drew attention to two decades of harmful experiments, often conducted on vulnerable populations, without appropriate consent. Pappworth's (1962/3) short article in the popular journal *Twentieth Century* and his book entitled *Human Guinea Pigs: Experimentation on Man* (1967) sparked public and professional debate and demonstrated that the Nuremberg Code's principle of informed consent had become part of broad public consciousness. It appears from the debate that surrounded Pappworth's publications that trust, so important in pre-War understandings of research relationships, was giving way to a more symmetrical relationship of informed consent.

On the other side of the Atlantic, a hugely influential publication in the *New England Journal of Medicine* by Harvard University's Henry K. Beecher (1966) presented a series of shocking findings. Beecher was a highly regarded anaesthetist who became concerned in the 1950s about ethics in research (Harkness et al., 2001) and the heightened financial and professional pressures on researchers to behave unethically. Beecher recognized that accepted standards for treatment of human 'subjects' such as those set out in the Nuremberg Code were being systematically ignored in Federally funded research in American facilities. His paper, regarded by some as the single most influential paper ever written about experimentation involving humans, outlined 22 studies in which 'subjects' had been unethically engaged in research, usually without their knowledge or without knowledge of the harm they risked. It made suggestions about: informed participant consent; informed, compassionate and responsible investigators; and developed a calculus to make research benefits commensurate with risk. These ideas were adopted by the National Institutes for Health and the Food and Drug Administration in the United States. Indeed, Harkness and his colleagues (2001) suggested that Beecher's paper laid the groundwork for United States ethical codes and ethics review committees. Beecher's ideas were also taken up outside his home country (Medical Research Council of South Africa, 2001).

A series of scandals kept issues of (un)ethical behaviour in high public and professional relief: the Tuskegee study, in which African American men in Alabama were denied treatment for syphilis from 1932 to 1972; a chronic disease study involving elderly Jewish patients unknowingly injected with cancer cells; experiments where children institutionalized at Willowbrook State School in New York were used in hepatitis vaccine trials (Adair, 2001; Oakes, 2002); and a San Antonio contraception study where women attending a clinic were not told that they were involved in a research study or might be receiving placebos rather than contraceptives (Levine, 1988). This is not an exhaustive list. Sadly, other unethical experiments from that period have surfaced more recently: between 1946 and 1948, the United States Public Health Service deliberately exposed over 1,300 Guatemalan prisoners, soldiers, psychiatric patients and sex industry workers to sexually transmitted diseases (Presidential Commission for the Study of Bioethical Issues, 2011a); in the early 1930s, academics at Northwestern University subjected indigent and other vulnerable subjects to interventions that included surgery, deprivation of oxygen, overhydration and dehydration, and snake venom (Dwyer, 2012). Not all of the ethically controversial work was of a biomedical character. Two social studies that came to the public's attention were Milgram's studies of obedience to authority and Humphrey's covert observations of the sexual practices of homosexual men. These two American investigations, together with that of Zimbardo (see Chapter 5), are regularly trotted out to justify regulation of all social science research, everywhere:

> The retelling of these horror stories builds an ethics lore, and socializes any novice ethics committee member into these worst-case scenarios, simultaneously legitimatizing ethics review. (Tolich, 2014)

Psychologist Stanley Milgram (1974) conducted experiments during the 1960s to explore people's obedience to authority. Research participants were led to believe they were administering electrical shocks of increasing intensity to another person when that person failed to meet learning objectives (a series of word association tests). 'Learners' were, in fact, confederates of Milgram.

They could be heard but not seen by the subject. Learners complained of pain and distress to the person applying the 'shocks'. They pounded on walls and ultimately stopped all activity, with the intention of convincing the experimental subjects that they had died. To Milgram's surprise, and to the participants' considerable dismay and psychological distress, many participants applied what they believed to be shocks of 450 volts to 'learners' (Blass, 2004). Milgram's experiments were repeated in Italy, South Africa, Germany, Spain and Australia. Burger (2009) partially replicated the study, while paying far greater attention to the welfare of the participants. Tolich (2014) argued that rather than using the Milgram experiments as a horror story of past ethical misconduct, it could be dissected prospectively. As a result, he suggested the research might be used to help contemporary researchers and ethics reviewers recognize the value both of following up participants who had been identified as being distressed in order to reduce the harm that had been caused, and of providing access to counselling.

However, the story of these experiments does not end there. Forty years after Milgram's work, Gina Perry (2012) interviewed various participants and experimenters who had taken part in the Milgram studies, tracing the impacts that the studies had had on these people, and outlining the ways accounts of the study and the nature of the results had been shaped by both supporters and critics. Among other things, Perry found some participants had been subjected to far greater pressure to continue than Milgram had reported, and remembered little of the debriefing his account had suggested. Any prospective dissection along the lines suggested by Tolich ought to take into account Perry's findings.

In 1966–7, and as part of a study of homosexual behaviours in public spaces, Laud Humphreys acted as voyeuristic 'lookout' or 'watch queen' in public toilets (the 'tearoom'). As a 'watch queen' he observed homosexual acts, sometimes warning men engaged in those acts of the presence of intruders. In the course of his observations Humphreys recorded the car licence plate numbers of the men who visited the 'tearoom'. He subsequently learned their names and addresses by presenting himself as a market researcher and requesting information from 'friendly policemen' (Humphreys, 1970, p. 38). One year later, Humphreys changed his appearance, dress and car and got a job as a member of a public health survey team. In that capacity he interviewed the homosexual men he had observed, pretending they had been selected randomly for the health study. This latter deception was necessary to minimize the risk associated with the fact that most of the sampled population were married and secretive about their homosexual activity. After the study, Humphreys destroyed the names and addresses of interviewees in order to protect their anonymity. His study was subsequently published as a major work on human sexual behaviour (Humphreys, 1970). There is no question

Humphreys deceived his subjects about the real purpose of his presence in the 'tearoom', that he failed to get informed consent from them and that he appears to have lied to police officers. However, the behaviour he observed occurred in a public place, he invested considerable effort in protecting participants' identities and, despite the received wisdom that this was a scandalous piece of research, it is unclear what harm resulted from the study.

These revelations, together with Pappworth's and Beecher's work, supported those arguing that researchers needed to pay careful attention to ethical matters and that their plans be subjected to review by their home institutions. It was in the United States that some of these developments first occurred. In July 1974, the United States' National Commission for the Protection of Human Subjects of Biomedical and Behavioral Research (NCPHSBBR) was created as part of the United States National Research Act. The 11 Commissioners were empowered to monitor Institutional Review Boards (IRBs), and charged with identifying basic ethical principles that should underpin the conduct of biomedical and behavioural research involving human 'subjects', as well as developing guidelines for ethical practice. The Commissioners included three medical doctors and two psychologists. There were no other social scientists.

The Commission worked by examining key cases, and generalizing from these by way of casuistry (Beauchamp, 2008). Its key ideas were summarized in a landmark 1979 document known as the Belmont Report (named for the Smithsonian Institute's Belmont Conference Center at which the Commission held key meetings in 1976). The Belmont Report: Ethical Principles and Guidelines for the Protection of Human Subjects of Research (National Commission for the Protection of Human Subjects of Biomedical and Behavioral Research, NCPHSBBR, 1979) was a statement of basic ethical principles and guidelines intended to assist in resolving ethical problems associated with research involving human 'subjects'. For Tom Beauchamp, the Report rested grandly on the presumption that 'no responsible research investigator could conduct research without reference to these principles; these principles form the core of any policy worthy of the name "research ethics"' (2008, p. 152).

The Report referred to earlier approaches to ethics, most notably the Nuremberg Code (though not the Helsinki Declaration), noting that codes often provided rules intended to guide investigators' appropriate conduct. However, 'such rules are often inadequate to cover complex situations; at times they come into conflict, and they are frequently difficult to interpret or apply' (NCPHSBBR, 1979). The authors argued therefore that broader principles offered a basis on which specific rules might be devised, criticized and interpreted. To that end, the Report set out three principles – respect for persons, beneficence and justice – intended to help understand the ethical issues associated with research involving human subjects. These three principles have been of fundamental importance in the development of many subsequent approaches to research ethics governance.

Respect for persons

Like the Nuremberg Code and the Declaration of Helsinki, the Belmont Report gave great emphasis to autonomy, incorporating convictions that, where possible, individuals should be treated as autonomous agents and that those with diminished autonomy (for example, the mentally disabled) are entitled to protection. The Report defined autonomy and set out the significance of failure to observe it:

> An autonomous person is an individual capable of deliberation about personal goals, and of acting under the direction of such deliberation. To respect autonomy is to give weight to autonomous persons' considered opinions and choices, while refraining from obstructing their actions, unless they are clearly detrimental to others. To show lack of respect for an autonomous agent is to repudiate that person's considered judgments, to deny an individual the freedom to act on those considered judgments, or to withhold information necessary to make a considered judgment, when there are no compelling reasons to do so. (NCPHSBBR, 1979, B. 1)

The Report observed that people's capacity for autonomous decision-making altered throughout their life-span and that in some cases individuals have diminished autonomy as a result, for example, of illness, disability or circumstances in which their liberty is restricted. As a result, protection must be offered depending on the risk of harm and the prospect of benefit. Also, of course, it is necessary to reconsider a person's level of autonomy from time to time. The Commission additionally stated that the principle of respect required that people enter into research relationships 'voluntarily and with adequate information' (NCPHSBBR, 1979, B. 1).

Beneficence

Beneficence, the second of the Belmont Report's basic ethical principles, was understood to go beyond acts of charity or kindness with which the term is sometimes associated. It was, instead, a responsibility to do good. The Commission made it clear that beneficence included ideas of avoiding harm (sometimes extrapolated to constitute another ethical principle, that of non-maleficence) and maximizing possible benefits, with the intention of ensuring people's well-being. In its discussion, the Commission included a lengthy review of the fraught area of risk–benefit relationships. For example, the

Report pointed to the difficulties associated with risky research involving children that had little immediate prospect of improving the lives of those children, but which might prove enormously rewarding to children in the future. In the end, the Commission observed that 'as with all hard cases, the different claims covered by the principle of beneficence may come into conflict and force difficult choices' (NCPHSBBR, 1979, B. 2).

Justice

In its discussion of the third principle of research ethics, justice, the Belmont Report drew on incidents such as the Tuskegee syphilis study and the exploitation of prisoners in Nazi concentration camps as examples of patently unfair treatment, pointing out that selection of participants in these cases had more to do with their availability and compromised position than with their relationships to the matters being studied. Members of the Commission considered the distribution of benefits and burdens of research, saying it would be unjust, for example, if someone were denied benefits to which they were entitled or if they bore a burden undeservedly. They suggested the principle of justice could be understood as the notion that equals should be treated equally. They pointed out, however, that this raised questions about how we work out equality in the face of differences such as age, gender, competence and status. The Report acknowledged notions of distributive justice as different bases for the division of benefits and burdens. Distribution to each person could occur on the basis of: an equal share or according to their individual need, individual effort, societal contribution or merit.

The Belmont Report also set out applications of these three principles as requirements for the conduct of ethical research. These included: informed consent, containing elements of sufficient information for participants, participant comprehension and voluntariness; assessment of risks and benefits, yielding a favourable risk–benefit assessment; and selection of subjects by fair procedures and yielding fair outcomes. Carol Levine (1996) later described the basic approach as 'born in scandal and reared in protectionism'.

Although the Belmont Report is not without its detractors (Miller, 2003; Weijer, 1999b), its articulation of ethical principles and applications has been very influential, providing the bases by which research ethics committees commonly evaluate proposed research (Sieber et al., 2002). Kimmelman (2006, p. 589) was able to claim that 'rules for human experimentation set out in the report have withstood almost three decades of challenge and change'. The Belmont Report has assumed a 'near canonical role' (Beauchamp, 2008, p. 29) for regulators in the United States and has been used by at least 17 Federal agencies in their development of research policies (Striefel, 2001). Nevertheless, Beauchamp himself acknowledged that the principles were perhaps 'more revered than they are understood and practiced' (2008, p. 30).

Despite the National Commission's role to identify principles underpinning both biomedical and behavioural research, the biomedical focus of regulations has posed problems for social scientists. The needs of social sciences were never addressed properly. In 2005, two of the Report's leading authors were invited to reflect on their work. They continued to disagree about the ambit of the Report. Albert Jonsen (2005), one of the original commissioners charged by Congress with identifying basic ethical principles and the only one with experience in social sciences, acknowledged that principles developed for medical research could not be universally applied but needed 'responsible interpreters who can make its words come alive in the particular circumstances of particular protocols, public policy, and the changing research enterprise' (p. 11). However, Tom Beauchamp (2005) who had been on staff with the Commission insisted the principles were universal 'norms shared by all morally decent persons' (p. 15) even if they might work out differently depending on context.

Zachary Schrag (2010a) rued the fact that the authors of the Report 'were willing neither to listen to social scientists nor to leave them alone' (p. 79) and this led to an outcome which might have been of significant value to biomedical science but perversely threatened to encourage ethical malpractice among social scientists (Reiss 1976, cited in Schrag, 2010a). Schrag saw nothing wrong with the basic principles. After all, who could argue against such 'fairly vapid' terms (Jonsen, 2007, cited in Schrag, 2010b). However, Schrag suggested 'A humbler commission could have acknowledged its lack of expertise in the problems of social science research and declined to make recommendations not grounded in careful investigation' (p. 95).

Council for International Organizations of Medical Sciences

The fourth major research ethics code of international significance to emerge was the International Ethical Guidelines for Biomedical Research Involving Human Subjects (Council for International Organizations of Medical Sciences (CIOMS), 2002). This code is known most commonly as CIOMS after the Council that drafted it. The Council was established in 1949 by the World Health Organization (WHO) and the United Nations Educational, Scientific and Cultural Organization (UNESCO) to prepare advice on health and research ethics.

Published first in 1982 as proposed guidelines, and revised in 1993 and 2002, CIOMS applied principles of the Helsinki Declaration to developing countries, while attempting to take account of their diverse socioeconomic conditions, cultures, religions, legal circumstances, laws and bureaucratic arrangements (Levine, 1993; Ringheim, 1995). The Guidelines dealt with the significance of multinational or transnational research in which people from low-resource countries might be involved as partners. CIOMS indicated in 2012 that it intended to revise its 2002 Guidelines.

Unlike Nuremberg, Helsinki and Belmont, CIOMS grappled explicitly with the application of 'universal' ethical principles in a diverse and multicultural world and declared that research should not violate any universal standards. The Guidelines gave special attention to matters of autonomy and protection of the dependent and vulnerable, while acknowledging the need to consider different cultural values (Council for International Organizations of Medical Sciences, 2002). As one of the drafters from Cameroon observed, 'The spirit of the guidelines was to promote essential, scientifically sound and ethical research that is responsive to the needs of diverse countries and communities' (Tangwa, 2004, p. 65). Some of these ideas found their way into the 2013 version of the Declaration of Helsinki.

The Guidelines were founded on the same three principles as the Belmont Report. Although the principles have equal moral status, in CIOMS the Guidelines provided an extended discussion of justice, to take account of the relative vulnerability of the least developed countries and their residents. The Guidelines suggested research investigators should not: engage in practices that make unjust conditions worse; take advantage of the inability of vulnerable populations to protect their own interests; or exploit international regulatory differences for personal and commercial gain. Instead, research should leave low-resource countries better off or at least no worse off than before, be responsive to the health needs of local communities (Guideline 10), and contribute to local capacity to design, conduct, review and monitor biomedical research (Guideline 20).

Despite the limited disciplinary ambit suggested by its title, CIOMS set out research guidelines that included the need for *all* proposals for research involving humans to be subjected to independent review of their merit and ethical acceptability and the requirement for researchers to gain the voluntary informed consent of research participants. Overall, these guidelines paid particular attention to matters of informed consent, research with vulnerable groups and women as research participants. CIOMS also gave detailed consideration to ethical review mechanisms:

> All proposals to conduct research involving human subjects *must* be submitted for review of their scientific merit and ethical acceptability to one or more scientific review and ethical review committees. The review committees *must* be independent of the research team, and any direct financial or other material benefit they may derive from the research should not be contingent on the outcome of their review. The investigator *must* obtain their approval or clearance before undertaking the research. The

39

ethical review committee should conduct further reviews as necessary in the course of the research, including monitoring of the progress of the study. (Council for International Organizations of Medical Sciences, 2002, Guideline 2; emphasis added)

The Commentary associated with this Guideline discussed the expected competence, composition and role of ethics review committees. For instance, committee membership should comprise men and women and include physicians, scientists, lawyers, ethicists and clergy 'as well as lay persons qualified to represent the cultural and moral values of the community and to ensure that the rights of the research subjects will be respected' (Council for International Organizations of Medical Sciences, 2002, Commentary on Guideline 2).

Universal Declaration on Bioethics and Human Rights

In 2005, UNESCO adopted the Universal Declaration on Bioethics and Human Rights. The preamble stated: 'It is necessary and timely for the international community to state universal principles that will provide a foundation for humanity's response to the ever-increasing dilemmas and controversies that science and technology present for humankind and the environment'. These included identifying the moral conditions under which scientific research might be conducted. The Declaration was expressly concerned with designing national research ethics policy for medicine, life sciences and associated technologies, and pushed beyond previous documents in linking bioethics explicitly to human rights law and to broad social concerns such as social exclusion, poverty and illiteracy. Unlike the Declaration of Helsinki and CIOMS which were generated by non-government agencies, the UNESCO Declaration was an international, intergovernmental agreement on bioethics, and therefore the first of its kind. It remained non-binding on member states and required members to incorporate its provisions into local legislation and regulation, while recognizing that this might require some adaptation of its 15 somewhat abstract principles, in part to meet the principle of cultural diversity and pluralism (Article 12). The Declaration allowed such adaptation as long as it did not compromise human dignity, human rights and fundamental freedoms. The International Bioethics Committee of UNESCO (2008) subsequently produced further elaboration of the material on consent.

The UNESCO Declaration has been applauded for promoting moral reflection (Kopelman, 2009) and improved governance. However, the universalist and apparently self-evident nature of the claims made by the Declaration has been contested by secular and religious ethicists (Cherry, 2009; Hedayat, 2007; Landman and Schuklenk, 2005) and, like principlism, the Declaration has also been criticized for failing to resolve tensions between principles. It has been condemned both for being too vague and for being open to abuse by those seeking to justify coercive legislation. Article 21 addressed the need for research ethics review in member nations but failed to explore how this might be achieved. Based on interviews with research ethics committee members in Kenya and South Africa, Adèle Langlois (2008) concluded 'Working out how to apply such principles in particular social and economic contexts is arguably as challenging as reaching agreement on how they should be constituted in the first place' (p. 49).

Towards a Declaration for the Social Sciences

None of these codes and guidelines were conceived with the methodologies and issues that concern social scientists in mind. Social scientists were rarely involved in their drafting, they were not consulted and they did not consent. Yet, these documents have shaped the governance of research ethics in the social sciences. As I examine in the next chapter, many national regulations have been based on principles and practices developed by the Nuremberg Code, the Declaration of Helsinki, CIOMS and the UNESCO Declaration. Initially prepared to regulate biomedical researchers, their ambit has often expanded to encompass social scientists.

In criticizing the absence of social scientists from the drafting process, it is worth considering what national guidelines might have looked like if social scientists *had* been involved. Robert Dingwall (2012) noted that before the intervention of the National Institutes of Health in the mid-1960s, some ethical 'conventions' had been established within the social sciences. Classic studies by the Chicago School of sociology from the 1930s onwards maintained anonymity by using pseudonyms and masking geographical locations. Anthropologists often gave tribal members pseudonyms, even if they were willing to identify the name of the tribe. Both disciplines confronted the ethics of covert observation, as well as cooption by the military and defence agencies – matters to which I return in Chapters 5 and 7 – and, where these conventions were challenged, Dingwall argued 'the community was capable of self-policing and articulating a professional consensus that was responsive to external criticism' (p. 11).

Hammersley and Traianou (2012) suggested we might gain some insight into what might have happened if the social sciences had been left to their own devices from the codes adopted by discipline-specific professional associations. Hammersley and Traianou identified the first social science code of ethics as the document created by the Society for Applied Anthropology in 1948. This code was drafted in response to American anthropologists' connection to the internment of ethnic Japanese residents by the United States during the

Second World War (Price, 2008), and discussed the responsibility of applied anthropologists to avoid adversely affecting the health of groups and individuals, or the broader system of social relations. Scholars were also expected to respect human personality and cultural values, protect informants, and 'advance those forms of human relationships which contribute to the integrity of the individual human being' (Society for Applied Anthropology, 1948/1951). Reaction to academic involvement in covert military and intelligence operations in South-East Asia in the 1960s (Horowitz, 1967), prompted the American Sociological Association (1970) and the American Anthropological Association (1971) to create their own codes of ethics. Like the Society for Applied Anthropology, the latter also considered scholars' responsibility to research subjects, and the duties to protect them from harm, and to avoid clandestine work for home or host governments. According to Pat Caplan (2003), the 1971 Code formed part of a radical challenge to traditional anthropology. Other early codes, such as that of the American Psychological Association (1963) and the British Sociological Association (1968), focused on defending academic freedom and professional standards, with the psychologists adopting sanctions for those who transgressed their code. Interestingly, we see in these documents a greater sensitivity to structural issues and broader social responsibilities than can be found in the biomedical statements of those times. The Associations tended to avoid excessive claims to universality and were sometimes able to demonstrate the support of their membership for their Codes through polling and ratification processes (Schuler, 1969).

However, not surprisingly, their content and nature were contested (Galliher, 1973) which makes it harder to support Dingwall's argument that there existed much in the way of consensus around ethical conventions. Letters written in 1964 by Howard Becker and Eliot Freidson, two eminent sociologists, rejected an early draft code for the American Sociological Association. Freidson argued codes could not work in sociology as they could do no more than identify and then distort and oversimplify complex issues (1964, p. 410), and Becker believed the diversity in approaches to ethics demonstrated by sociologists meant there could be no agreement on a code:

> The code is equivocal or unenlighteningly vague in dealing with most of the problems distinct to social science ... because there is no consensus about such problems ... (1964, p. 409)

Of course, Becker and Freidson's opposition was subsequently overcome and for a while the codes of ethics adopted by professional associations were significant markers of appropriate behaviour and, in some cases, the very act of drafting the codes may have encouraged collective ethical reflection. Nevertheless in many countries, as I discuss in Chapter 4, the influence of professional associations over ethics has now been largely ceded to research institutions and research councils, although there may be some opportunities for professional associations to reassert themselves (Iphofen, under review). The problem may have been less a lack of ethical authority accorded to professional associations' codes but rather, according to Rena Lederman (2007), that their very diversity that could not be tolerated by regulators. As a result, contemporary materials produced for social sciences by institutions and research councils around the world seem to echo the concerns of bioethical codes considered in this chapter.

In 2012, the Social Sciences and Humanities Research Council of Canada funded 'Ethics Rupture', a gathering of 30 academics from North America, Europe and Australasia (van den Hoonaard, 2013a). Following the summit, we drafted the New Brunswick Declaration (van den Hoonaard, 2013b). This series of positive statements articulated a social science ethical sensibility. The Declaration was intended to support a constructive dialogue between various groups with an interest in nurturing ethical research and complementary regulatory practices. In particular, we hoped it might offer some international support to researchers seeking to influence future regulatory practices in their own institutions and jurisdictions.

The Declaration was designed to reflect the concerns of signatories without over-generalizing from the negative experiences of a particular jurisdiction or institution at a specific time. While constructed to be aspirational, the Declaration sought to avoid excessively burdensome commitments that might be difficult to sustain. The Declaration articulated many of the themes with which social scientists have struggled including: 'Encouraging a variety of means of furthering ethical conduct involving a broad range of parties' (Article 4); 'Encouraging regulators and administrators to nurture a regulatory culture that grants researchers the same level of respect that researchers should offer research participants' (Article 5); and the need to 'Commit to ongoing critical analysis of new and revised ethics regulations and regimes' (Article 6). Noting a suppression of the ethical imagination by a combination of principlism and conservative review committees, Gontcharov (2013) generously described the Declaration as offering the 'possibility for restarting the conversation on the principles of ethical governance in academic research' (p. 156).

Conclusion

Since 1945 key efforts to formulate principles for ethical research have been reactive, variously motivated responses to questionable practice. Most of the dubious behaviour that has sparked significant response has occurred in biomedical settings. This does not mean social sciences were immune to wrongdoing. Instead, the miserable physical and social face of biomedical misconduct has ensured problems in that area take high relief. In response, scientists and government agencies working nationally and internationally have developed codes and principles for biomedical application which have tended to coalesce around the key principles of respect for persons, beneficence and justice, and commonly include explicit consideration of matters such as informed consent and confidentiality. Most of these codes have been firmly based in a Western tradition and, given their aim of universalizing that paradigm, have invoked deep suspicion in other communities (Tangwa, 2004). The more recent Declaration of Helsinki, CIOMS and UNESCO Declaration have started to tackle the difficulties of applying universal principles in a range of countries. However, the charge of 'ethical imperialism' has not been limited to geography. Despite the particular disciplinary contexts from which they emerged, bioethical principles and, significantly, their associated practices, have been applied not only to biomedical research but have also been translated into social science research practice – with varying degrees of scrutiny and success. These are matters I take up in the next chapter.

FOUR

Regulating Ethics

In Chapter 3 I discussed the development after 1945 of key biomedical ethical codes and principles. This longer chapter changes scale to describe the origins and character of more specific ethical regulation of social sciences in the developed countries of North America, northern Europe and Australasia, and the more recent spread of bioethics-focused review to the global South, largely (but not exclusively) comprising the low- to middle-income countries of Latin America, Africa and Asia. For many countries, there is little to say about research ethics governance in the social sciences. This may be because social science has not yet established a professional footprint (UNESCO and International Social Science Council, 2010). In a diminishing number of cases, there are no national guidelines, or any local committees that exist that do not regulate the social sciences. In some cases, material developed in local languages remains largely invisible to an international audience. In other jurisdictions, there is no published information or evaluation, and certainly little available on the internet. There is some irony where a research community has failed to analyse the nature or impact of the governance of research in its own country. Perhaps this is seen as relatively unimportant or even a little self-absorbed. However, where regulation has been more pervasive, there is evidence that it has distorted the research programmes of many disciplines.

Of course, this chapter reveals diverse regulatory experiences between jurisdictions. Nevertheless, it is possible to point to some recurrent themes. First, many early regulatory initiatives were responses to crises, often caused by biomedical research malpractices. More recently, ethical regulation has emerged as part of broader social trends in the global North towards individual and organizational 'accountability', public scepticism towards science and authority, and institutional risk-driven anxieties. Second, in the majority of the countries I discuss, ethical review strategies based on biomedical experience are being applied to the work of social scientists. This has been achieved either via national legislation or through the actions of major funding agencies extending irresistible conditions to their support for research. Cynically interpreted, funding support has been used coercively by biomedical agencies to apply their views of the world to other disciplines. Third, approaches to ethical regulation appear to have been dominated by either a 'top-down' (the United States, Canada, Australia, Norway, Nigeria, Uganda, Brazil, Qatar) or a 'bottom-up' or 'middle-out' (the United Kingdom, New Zealand, South Africa, Denmark) character. In the former, national strategies set out legislatively or by major government bodies and research organizations are common. In the latter, professional organizations and individual institutions (and even individual researchers in the case of Denmark) drive a multiplicity of ethical approaches. However, developments in South Africa and the United Kingdom suggest a shift away from 'bottom-up' arrangements to more uniform national regulation. The future may hold even more broadly applied regulation with the emergence of new supranational approaches (for example, the European Research Area) and as nations at the vanguard of ethical regulation establish international 'benchmarks' and export training packages for ethical research conduct, through the deployment of discourses of aid and development. Finally, debates about research ethics largely: are produced and conducted in the global North; are based on universalist claims about ethics and the primacy of the individual; exclude other belief systems; and erase colonial and neo-colonial experiences.[1]

United States

Following the Second World War, the scope and scale of biomedical research expanded enormously. Heeding the issues that had emerged from Nuremberg, many United States biomedical organizations established voluntary ethics review mechanisms. Despite such provisions, various scandals (see Chapter 3) led the United States Public Health Service (USPHS) to develop a policy in 1966 to protect human research participants. The policy embraced social and behavioural work. Its requirement that 'every research institution receiving grant dollars from the agency establish a committee to review Federally funded research projects for conformance with human participant protection' (Citro et al., 2003, p. 61) was to become a foundation-stone for United States ethics review structures.

Confusion about, and variable application of, the USPHS policy led the Department of Health, Education and Welfare (DHEW) to publish *The Institutional Guide to DHEW Policy on Protection of Human Subjects* (the 'Yellow Book'). This 1971 Guide provided help to review committees by defining risk and setting out issues of harm – including those that might be associated with common social science research methods. In 1974 DHEW stated that it would not support any research unless first reviewed and approved by an Institutional Review Board (IRB).

In the meantime, public outrage about unethical studies such as those at Willowbrook and Tuskegee (see Chapter 3) sparked other action, including passage of the National Research Act in 1974. The Act approved DHEW's new IRB regulations and established the National Commission for the Protection of Human Subjects of Biomedical and Behavioral Research (NCPHSBBR). Among other things, the Commission was charged with reviewing the IRB system.

The Commission identified a variety of other cases in which vulnerable 'subjects' had been subjected to medical risks without consent or the permission of next of kin. The problems observed in the social and behavioural sciences were not of great magnitude, but they were held to be similar in character to those of the biomedical sciences. Not surprisingly then, the Commission's 1978 report supported the IRB system and 'recommended that DHEW should issue regulations applicable to all research over which it had regulatory authority ...' (Citro et al., 2003, p. 64) – a recommendation that was to be another key element of regulations in the United States (Heath, 2001).

The Commission also set forth principles and recommendations concerning human research in the so-called Belmont Report (National Commission for the Protection of Human Subjects of Biomedical and Behavioral Research, 1979). As I noted in Chapter 3, these were: respect for the autonomy of persons and for the well-being of non-autonomous persons, beneficence and justice. In addition to these general principles, the Commission identified key areas of sensitive research – research on prisoners, pregnant women and foetuses, and children. The Belmont principles were translated into six norms of scientific behaviour: valid informed consent; competence of researcher; identification of consequences; equitable and appropriate selection of 'subjects'; voluntary informed consent; and compensation for injury.

On the basis of the National Commission's recommendations, in 1979 DHEW set out guidelines using the National Institutes of Health (NIH) Office for Protection from Research Risks (OPRR). These guidelines required that all research conducted in institutions receiving DHEW funds be exposed to an IRB review comparable with that applying to biomedical work – irrespective of the funding source for an individual piece of research. Social scientists were outraged. They had not been consulted in this matter and variously believed the new provisions were overbearing, ill-considered and violated constitutional rights. As Oakes (2002, p. 448) noted, 'From the very beginning, social scientists were required to comply with rules they were essentially excluded from developing'. A year later, DHEW became DHHS (Department of Health and Human Services) and in 1981 released major revisions to its 'human subjects' regulations that 'permitted exemptions and expedited review procedures that satisfied many social and behavioral science researchers' (Oakes, 2002, p. 448).

During the 1980s, the DHHS regulations presented problems to social scientists because of their biomedical focus, but IRBs tended to be sufficiently flexible to accommodate the conduct of social and behavioural work. The 1980s also saw a series of policy proposals sparked by a recommendation of the 1981 'President's Commission for the Study of Ethical Problems in Medicine and Biomedical and Behavioral Research' that a Common Rule for all Federally funded research involving human participants be developed. Ten years of work towards this end culminated in June 1991, when a common Federal policy (Title 45 of the Code of Federal Regulations Part 46 (45 CFR 46), Subpart A), known as 'the Common Rule', was published. The policy converted the Belmont principles into regulations for human research funded by DHHS and also provided the regulatory procedures for 'all research involving human subjects conducted, supported or otherwise subject to regulation by any Federal Department or Agency which takes appropriate administrative action to make the policy applicable to such research' (45 CFR 46.101 (a)). The Common Rule was followed by 18 Federal agencies, including the National Science Foundation, the Department of Education and the Department of Agriculture but, interestingly, not the National Endowment for the Humanities, whose work focused on preserving and providing access to cultural resources. The Common Rule prescribed a variety of institutional structures, review mechanisms and policies for research involving human 'subjects'. Research institutions had to comply with the Common Rule for all research in order to remain eligible for funding provided by those government agencies subscribing to the Rule.

Although the regulations applied to activities sponsored by a range of Federal organizations, they were written primarily with biomedical research in mind, on the basis that the greatest risk to human 'subjects' was typically associated with work of that type.

> There was some debate concerning whether to have a separate set of regulations for social and behavioral research. The authorities decided to have just one set of regulations. To accommodate social and behavioral research (which is often but not always of minimal risk) under the same regulations, IRBs were given the prerogative of formally exempting some research from the regulations, of conducting expedited review, and of waiving the requirement of signed consent under certain reasonable circumstances. However, these provisions are not particularly easy to interpret. (Sieber et al., 2002, p. 1)

In the meantime, the regulatory context of research changed to the extent that IRBs seemed less than willing to exercise their prerogatives of exemption and expedited review. Concerns about institutional risk, at least in part, underpinned apprehension about ethical process and conduct. For instance, charged with ensuring that research-related risks to participants were minimized, DHHS offices such as the Office for Human Research Protections (OHRP) have suspended Federally funded research in institutions that have failed to comply with Federal regulations. The effect has been to raise levels of institutional anxiety and internal regulation and to encourage organizations dependent on Federal funding to follow the 'letter of the law', rather than the spirit of the Belmont principles. These same outcomes have also been promoted by threatened or commenced legal suits against researchers accused of ethical misconduct. It seems likely too that problems of 'heavy IRB workloads, lack of expertise on IRBs to review complex research ... and lack of adequate facilities and support for IRB operations' (Citro et al., 2003, p. 73) have conspired to encourage simple rule-following strategies on IRBs rather than complex, ethical reflection.

By the early 2000s, roughly three-quarters of the largest United States research institutions – notably research universities and their hospital affiliates – had voluntarily expanded the IRB system to embrace *all* research involving human 'subjects' (American Association of University Professors, 2001) and many IRBs seemed to regard all social research as if it posed the sorts of physical risks sometimes associated with biomedical research practices.

> They interpret the Common Rule as literally as possible, ignoring any cultural or procedural inappropriateness this may entail, and generating an extensive paper trail to prove that they have done what they construe the Common Rule to require. Inappropriate demands are placed on researchers and subjects that do not address what should be the focus of the enterprise: the protection of participants in research activities. Some results of this environment of fear include (a) a self-defeating quest for entirely risk-free research in a world where nothing is risk-free, (b) long delays in approving protocols, and (c) extremely bureaucratic interpretations of the requirement for informed consent. (Sieber et al., 2002, p. 3)

Such interpretations and consequences of the Common Rule together with the associated 'creep' of institutional ethical review have been the subject of a good deal of critical and somewhat resentful attention in recent years (see, for example, Gunsalus et al., 2007; Schrag, 2010a; Sieber et al., 2002; Social Sciences and Humanities Research Ethics Special Working Committee, 2004). In general, social and behavioural scientists are disenchanted with Federal regulations that entail scrutiny of proposed research. Schrag (2010a), for example, concluded that regulations had been extended to cover social sciences on the basis of 'ignorance and power' (p. 9), 'haste and disrespect' (p. 192). Federal officials, he observed, had little understanding of the practices of social sciences and demonstrated scant interest in rectifying the situation. Social sciences had rarely been invited to contribute to the development of regulations that covered their work. Instead, they were 'left howling outside the door' (p. 4). Where they were invited into the room, their input was ignored or misrepresented, their complaints 'papered over' (p. 75). The pattern has been for jurisdiction to be extended without consultation, and for disciplines to be caught off-guard by a metanarrative of ethics governance that they did not understand and by regulations couched in language that initially appeared not to include them.

A Panel on Institutional Review Boards, Surveys and Social Science Research was charged in 2001 by different standing committees of the National Academies' National Research Council to examine the impact of the 'structure, function, and performance of the IRB system' on social and behavioural research and to 'recommend research and practice to improve the system' (Citro et al., 2003, p. 11). The Panel released its report and recommendations in 2003. It acknowledged the key role of IRBs but expressed concern about excessive interference in research designs, unnecessary delays, an overemphasis on formal rather than substantive informed consent procedures, and a lack of attention to the ways new information technologies might challenge the confidentiality of research data.

Similarly, Charles Bosk and Raymond De Vries (2004) argued social scientists in the United States needed to lobby for change in existing review arrangements. They pointed out that while current processes might cause more harm than benefit, it would be hard to imagine turning back the clock. Consequently social scientists should:

> find ways to work within the system at the same time that they work to change it ... Given this, a spirit of cooperation rather than belligerence seems the appropriate way to respond to our colleagues who have either volunteered or had their arms twisted to perform this onerous task. (p. 260)

In 2011, the Obama administration signalled its intention to revise the Common Rule, the first general revision since it came into force in 1981, but progress so far has been slow. The Presidential Commission for the Study of Bioethical Issues (2011b) called for new research regulation to be underpinned by ethical principles, a database of empirical research with which to assess the effectiveness of human 'subject' protections, and for ethics review pathways to be calibrated so that the level of scrutiny be commensurate to risk. The Commission also noted that United States agencies often insisted other countries met both the spirit and the letter of United States regulation instead of recognizing the existence of equivalent or even better protection. In 2014, the National Research Council called for a narrower focusing of research that should fall within the jurisdiction of IRB review. However, while changes seem likely, even Greg Koski the former Director of the OHRP was reported as being pessimistic they might prove sufficient to meet current challenges, as they were:

simply tinkering around the edges of a system that the bioethics community, the investigator community, and virtually every other community see as being somewhat dysfunctional and not achieving the goals for which it was originally intended. (Dahl, 2012)

Canada

Work towards the articulation of general ethical principles and the establishment of ethical review committees was under way in Canada through the 1970s. During that decade, the Medical Research Council developed research ethics guidelines. In 1978, a Consultative Group of the Canada Council released its own recommendations which were adopted by the Social Sciences and Humanities Research Council.

According to Adair (2001), Canadian initiatives have either been a reaction to developments in the United States, or they have emerged as a response to public scandal, associated largely with researchers' integrity. A key incident involved Concordia University engineering professor Valery Fabrikant. His complaints to his university and to the Natural Sciences and Engineering Research Council (NSERC) of demands from colleagues for undeserved coauthorships, and other improper scientific conduct went unanswered, so he took matters into his own hands. He murdered four of his colleagues in their offices one afternoon in 1992. As a consequence of this terrible episode, Canada's three key research councils released a 1994 Statement on Integrity in Research and Scholarship. Four years later, following other incidents involving academic dishonesty, the same group released the Tri-Council Policy Statement: Ethical Conduct for Research Involving Humans (Tri-Council, 1998). This policy, abbreviated as TCPS, described standards and procedures for research involving humans and made clear that research councils would provide funding only to those individuals and institutions able to 'certify compliance with this policy regarding research involving human subjects' (p. 1.1).

Canadian ethics review 'involves the application of national norms by multidisciplinary, independent local REBs' (Research Ethics Boards) to safeguard the ethical standards of research developed within their institutions (Tri-Council, 1998, Article 1.1). With few exceptions, all proposed research involving living human 'subjects' must be scrutinized prospectively by an REB. TCPS sought to avoid the imposition of one disciplinary perspective on others and to harmonize ethics review processes across Canada to the benefit of researchers, research 'subjects' and research ethics boards (Tri-Council, 1998, p. 1.2). In 2001, the research councils created the Interagency Advisory Panel on Research Ethics, known as PRE. In turn, PRE established the Social Sciences and Humanities Research Ethics Special Working Committee (SSHWC) to examine issues in TCPS of relevance to social science research. SSHWC released a substantial report on TCPS entitled *Giving Voice to the Spectrum* in 2004 (Social Sciences and Humanities Research Ethics Special Working Committee, Canada (SSHWC), 2004). The report's title reflected the Committee's concerns that Canadian granting agencies' regulatory structures – drawing largely from positivist, experimental and clinical approaches to research – did not respond well to the full range of research experiences and approaches embraced in social and behavioural research. The Committee noted a range of deleterious effects of the TCPS, which included: research students having to pay additional semesters' tuition fees as a result of lengthy ethics review procedures; ethics committees unfamiliar with social science research methods placing obstructions to good practice; and scholars changing research areas rather than engaging in futile disputes with REBs about (in)appropriate practices. The Committee concluded that substantial changes to the TCPS and ethics review were required so that a unified system could recognize the specific characteristics of social and behavioural research. The chair of the Committee later described 'a fourteen-year paradigmatic hiatus in the life of the *TCPS* which allowed ethics-review committees to look askance at qualitative research' (van den Hoonaard, 2011, p. 259). The activities of the PRE and its committees offered the research councils the opportunity to build policy on the basis of expert advice and community participation. However, Onyemelukwe and Downie (2011) argued that funders of researchers should not also be the regulators of research and that Canada deserved an independent body to develop research ethics policy (Experts Committee for Human Participant Protection in Canada, 2008).

In 2010, the research councils revised their policy (Tri-Council, 2010). At 200 pages, TCPS 2 was double the length of its predecessor. It was structured around respect for human dignity by accentuating respect for people, concern for welfare and justice. It drew on consultation with Canadian researchers, research ethics stakeholders and communities, and included chapters on qualitative research and research with Aboriginal communities. Some social scientists greeted TCPS 2 with cautious optimism. After all, TCPS 2 adopted the language of 'research participant' rather than 'human subject', and engaged with the ethics of online research and working with Indigenous communities. Ted Palys and John Lowman (2011) applauded its attention to qualitative research and emergent research designs, and to the relationship between law and ethics when tackling privacy and confidentiality, areas that they had found some REBs to have woefully misunderstood:

> Will this significant expansion help create the 'culture of ethics' to which the original authors of the TCPS aspired? Or will it further bureaucratize an already bureaucratically intensive process that, at its best, provides a light, selective, independent and thoughtful oversight – but at its worst is a vehicle for epistemological imperialism, liability management and institutional censorship? No doubt it will provide some of both ... (p. 9)

Clearly, in some respects, TCPS 2 was a marked improvement on its predecessor. As such, it offered hope to social scientists around the world that, where regulators allowed consultation with and showed a willingness to learn from social scientists, positive changes could be effected. To the extent that TCPS 2 represents better practice, its terms can be used to ratchet up similar provisions elsewhere when it comes to revising other regulations. Nevertheless, TCPS 2 certainly did not break the mould of regulation, some of its changes were symbolic rather than fundamental, and it may even have entrenched the excessive caution adopted by some Canadian REBs by only accommodating long-standing social science practices as allowable exceptions that needed to be justified in relation to a standard positivist model (Bell, under review; Gontcharov, under review; van den Hoonaard, 2011).

Australia

Don Chalmers (2004) noted that Australia has a comparatively good record in human research ethics, blemished only by a number of biomedical incidents in the post-1945 era (Australian Health Ethics Committee, 2002). Chalmers suggested that rather than scandal-driven change, it is arguably an age of scepticism, with its calls for accountability and transparent processes, that has underpinned shifts to increasingly formal ethical regulation in Australia.

For the most part, regulation has had a biomedical impetus, being led by the National Health and Medical Research Council (NHMRC). For instance, soon after the release of the Declaration of Helsinki, the NHMRC (National Health and Medical Research Council, Australia, 1966) promulgated its Statement on Human Experimentation and Supplementary Notes. This Statement, together with subsequent Supplementary Notes, became the standard for the institutional review of medical, and eventually social and behavioural, research. Revisions to the Statement extended the scope of review in 1976 to include experiments on human behaviour, but without commensurate amendments to the constitution of those groups involved in the review process.

In 1985, the NHMRC tied research funds to institutional compliance with the Statement, compelling universities and other organizations to establish ethics review committees. In some research institutions, the NHMRC's conditions and procedures for research scrutiny were also adopted as models for social and behavioural research and, by 1988–9, social and behavioural science projects made up one-fifth of the workload of institutional ethics committees (McNeill et al., 1990). Different institutions chose to deal with social science research in a variety of different ways (Dodds, 2000), meaning that some researchers faced little or no review and others confronted committees that regarded their work within a medical research paradigm.

A review of the ethics committee system in 1996 recommended the Statement be revised. The revision was led by the NHMRC and, late in the process, the Australian Research Council (ARC) and the nation's learned academies were asked to endorse it. The 1999 National Statement on Ethical Conduct in Research Involving Humans was 'recommended for use by any individual, institution or organization conducting research involving humans as an inclusive, reliable and informative guide to the ethical considerations to the review of that research' (National Health and Medical Research Council, Australia, 1999, p. 3). The National Statement drew heavily on the Belmont Report for its three ethical principles: respect for persons, beneficence and justice, but it did make one notable departure. The Belmont Report had given considerable significance to individual autonomy. In contrast, the Australian National Statement acknowledged that in many societies individuals' rights are 'complicated and constrained' (p. 3) by the authority of others. The 1999 Statement also required:

> all institutions or organizations that receive NHMRC funding for research to establish a Human Research Ethics Committee (HREC) and to subject *all* research involving humans, whether relating to health or not and whether funded by the NHMRC or not, to ethical review by that committee. The NHMRC expects this Statement to be used as the standard for that review. (National Health and Medical Research Council, Australia, 1999, p. 3; emphasis added)

The ARC followed suit. Many HRECs somewhat uncritically followed principles, initially associated with bioethics, relating to confidentiality, informed consent, harms and benefits, and relationships, to the extent that some common methodologies used in social science research were significantly restricted.

Aboriginal and Torres Strait Islander communities and researchers made it clear that there was a need for a separate but complementary set of guidelines covering Indigenous research. The Guidelines for Ethical Research in Australian Indigenous Studies (GERAIS) produced by the Australian Institute of Aboriginal and Torres Strait Islander Studies (2012) contain 14 principles that espouse the values of Indigenous rights, respect and recognition; negotiation, consultation, agreement and mutual understanding; participation, collaboration and partnership; benefits, outcomes and giving back – marking a significant move away from the traditional principles of medical ethics.

Today, Australia has a model of ethics review that lies between a completely legislated system and voluntary self-regulation. It features three tiers. At the first level, individuals are expected to behave ethically in their research relationships, being guided by principles such as respect, integrity and beneficence as set out in the National Statement. In the middle, lie the HRECs. The highest level is the Australian Health Ethics Committee (AHEC), a body established under the terms of the 1992 National Health and Medical Research Council Act and charged with overseeing the operation of every

HREC in Australia. The strong biomedical emphasis at this level is apparent, for while at least half of AHEC's membership must comprise specialists with biomedical backgrounds (such as experience in medical research, experience in nursing or allied health practices), only one specialist social scientist is required.

Over time, the way some HRECs interpreted the National Statement incensed social scientists. Bamber and Sappey (2007) suggested the requirement by some local committees that researchers of the workplace obtain written consent from various levels of management would have blocked the development of seminal studies in industrial sociology, leaving industrial sociologists as 'servants of power' (p. 34). Johnson (2004), an anthropologist, questioned the assumptions of a medical model that imagined the Australian researcher as always in a position of power in relation to research 'subjects', a position she argued was poorly theorized, naive, blind to gender and often contested by the women in New Caledonia with whom she worked.

In 2004, the NHMRC invited AHEC, the ARC and the Australian Vice-Chancellors' Committee to create a joint working party to revise the National Statement. For the first time, social scientists were included in the redrafting process from the beginning. The 2007 National Statement on Ethical Conduct in Human Research (National Health and Medical Research Council, Australia, 2007b) updated and extended the previous Statement and attempted to correct both some of the mistakes and some of the mistaken applications of the 1999 document. It provided some well-prepared social scientists with additional tools for challenging the decisions of those HRECs that had proved incapable of handling qualitative or emergent research designs. For example, committees that had insisted all researchers obtain signed consent forms found the new National Statement unsympathetic to their stance. The definition of research participant was narrowed and participants were only to be afforded protection from harm 'wherever it would be wrong not to do so' (p. 9). So, covert research was recognized as justified in some circumstances, which opened up the possibility of preserving traditional approaches in industrial sociology. Indeed, the new National Statement challenged the notion that an HREC might be the only way of undertaking research ethics review by enabling the adoption of review processes that were commensurate with risk and devolved to a point that could be more responsive to distinct disciplinary traditions and practices. The ability and willingness of institutions to take advantage of this has been uneven:

> If Australia diverged from the United States in avoiding scandal, it followed a remarkably similar path in extending a medical model of research ethics to non-medical research without considering what such a system might really need, without consultation, and with little commitment to negotiation. Like the United States, this established a pattern in Australia that has continued to dog the governance of research ethics. (Israel et al., under review)

While clearly a vast improvement for social scientists on the 1999 version, the document revealed its origins in the medical research tradition. It also extended the remit of the review process to all of humanities and the creative arts. Many social scientists remained unconvinced the National Statement might meet the needs of their disciplines. Anthony Langlois, a political scientist and head of his own institution's HREC, wrote of concerns the new arrangements would lead to:

> research findings being potentially skewed; research going underground or being undertaken in ways which diverge from what has been approved by committees; self-censorship; disengagement from institutional research governance procedures; the generation of risk for researchers who are operating outside institutional approvals because they feel they 'have to'; the construction of unnecessary prejudice against the legitimate aims of research ethics review procedures; and, finally, and most disturbingly, important and legitimate research not being undertaken. (2011, p. 141)

New Zealand

By the 1980s, social scientists in New Zealand faced growing examination of the ways in which their research was conducted, the result of pressure from external funding agencies (Roche and Mansvelt, 1996) and the fallout from medical scandals. Public revelations about experiments conducted on women at the National Women's Hospital in Auckland between 1966 and 1982 (Coney and Bunkle, 1987; McIndoe et al., 1984) prompted the Minister of Health to establish a Commission of Inquiry. The Cervical Cancer Inquiry, also known as the Cartwright Inquiry, completely changed management of research ethics (Tolich, 2001). The Inquiry recommended: all 'human subject' research be approved by an ethics committee comprising a balance of academics and lay people; 'subjects' be fully informed about the research and what it implies for them; and participants' written consent be obtained. Subsequent changes to strengthen and streamline research ethics governance reflected further medical misadventure, poor research ethics committee decision-making, and the need to facilitate clinical trials (Moore, 2011). Ethics review is only mandated by law for health and disability research, and research conducted in tertiary education, and review committees exist for each. Documents created by the National Ethics Advisory Committee (2012) in relation to observation-based research expected health researchers to meet the Belmont principles of respect for people, beneficence and non-maleficence, and justice, and consider the needs of integrity, conflict of interest, diversity and Māori. In each case, the focus was medical research and social scientists played little role in developing guidelines.

As a result, New Zealand has no national regulation or policy statement providing a research ethics framework for social science. University-based social scientists face institution-specific review, and government-based social science research is exempt from review. In universities, social scientists need to satisfy institutionally based ethical requirements determined by a university ethics committee as well as legislation such as the Privacy Act 1993, Health and Safety in Employment Act 1992, Human Rights Act 1993 and the Education Act 1989 (O'Brien, 2001). There has been no systematic attempt to harmonize policies between universities. However, guidelines adopted by different universities focus on principlism as well as the other matters addressed by the National Ethics Advisory Committee. Of course, researchers are also expected to uphold the ethical standards set down by relevant professional bodies and to abide by the laws of the country within which the research is undertaken. Attention is also given to obligations associated with the 1840 Treaty of Waitangi between the British Crown and the Māori people of Aotearoa/New Zealand.

In 2010, Māori members of research ethics committees (Hudson et al., 2010) drafted *Te Ara Tika*, Guidelines for Māori Research Ethics, for the Health Research Council of New Zealand. Māori committee members are charged with responsibility both for acting as ethical reviewers and for acting as guardians and advocates (*kaitiaki*) for Māori ethical concerns, ethical issues and interests. While drafted with the needs of health and disability research ethics in mind, the framework could be relevant to all research in New Zealand. However, the document has no formal standing with ethics committees or the Ministry of Health. *Te Ara Tika* calls for *tikanga Māori* (locally specific Māori protocols and practices) to encourage research that sustains relationships and preserves justice and equity. The authors argued this would be best achieved by research that is informed by *kaupapa Māori* which seeks 'to restructure power relationships to the point where partners can be autonomous and interact from this position rather than from one of subordination or dominance' (Bishop, 2008, p. 440). In *Te Ara Tika*, this is envisaged as research where Māori are significant participants, the research team is typically all Māori, Māori research methodologies are adopted where appropriate, and which produces Māori knowledge. They called for research that was informed by ideas of respectful conduct, where tangible outcomes are achieved for Māori communities, and those communities are able to assume power in the research relationship and responsibility for the outcomes of a project.

United Kingdom

British social scientists have been enmeshed in a tangled web of professional codes and patchy institutional requirements. Often, those research ethics governance frameworks that did exist were not designed to meet their needs, having been dominated since the 1960s by biomedical interests (Lewis et al., 2003). Even when applied to medical research, these review pathways were excessively complex and bureaucratic, disproportionate to risk, inconsistent and antagonistic to some high quality research (Academy of Medical Sciences, 2011).

One strand of the uncoordinated network for social science research ethics was provided by professional associations such as those associated with educational researchers, sociologists, psychologists and criminologists, all of which developed their own ethical guidelines or codes. In 2013, Emmerich found the 43 Learned Societies within the Academy of Social Sciences together had 17 current statements relating to research ethics. A second strand relating to health research was created for the National Health Service and run by the National Research Ethics Service and then the Health Research Authority. Medical research had been subject to review by committees since 1968, but a specialist committee for social sciences was established in 2009 to enable review of research in social care contexts. While several social researchers claimed these committees were hostile to the social sciences (Burr and Reynolds, 2010), others identified more thoughtful behaviour (Hedgecoe, 2008; Jennings, 2012). In a third strand, many British universities established codes of practice, set up ethics committees or offered ethical guidance (Tinker and Coomber, 2004).

Britain's leading social and economic research agency, the Economic and Social Research Council (ESRC), took up the challenge presented by a lack of national coordination and the possibility that inappropriate bioethical regulations would be imposed across the research spectrum. The suitability of the ESRC to act an arbiter of ethics had been tarnished by apparent willingness to accept funding from the British Foreign Office to investigate Islamic fundamentalism as part of the response to terrorism (Attwood, 2007). Nevertheless, the ESRC shifted the locus of power in research ethics governance 'from being endogenously controlled by communities of disciplinary practice to exogenously determined regimes of control in the form of new ethical bureaucracies' (Boden et al., 2009, p. 736).

The ESRC released its Research Ethics Framework (REF) in 2005 (Economic and Social Research Council, 2005), subsequently replaced by the Framework for Research Ethics (FRE) in 2010, revised in 2012 (Economic and Social Research Council, 2010). The frameworks set out the ESRC's expectations for work it was asked to fund, and identified good practice for all social science research. The REF claimed to: preserve researchers' disciplinary affiliations; emphasize their ethical reflexivity and responsibilities; and seek a thoughtful, consistent structure for social science ethics scrutiny. However, the REF was criticized for being wrong both in principle and in practice by fashioning narrow and overly prescriptive requirements more concerned with institutional risk and reputation than with fostering an ethical research culture (Dingwall, 2012; Hammersley, 2009; Roberts and Lewis, 2009). The 2010 Framework extended the remit of research ethics committees and specified minimum requirements for their composition. It made review mandatory for those researchers seeking ESRC funding, removing exemption for those researchers engaging in arguably routine methods of research, and requiring full review for a broad range of 'sensitive topics' that included matters of gender and ethnicity or elite status, and for research occurring outside the United Kingdom or involving the internet or data sharing. Critics of the 2005 Framework found even less comfort in the new version, with Stanley and Wise (2010) describing the new document as 'bad in its entirety' (para. 1.4), based on an inadequate and, within its own terms, 'unethical' (para. 6.2) consultation process.

British research institutions responded to ESRC requirements and, by 2012, there had been a:

> revolution in ethics review in universities, with any university with a substantial research profile now having some sort of ethics review process. The quality of these reviews is likely to be patchy, but more problematically, there is no national system in place for evaluating the quality of consideration generated by such RECs. (Jennings, 2012, p. 94)

So, it remains difficult to have confidence that the same project would be treated consistently between different institutions. The ESRC seemed to lose interest in research ethics after the 2010 revision, but did cosponsor symposia in 2013 after which a working group circulated a set of generic principles, values and standards for social science research (Academy of Social Sciences Working Group, 2014).

Nordic Countries

A system of regional medical and health-related research ethics committees was established in Norway in 1985. Following the requirements of the Declaration of Helsinki, the remit of these committees was extended to include experimental psychology in the 1990s (Dalen, 2007). Other forms of social science research are not required to undergo review by a research ethics committee. The Norwegian approach is unusual in building an alternative structure to support ethical decision-making outside the biomedical realm. In 1990, the Norwegian Parliament approved the establishment of three national committees for research ethics, including the National Committee for Research Ethics in the Social Sciences and the Humanities (NESH). Each committee is expected to: 'provide competent advice in all fields of research; oversee and advise at the national level; provide advice to scientific communities, governmental authorities and the general public; and coordinate national activities and represent Norway in international fora' (National Committees for Research Ethics in Norway, 2005). NESH first drew up guidelines for the social sciences in 1993 and revised these at six-yearly intervals. The most recent version for cultural and social studies was published in 2006 (National Committees for Research Ethics in Norway, 2006). NESH acts as a 'national watchpost', informing and advising upon research ethics policy. It also gives opinions on specific research projects, and offers ethical education services. NESH's committee reports for 2013 point to its advisory work on the use of deception, working with Australian Indigenous communities, and researching disasters such as the 2011 right-wing terrorist attacks. Hvinden, a professor at the Norwegian University of Science and Technology, concluded in 2002 that NESH had 'helped to sharpen scientists' awareness of ethical considerations, although thoughtlessness, mistakes and violations still occur' (p. 138, original in Norwegian). There have been some suggestions that a separate research ethics body with appropriate experience be established to deal with research in relation to indigenous Sami peoples (Bull, 2002).

Denmark has taken an unusual approach to social science research ethics, explicitly determining in the mid-1990s that social science research ethics committees were unnecessary. While regional and national Research Ethics Committees (RECs) exist, they focus on the conduct of biomedical research – broadly defined. In the 1990s, the Danish Social Sciences Council and the Danish Humanities Research Council established a working group to investigate the need for ethics review within the social sciences and humanities. The group determined there was no need for committees.

> In the working group there was clearly a worry that RECs would mean a requirement for informed consent, which would be difficult to obtain in some social science and psychology projects. It was further argued by some members of the group that (some kinds of) social science are very important in policy formation in a modern society, and that they should therefore not be too constrained by ethical demands. Some also claimed that the potential for harming research participants in the social sciences is much lower than in the health sciences. After the report from the working group the discussion about RECs outside the health area has died down in Denmark. (Holm, 2001, F-10)

In the early 2000s, humanities and social science researchers proposing research for Swedish Research Council funding were simply asked to 'consider whether their research entails any ethical aspects' (Swedish Research Council, 2005) and invited to consider Ethical Principles for Scientific Research in the Humanities and Social Sciences (Swedish Council for Research in the Humanities and Social Sciences (HSFR), 1990/1999). This document was replaced by the Swedish Research Council's Expert Group on Ethics' more generic Good Research Practice guide (2011). However, from 2004, legislation governing Ethical Review of Research Involving Humans was applied to all research fields in all institutions, regardless of funding source. Applications for ethical examination of research were considered by regional committees under the supervision of a central committee. A 2008 amendment sought to clarify and extend the ambit of the 2004 Act. The Swedish Research Council's Expert Group on Ethics (2011) interpreted the Act as requiring review for

> all research on humans which concerns sensitive data, statutory offences and information on judgements in criminal cases, involves physical encroachment on research subjects, the measurement of physical or psychological influence, as well as research that carries an obvious risk of harming subjects physically or psychologically (p. 119)

Where review is not mandatory but researchers require a review for other purposes (such as satisfying the requirements of funders or publishers), regional committees can provide an advisory statement.

CODEX (the research ethics website maintained by the Swedish Research Council) concluded that social science research 'often takes place without requirements for research ethics review and reflection being brought to the fore'. Given the legislation, it would not be surprising if social science research not involving sensitive data or obvious risks were not submitted for review, particularly – as one qualitative health researcher suggested – if research ethics boards, initially constituted to deal with health research, are struggling to deal with unfamiliar methodologies like grounded theory:

> Since the experience of research methods that derail from the mainstream is still limited for the ethical review boards it is evident that CGT [classic grounded theory] studies are difficult to assess from an ethical perspective ... What is most important for an ethics research application to get through is to write the information to the participants according to a preformed default standard. By doing that the project has tackled the fundamental challenge of satisfying the committee members' urge for a mainstream application. Something they recognize as right ... (Thulesius, 2010)

Of course, the implication from CODEX that social scientists in Sweden do not engage in ethical reflection is more worrying.

The Finnish National Advisory Board on Research Integrity (TENK) traces its history to 1991. It published ethical principles specifically for the social sciences and humanities in 2009. These principles envisaged a departure from default positions of medical research codes in a range of ways relating to confidentiality, informed consent and non-maleficence and there is some irony that many countries are more wed than Finland itself to using the Helsinki Declaration across all disciplines. The Board recommended a regional review structure but left it to universities to decide how to respond. By 2013, almost all tertiary and research institutions had committed to complying with the voluntary guidelines and were therefore reviewing social science proposals where the Board had deemed that it was warranted according to a checklist of risks.

Other parts of Europe

Outside the Nordic countries, surprisingly little is published on the regulation of social sciences research ethics in much of Continental Europe. Robert Dingwall (2012) briefly reviewed the growth of ethics regulations and pointed out that 'major players in social science like France, Germany and Italy have made no moves to adopt such controls' (p. 21). Dingwall suggested this reflected a range of factors: limited connection to United States research structures; underfunding of university and research systems; and post-Fascist and post-Communist distrust of any apparent restriction of freedom of thought and expression. So the level and nature of review depends on the concerns of the particular research institution and professional association. However, the way such factors play out in each country is likely to be complicated. For example, the German Constitution specifically grants academic freedom (Art. 5, para. 3), understood as allowing researchers the right to study, conduct research freely, and publish the results of their work without prior approval. Yet, academic freedoms are not absolute and may be trumped by competing rights or statutory provisions for matters such as data protection. In fact, ethics committees do exist to review research supported by Federal grants. The professional associations for both psychology and sociology have their own ethics committees and, after the Fukushima nuclear disaster, an ethics committee for safe energy was established. The German Ethics Council, the Ethikrat, was established in 2008 and each year has a statutory remit to consider a small number of ethical, social, scientific, medical and legal questions in regards to research, especially in the life sciences, and their possible consequences and applications for individuals and society. In practice, most reports have been connected to biomedicine.

In The Netherlands, many hospitals set up medical ethics committees in the 1970s and 1980s. Following concerns about the ethics of medical research, a Central Committee on Human-Related Research was established in 1999 to oversee those committees. While the 1998 legislation governing ethics review appeared to be drafted with biomedical research in mind, it was sufficiently vague to be interpreted as incorporating all human research. As a result, various university faculties established their own review committees to cover social science research. However, Zwanikken and Oosterhoff (2011) reported that there were gaps in coverage: many of these committees did not review student research and medical research committees were not prepared to review research by Dutch researchers in developing countries.

Most countries of Eastern Europe and the Former Soviet Union (Kubar and Asatryan, 2007) started developing biomedical research ethics structures after 1990 as opportunities arose to join international research projects. However, the extension of national policy and local review processes to the social sciences is variable and difficult to track. In the three Baltic States, for example, Dranseika et al. (2011) noted that information on local committees was still 'scarce and sporadic' (p. 48). Nevertheless, they reported that there was no legal requirement for non-biomedical human studies to be reviewed, although review of sociological, anthropological or psychological research being undertaken within the healthcare context might have to occur. Instead, processes for dealing with social science research were determined at the level of the research institution or driven by funding bodies or research outlets.

After 1945, and particularly since the 1960s, various legal and institutional approaches to research ethics have been adopted within European nations. Different roots and historical backgrounds have promoted diversity in regulatory initiatives and the organizational arrangements and methods of operation associated with them (Institute of Science and Ethics, 2004). As European integration has proceeded, the European Commission has argued for greater consistency in regulatory approaches to research ethics. Directive 2001/20/EC required member states to establish national research ethics committees to review clinical drug trials according to internationally agreed principles. The 2005 Brussels Conference on Research Ethics Committees in Europe (European Commission, 2005) produced the EUREC Declaration as a basis for a European Network of Research Ethics Committees, and work commenced in 2011 on building such a network. The Network is intended to facilitate knowledge exchange, to conduct ethics-related research, to disseminate ethics teaching materials among members, and to be involved in discussion with the European Commission about the local implementation of directives (European Commission, 2005). Though an interesting development, the initiative has been dominated by biomedical interests.

For social scientists, one of the more promising supranational developments was RESPECT, a project of the European Commission's Information Society Technologies priority initiative conducted by the Institute for Employment Studies. RESPECT was to create a set of ethical and professional guidelines to serve as a voluntary code for socio-economic research across Europe and function as an aid to decision-making, rather than a prescriptive code. The guidelines, a blend of existing codes and European Union legal requirements, were founded on three principles: upholding scientific standards; compliance with the law; and avoidance of social and personal harm (Institute for Employment Studies, 2004). However, there is little evidence the RESPECT Code has influenced European or national approaches. For the time being, there exists an uneven range of separate and distinct nation-based approaches to research ethics governance in Europe, and initiatives such as those in the United Kingdom, Finland and Sweden appear to be uninformed by European developments. One exception has been the creation of a research ethics review process by multidisciplinary, multinational panels at the European level for European Research Council grants (Iphofen, under review).

Latin America and the Caribbean

The need to regulate research ethics in Latin America in the 1990s and 2000s was driven by a return to civilian government across the continent, regulations connected to Mercosur (the South American regional economic community), a growing capacity for research, and the uncovering of medical research scandals involving researchers from the United States experimenting on the poorest groups in low-income countries. Florencia Luna (2006) argued that Latin American bioethics was ill-prepared to respond to these issues with governments assuming a church-led 'homogeneity that does not exist, ignoring the reality of multiculturalism and moral and religious pluralism' (p. 10). In contrast, Luna identified in Argentina, Mexico, Chile and Brazil an alternative, secular view based on philosophy and, in particular, the principlism advocated by Beauchamp and Childress, and the Spanish bioethicist Diego Gracia (1995).

Brazil first issued guidelines for medical experimentation on human subjects in 1988. In 1996, the National Health Council in Brazil adopted Guidelines and Norms Regulating Research Involving Human Subjects (Conselho Nacional de Saúde, 1996, Resolution 196/96). The document extended its ambit to all research involving human participants, confirmed the importance of the ethical principles of autonomy, beneficence, non-maleficence, justice and equity, and led to a system that included a set of research ethics committees under a National Commission for Ethics in Research (CONEP) with consultative, deliberative, normative and education roles. By 2010, 596 committees had been registered with CONEP and about two-thirds of these reviewed projects in the social sciences (Hardy et al., 2010).

Brazilian authorities strongly supported the deployment of a universal set of research ethics standards for all human research. Indeed, the Declaracion de Cordoba, drafted by Latin American ethicists, advised countries to reject the 2008 revision of the Helsinki Declaration because of its retreat from universalism. In resisting the development of a 'double standard' between developing and developed nations, the Brazilian regulations enabled the colonization of social sciences research ethics by bioethics. Resolution 196/96 privileged one form of research – positivist and medical. It 'arbitrarily imposes a local, biomedical view on research practice, or on ethics in research practice, as if it were universal' (Oliveira, 2004, p. 33, original in Portuguese). In the words of Brazilian anthropologists, it made little distinction between the collection of myths and the collection of blood (Ramos, 2004) and risked promoting a bureaucratic process that rested on authoritarian foundations (Figueiredo, 2004). CONEP assumed a hierarchy of power and knowledge production between researcher and researched rejected by Brazilian critical scholars in the social sciences. Langdon and her colleagues responded: 'our method is not a matter of "application" of a series of procedures (as seems to be understood in many Committees), but it is above all the adoption of a reflective and critical stance with regard to [our] own research' (Langdon et al., 2008, p. 144, original in Portuguese).

The bureaucratic apparatus has been unable to grapple with the complexities of social research. For example, the 1996 Resolution gave 'special' status to Indigenous groups and required that all research involving them be reviewed by both CONEP and the National Indian Foundation (FUNAI). Resolution 304/2000 subsequently required research on Indigenous peoples 'serve the needs of the individuals or groups that are the subjects of study, or of similar societies, and/or the national society ...'. While acknowledging the importance of giving Indigenous people a voice in research governance (Santos, 2006), social scientists have found their work on health with Indigenous Brazilians 'hampered' by these resolutions which failed to provide appropriate protections while blocking entirely reasonable research proposals.

The Brazilian system has been resisted by psychologists (Trindade and Szymanski, 2008), anthropologists (Langdon et al., 2008) and other social scientists. In 2006, qualitative researchers met in Guaruja (Coimbra et al., 2007) and called for guidelines and review committees sensitive to the needs of different disciplines (Guerriero and Dallari, 2008). They complained their work was being reviewed by committees as if all research were synonymous with experimentation conducted with established sample frames and predetermined sample sizes. They were also concerned Western conceptions of individual autonomy were displacing any sense of the social. Although the 1996 Resolution of the National Health Council claimed 'to respect the cultural, social, moral, religious and ethical, as well as the habits and customs when research involves communities' (Conselho Nacional de Saúde, 1996, III.3 l), demands were being made by CONEP that completely misunderstood the local context (Bento et al., 2011). For example, one researcher had been asked by a committee to obtain signed informed consent from individual participants using documents translated into Xavánte, an indigenous language. The requirement compromised a strong tradition among the Xavánte of community decision-making through ritualized daily meetings, and ignored the lack of a standardized written form for their language, and a relatively high level of bilingualism among the population. The meeting in Guaruja called for national guidelines that dealt with the concerns of the social sciences and humanities, and with qualitative methodologies in particular.

In 2012, the National Health Council adopted Resolution 466/12 which provided new guidelines and rules for research involving humans, identifying the rights and responsibilities of the state, researchers and research participants. The Resolution pointed to the principles of autonomy, non-maleficence, beneficence, justice and equity, albeit 'among others' (s I). The 2012 Resolution envisages a special resolution for social sciences and humanities but, until that is published, Resolution 466/12 as it currently stands covers those fields (Guerriero, under review). While some of its provisions may be more accommodating of qualitative research, the default position remains positivist. For example, the Resolution requires free and informed consent to be formalized in a Statement of Consent that must include details of reimbursement and an 'explicit guarantee of indemnity for any damage arising from the research' (IV.3 (h), original in Portuguese) with two documents to be 'initialed on every page and signed at its end' by participants and researchers (IV.5 (d)). The Resolution goes on to allow researchers to request a waiver of this requirement from CONEP and the research ethics committees (IV.8). The difficulty with requiring a waiver is that it portrays a large swathe of social science research as a departure from the norm, and requires researchers to request the waiver from a system that has already demonstrated little interest in their research methodologies. Not surprisingly, Resolution 466/12 was rejected by associations of Brazilian anthropologists, sociologists and political scientists who are working with CONEP towards a new draft for social scientists (Associação Nacional de Pós-Graduação e Pesquisa em Ciências Sociais, 2013).

Most other Latin American countries have national regulations covering clinical research. However, many Latin American and Caribbean countries do not have a comprehensive system of research ethics committees, and those that do may not have guidelines for overseeing and regulating research, relying on committees with overlapping jurisdictions and inconsistent approaches. Little has been published on whether or how these committees have had an impact on health research (Rivera and Ezcurra, 2001) and, even where this has happened as in Colombia, Peru, Mexico, El Salvador and Grenada, there is no mention of the social sciences. In the face of bureaucratic failure, Aultman suggests health researchers 'may ignore the review process and conduct research without proper review and oversight with little, if any, repercussion' (2013, p. 365). As a result, the Brazilian system has been viewed with favour by regulators in other parts of Latin America, with calls for national systems to be adopted in Argentina, Uruguay and Peru (for example, Barboza et al., 2010). Given the difficulties Brazilian social scientists have had, their colleagues in other parts of Latin America ought to be concerned.

Acknowledging the suffering and injustice faced by the poor in Latin America, Barchifontaine (2010) noted that it would be far less confronting to work with an imported notion of ethical reflection. However, he argued that the individualism, paternalism, ethical imperialism and ethical fundamentalism of dominant views in bioethics served Latin America badly, undermining more appropriate responses to ethical questions. While there is a possibility that the Brazilian or United States models may be introduced elsewhere, most social science research currently falls outside national regulation, and should Brazilian social scientists challenge the current orthodoxy, this may encourage further demands for more responsible and responsive regulation.

Very little has been written about research ethics in the Caribbean, though there are hints social scientists studying health issues may face review committees with little experience of non-biomedical research (Ministry of Health, Jamaica, 2012) and other social researchers proceed without formal review. For example, Pat Sikes (2013) drew on the experiences of education students enrolled in a British professional doctorate in Trinidad and Jamaica to conclude that 'formalised ethical review procedures are as much of a novelty in Caribbean universities and colleges as they were in the UK a decade earlier' (p. 526).

Africa

Most countries in Africa do not have national research ethics guidelines, though several have recently created review processes. The constitutions of countries such as Cameroon, Mozambique, South Africa and Tanzania require research participants provide informed consent to scientific experimentation, but overall governance has not kept pace with the growth in research activities. In the face of health research scandals, the World Health Organization Regional Committee for Africa (2001) drew attention to the inadequacy of research ethics review processes for health-related studies on the continent.

Kirigia and his colleagues argued that 'every country, whatever its level of economic development, should have a functional research ethics review system for protecting the dignity, integrity and health safety of all its citizens participating in research' (Kirigia et al., 2005). Two institutions established a committee at an early stage: the University of the Witwatersrand in South Africa in 1966 and the Medical Research Council in then Rhodesia in 1974. However, by 2003, only 18 out of 46 countries confirmed that they had a national research ethics committee to deal with health research while ten countries – and probably many more – still had none. Even where committees existed, this did not necessarily mean they could do the job expected of them (Tindana and Boateng, 2008). Nevertheless, a combination of pressures ranging from the requirements of international funding, collaborative partners, and African and international journal policies stimulated the establishment of more committees. By 2009, most institutions across sub-Saharan Africa had established research ethics committees, though flaws remained in membership, training, resourcing, and the consistency of decision-making processes and outcomes (Nyika et al., 2009). The University of Botswana drew on support from the Johns Hopkins–Fogarty African Bio-ethics Training Program to create its own research ethics review structures; however, these operate in a country that, despite its economic development and political stability, had:

> no national guidelines ... specifically pertaining to research ethics and no laws that regulate the operation of interest groups that may influence the conduct of research. The regulation of human subjects research is ... inadequately covered by the older law for anthropological research, though at the time of writing efforts are underway to draft a new law. There are no national training programs or accreditation processes for the constitution of IRBs. While human subjects oversight is provided by the Ministry of Health, there are no enforcement mechanisms to ensure adherence to those guidelines for ethical research. (Hyder et al., 2013, p. 12)

In 2011, the Mapping African Research Ethics Review and Drug Regulation Capacity (MARC) project identified 155 research ethics committees across the continent, with more committees per head of population in Southern and Anglophone Africa, and the strongest structures emerging in countries such as Botswana, Gambia, Ghana, Kenya, Malawi, Nigeria, South Africa, Tanzania, Uganda and Zimbabwe, and fewer in Central and Lusophone Africa (IJsselmuiden et al., 2012). However, deficiencies in the operation of the committee system remained. Kass et al. (2007) also pointed to the pressures on African research ethics committees that might be associated with widespread poverty and corruption.

Like in the rest of the continent, research ethics regulation in South Africa has been driven by bioethics. South Africa became one of the first countries to respond to Beecher and Pappworth's concerns about questionable biomedical research practices (see Chapter 3). In 1977, the Medical Research Council of South Africa produced its Guidelines on Ethics for Medical Research, the most recent edition of which was published in 2002. Moodley and Myer (2007) reported the ethics review system in South Africa was functioning reasonably, but found wide variation in capacity to conduct reviews in a timely and informed manner between committees, depending on their geographical location and institutional history. Membership was dominated by white males, scientists and clinicians, and failed to contain adequate representation from those communities from which participants might be drawn (Moodley and Rennie, 2011). As a result, committees might be seen as reinforcing 'the asymmetrical power relationship that already exists between predominantly white researchers and predominantly black participants' (Moodley and Myer, 2007).

Before 2004, there was clearly no statutory national requirement that social science research be subject to ethics review. However, nationally binding ethical guidelines for health research were published by the Department of Health in 2004 (Van Zijl et al., 2004) and s72(6)c of the 2004 Health Act implied that all research with humans fell within the Act's purview. Universities responded by expanding review to cover social sciences and humanities. Where this occurred, review processes were initially resisted by some researchers (Louw and Delport, 2006) and regarded negatively by others. For example, Mamotte and Wasenaar (2009) surveyed social scientists at one university and one research organization. In the former, 60 per cent of researchers reported only negative experiences of the research ethics committee, though the low response rate of 10.1 per cent from the combined sample means that any interpretation should be cautious. Researchers in the university were frustrated by the 'slowness of review, inadequate review, and problems that arose as a result of the centralization of review, the review of student research and researcher naivety about research ethics and ethics review' (Mamotte and Wasenaar, 2009, p. 74). The Health Act also established the National Health Research Ethics Council (NHREC) with responsibility for the oversight of local RECs and researchers.

Startlingly, given the depiction of Eurocentric research methodologies by many African scholars as neo-colonial, many of the guidelines used in Africa have been international documents, or only slightly modified versions of them. There is limited evidence that governance structures have sought to generate and disseminate understandings of ethical research conduct that are sensitive to local cultural, social and economic contexts, a need remarked upon by commentators on bioethics in Nigeria (Fadare and Porteri, 2010) and Cameroon (Andoh, 2011), and social research ethics in Botswana (Ntseane, 2009):

> Some researchers from developed countries, still operating with colonial tools of manipulation and power to access, control and own all types of data from the former colonies, write over, erase, and relegate to marginal and irrelevant the ethical guidelines from former colonized societies. Still others are compelled by research funding agencies ... to enter into contract agreements that privilege Euro-Western ethical frameworks. (Chilisa, 2009, p. 410)

Bagele Chilisa argued there were viable alternatives (Chilisa and Preece, 2005) and suggested an African research ethics could combine the African concepts of *Ma'at* and *Ubuntu* (Metz, 2013) which in the context of research would mean that scholarship should pursue truth and justice, act in harmony with local culture and, among other things, respect the importance of consensus, interconnectedness and community.

There is some recognition that international guidelines may not transplant well. Training and Resources in Research Ethics Evaluation (TRREE) for Africa acknowledged in its training materials that 'in some tribes in Tanzania such as the Maasai, Sukuma and Kurya, an unmarried girl, even if she is of the age of majority, is regarded as incapable of giving her consent. Equally in some of the Islamic communities an adult wife cannot give her consent without the permission of the husband' (Training and Resources in Research Ethics Evaluation, 2014, s. 2.2.6.1.2), but this only hints at the difficulties that might be faced by researchers seeking to work directly from international protocols. Returning to Sudan after graduating from a Fogarty-sponsored programme in Toronto, Hussein concluded that 'While the adoption of Canadian models is tempting because it would be easier, it does not necessarily fit within local contexts, especially when it comes to Islamic bioethics' (2008, p. 293).

Less surprisingly, almost no regulatory materials have considered the needs of researchers working outside the health field and, by and large, these do not exist or are assumed to be the same as those developed in the bioethics field. The 2007 Mozambique Science and Technology Ethics Code (Government of Mozambique, 2007) and the 2009 Senegal Code of Ethics for Health Research (Government of Senegal, 2009) apply to all types of research in those countries. Despite a call in 1996 for Botswana to develop a research ethics policy outside health and the work of the Botswana Educational Research Association in establishing its own code of ethics, nothing had emerged at a national level by 2006 (Mazonde and Msimanga-Ramatabele, 2006). In 2006, Nyamnjoh suggested 'Few Africans or Africanists have contributed to the ethical debate' (p. 5) around social science research. Since then, a small number of social scientists in Africa have invested considerable time in building a high-quality empirical base to support evidence-based practice in research ethics and I shall be returning to that work at various points through this book.

Asia

Given wide economic disparities, and the broad range of social, political and cultural traditions in Asia, it is hardly surprising that arrangements for research ethics governance also vary widely. In the Middle East, there is a clear division between the well-funded research and health structures of the Gulf countries and most of their Arab neighbours – Saudi Arabia, Qatar, Bahrain, Kuwait, the UAE and Jordan all have national research ethics guidelines governing biomedical research while Syria, Iraq, Oman, Palestine and Yemen have none (Alahmad et al., 2012). Qatar's Guidelines, Regulations and Policies for Research Involving Human Subjects were published by its

Supreme Council of Health (Qatar Supreme Council of Health, 2009). The Qatari policies established a set of rules and a review mechanism to cover all research but offered exemptions to some low-risk social science research. A 2010 law establishing Saudi Arabia's System of Ethics of Research on Living Subjects is one of the few documents to refer to respect for Islamic perspectives but it only did so at the level of a general statement (Art. 18). It defined research in terms of 'Systematic experimental survey that aims at achieving advancement of biosciences or enrichment or development of general Knowledge' by using, among other creatures, a human being (Art. 1). The law's ambit is unclear as, not surprisingly, much of social science would not choose to depict its work in this way.

Fifteen countries in the World Health Organization's Eastern Mediterranean region (the Maghreb and Middle East) reported to Abou-Zeid et al. (2009) that they had national ethics committees, but many acknowledged they met infrequently, had members lacking formal ethics training, and had insufficient financial and administrative resources. Only four of these committees included a social scientist among their members. Eight committees pointed to the need to develop guidelines that were sensitive and relevant to the local context. Several committees reported that it was possible to conduct even medical research without any ethics approval. Earlier research in the same region had found that many health researchers engaged in qualitative research thought it unnecessary to gain ethical clearance for interviews, focus groups or questionnaires on the basis that they did not involve an intervention, an invasive procedure or the administration of drugs (Abdur Rab et al., 2008). Abou-Zeid et al. did not explore whether governance structures operated outside the health field. Hints from researchers' own publications suggest that research ethics policies did not, or were not being used to, cover social sciences in some jurisdictions. For example, one British researcher based at the University of Damascus was not directed to the apparently relevant Ministry of Higher Education guidelines: 'we were never referred to these or required by the university to adhere by them. Indeed, we only learned of their existence late on in our research' (Hett and Hett, 2013, pp. 502–503).

While the first review committee in Pakistan was established in 1987, committees remained rare until the National Bioethics Committee was created in 2004, and even after that local committees remained without registration, accreditation or regulating processes. As a result, in 2013, Shamim and Qureshi noted the majority of universities did not have 'a requirement for ethical clearance by their students or staff' (p. 466). Even if they did, however, Sheikh (2008) argued it would be difficult for researchers and research committees to pursue ethical conduct in a highly corrupt political culture where 'openness is discouraged, leading to mistrust in all spheres of the community' (p. 285). Reflecting on interview work by the University of the Punjab with lost, kidnapped and runaway children in 1999, Jabeen (2009) recalled that their consent was not sought as it 'never occurred to the research team that children should have a right to be asked and to say "No"' (p. 415).

India developed its research ethics policy in 1980 when the Indian Council of Medical Research (ICMR) published a Policy Statement on Ethical Considerations Involved in Research on Human Subjects. Twenty years later, the ICMR (2000) produced Ethical Guidelines for Biomedical Research on Human Subjects, subsequently revised in 2006 as Ethical Guidelines for Biomedical Research on Human Participants. These documents reflect the globalization of bioethics rather than the application of Indian philosophical traditions to new areas. Chattopadhyay (2011) dubbed this work as 'bio-bureaucracy' with its 'top-down approach, limited participation, and little, if any transparency' (p. 31).

A non-government organization, Centre for Enquiry into Health and Allied Themes (CEHAT), based in Mumbai created ad hoc ethics committees for two large social science projects it ran in the late 1990s. These committees later merged and evolved into an Institutional Ethics Committee with responsibilities across the research of the organization (Madhiwalla et al., 2005). While the number of ethics committees in India has increased, each one is owned by a particular institution, often following the ICMR Guidelines, but operating without any independent supervision of its activities. The advent of research ethics committees for health placed Indian social scientists under little pressure to formalize a review process or even defend their practices. Most social scientists, even those involved in health research, have escaped scrutiny by bioethics committees concerned largely with the high levels of risk more commonly associated with biomedical research, and Jesani and Barai-Jaitly (2005) reported finding 'almost no documentation of ethical dilemmas faced by social scientists in our country' when reviewing the field in the late 1990s.

The situation changed when research was published on sexual behaviour and HIV transmission in five villages in Uttaranchal. Based on interviews, surveys and discussions with villagers, the report outlined prostitution, incest and multiple sexual relations. The work was caught in a local political fight over statehood (Kapur, 2005) and triggered 'right-wing political mobilisation against the activist/researchers, vandalising of their offices, and imprisonment of the office bearers of the organisation for forty days on charges such as obscenity and pornography' (Jesani, 2004, p. 3). By then, the newly formed National Committee for Ethics in Social Science Research in Health (NCESSRH) (2000) had already created its Ethical Guidelines for Social Science Research in Health, with a view, among other things, towards improving the 'quality, legitimacy and credibility' (s.1.5.4) of social science research in health in an environment where ethics had barely entered social science curricula. The work was pitched as having immediate relevance to social scientists working in health, but as applicable to other areas of social science as well. Nevertheless, Jesani characterized the take up of formal review across the country by 2004 as 'very uneven and slow' (p. 4).

In Central, East and South-East Asia, as well as in the Pacific, most countries do not have national ethical review guidelines that cover the social sciences. The capacity and willingness to establish a coordinated approach differs according to a country's socio-political situation and research environment. A UNESCO project on bioethics in Central Asia reported in 2006 'insufficient educational programmes at undergraduate and postgraduate levels, no experience in ethical review of research projects, no regulations, and no financing among other issues' (Sarvmsakova, 2009, p. 169). Some smaller countries, including Cambodia, Fiji and Laos, established research ethics committees specifically to meet the requirements of international health research funding bodies, and did so without a national policy, legal framework or dialogue among national stakeholders. In Laos, this remit was extended by Ministerial Decree to cover all health research, whatever the methodology. Another group, which includes Malaysia, established health research ethics guidelines that appear to cover at least some social science research, albeit only by explicitly exempting some forms of low-risk research from review (Medical Review and Ethics Committee, 2006). A group of larger countries, including China, Japan and Vietnam, have guidelines drawn up for different purposes created by competing government departments (World Health Organization, 2013). Hong Kong institutions remain outside the research governance structures of China and are free to adopt their own policies until 2047. While institutional oversight is becoming more overt, Jordan and Gray (2013) found over half of the academics surveyed in human research disciplines at the University of Hong Kong were, at best, only 'somewhat familiar' with the key research ethics principles for human research found in the documents outlined in Chapter 3. Macfarlane and Saitoh (2008) interviewed 13 academics in a Japanese research-intensive university and were told research ethics was a 'relatively new concept in Japan and that for many of them this was the first occasion they had been asked to think about and reflect on such matters' (p. 185).

In South Korea, guidelines followed the international embarrassment of the Hwang fabrication scandal in stem-cell research which shattered a broader 'culture of unethical behavior' (Kim and Park, 2013, p. 375). From 2007, institutions receiving government research funding were required to adhere, at least in principle, to the requirements of the Ministry of Science and Technology's Guides for Securing Research Ethics. Further government orders followed and most journals and professional associations either adopted or adapted existing professional codes (Lee, 2008, cited in Kim and Park, 2013).

One of the few countries in the region to regulate social science research ethics explicitly was Thailand. However, even there, there was little attempt to engage with the different methodologies employed by social scientists. In 2007, the Forum for Ethical Review Committees in Thailand (FERCIT) drafted a bill to cover human research, and some universities have established research ethics committees. The Office of the National Research Council of Thailand created a short set of national guidelines in 1998. In 2007, FERCIT drew on international codes as well as the 1998 work of the Canadian Tri-Council to produce guidelines for research on human subjects (Sueblinwong et al., 2007). These unequivocally incorporated the social sciences, though most of the document was concerned with health research and, even in the social sciences section (s.7.3), two of the ten subsections attended specifically to medical records and the need to provide for health care. Despite the FERCIT Guidelines, a small-scale study of ten Thai doctoral theses that employed qualitative methodologies found little evidence that researchers were engaging with ethical issues (Joungtrakul et al., 2011).

Globalization or localization?

The global export of principlism forms part of broader international flows of capital, students and academics, as well as knowledge and ideology. The impact of global capital has had a long-standing impact on research ethics governance. Some of the earliest medical research ethics committees around the world were established to allow medical researchers to compete for United States health research grants. United States regulators have used this funding as leverage to ensure that both the spirit and the letter of American legislation are followed. More recently, pharmaceutical companies have sought to open up new markets and take advantage of cheaper sites for multi-centre drug trials (Dallari, 2008). Multinational research teams have looked to those countries with lower risks of litigation, low labour costs, pharmacologically 'naive' participants (Macklin, 2004, p. 7), weak ethics review and the absence of other regulatory processes. As a result, research in low- and middle-income countries in Asia, Africa and Latin America has burgeoned. Latin America has been described as 'the El Dorado for research' (Aultman, 2013, p. 359). Changes in the law led to a dramatic increase in pharmaceutical sponsors of clinical trials in India – from 29 in 2005 to 350 in 2009 (Ravindran and Nikarge, 2010). As developing countries struggle to keep pace, the Helsinki and UNESCO Declarations have created regulatory templates for those without the infrastructure to create their own, and a range of capacity-building initiatives in research ethics have encouraged researchers in developing countries to follow these models.

In Africa, for example, funds and training programmes have been provided by, among others, the World Health Organization, the Fogarty International Center of the United States National Institutes of Health, the Pan African Bioethics Initiative and Training and Resources in Research Ethics Evaluation (TRREE) for Africa. In some initiatives, researchers and administrators are brought to designated centres in the global North as groups for specific courses or within faculty exchange programmes. In other cases, regional fora are run in developing countries, often with the help of local returnees from courses in the developed world. South Africa acts as host for two regional research ethics capacity-building programmes – the International Research Ethics Network for Southern Africa (IRENSA) and the South African Research Ethics Training Initiative (SARETI).

These initiatives are often portrayed as unproblematic. However, some commentators have questioned whether the systems being supported are sustainable and whether they rely too heavily on professionals from the global North, are well-designed or accurate, or are appropriate in this, or even any, setting (Eckstein, 2004). De Vries and Rott (2011) portrayed some courses as less of a dialogue and more like 'missionary work', a one-way flow of western ideas and influence. For example, several international organizations have supported the development of research ethics capacity in Latin America, these include the United States Naval Medical Research Center Detachment–Peru, which ran bioethics courses and conferences in Lima and two regional centres, drawing attendees from 12 Latin American countries, and facilitated enrolment in a basic Collaborative Institutional Training Initiative (CITI) course. Not all training is necessarily valuable and some programmes may undermine an attempt to take research ethics seriously in a range of disciplines. Some United-States-based social scientists have been scathing in their assessment of 'McEthics' (Freyd, 2011) material in CITI courses, particularly when the course strays from biomedical research paradigms.

Encouraging student and academic international mobility has become a part of many countries' national development plans, either as a way of enhancing local intellectual capital or asset stripping other nations. Student mobility has also become an important source of income for those countries and institutions seen as favoured providers of education. Having enrolled in international degree programmes, students need to meet the requirements of those courses, even if they and their lecturers and supervisors share a common critique of the regulations. For example, a group of international postgraduate education students studying at one institution in the United Kingdom argued the imposition of British-based review on international projects risked reproducing neo-colonial practices as a system that

> arises out of the culture and institutions of a former coloniser ... sets the standards for good research ... measures what is to be thought of as ethical research ... by implicitly comparing the ways in which research would be rigorously and ethically engaged with in a British context against the ways in which research

would be conducted in [other] contexts. ... In presenting ethical encounters as a universal standard, an ethics review procedure applied outside of its designated context leaves itself vulnerable to criticisms of cultural reduction and irrelevance. (Allen et al. 2009, pp. 145–146, quoted in Sikes, 2013)

The same processes can occur through the offshore delivery of programmes by universities from the global North (Sikes, 2013). Not every research student and academic returns from the research heartlands to the research peripheries of the world, but those that do may ease international transfer of a range of research and education policies (Hsiung, 2012; Shamim and Qureshi, 2013).

I am wary of appearing to suggest the heterogeneous experiences of a multitude of societies can be collapsed into entities such as 'Asia', 'Africa' or 'Latin America'. The pattern of regulation in each country often displays a mix of global and local influences. In some parts of the world, there is an emerging critique and a distrust of the motivation for some of the funding for capacity-building in research ethics. In India, for example, Chattopadhyay (2011) questioned the threat of a 'neocolonial moral imperialism' which would deliver an American or European 'mantra of "universal" ethical principles' (p. 32):

> it is unfair to use and impose, either consciously or inadvertently, the dominant sociocultural/moral constructs of white Western bioethics ... and to override the values and goals of non-Western cultures and societies ... exporting Western 'moral imperialism' is *unethical.* (p. 35)

Researchers who fail to comply with imported ethical requirements risk forfeiting funding, having their papers rejected by publishers or losing their jobs. In Pakistan, Qureshi (2010) noted how researchers from 'developing countries' were alienated by the universalist assumptions of Western norms and, 'penalised for being too parochial and not following the internationally agreed principles of ethical research practices' (p. 90). Canadian and Australian social scientists may be frustrated that research ethics policies in their countries are dominated by biomedical assumptions. However, at least they have a seat at the table. It may not be the best seat and it may not be the top table, but they are able to have some impact on regulation. Where regulations are imported, there is little chance of influencing their formation. Where research infrastructure is underdeveloped, imported codes may even ossify as regulatory authorities may have neither the will, resources nor mandate to modify requirements as problems emerge.

When researchers resist the roll-out of universal ethical norms, they may be seeking guidelines that display greater cultural sensitivity. As we saw, Brazilian anthropologists were particularly incensed that Resolution 196/96 made it hard to engage in ethical research with Indigenous peoples. For, the application of global principles for research ethics 'requires contextual knowledge, particularly in terms of culturally appropriate norms of behaviour in a given research context' (Shamim and Qureshi, 2013, p. 465). The establishment of local research ethics committees appears to offer the promise of applying these principles wisely, by taking advantage of local knowledge:

> Except it just ain't so. Despite responsive elements, the system as a whole combines the rigidity and formalism of conventional bureaucracy with a distinctly limited appreciation of due process ... (Burris, 2008, p. 67)

Instead, research ethics committees in different parts of the world have been repeatedly attacked precisely for their failure to engage with the local context. However, for many, opposition to universalist claims is not simply targeted at insensitivity in application but draws on critical ethical traditions to challenge the universal basis for principlism, and calls for a deeper understanding of and engagement with how different societies, cultures and peoples understand ethics, research and ethical research.

Conclusion

There has been considerable variation in how different countries regulate social science research ethics. As I suggested at the outset, however, several major themes emerge. In many jurisdictions, approaches derived from biomedical sciences have been applied, sometimes coercively and typically with state sanction, across broad swathes of research enterprise. Ethical authority has been drawn from political authority, economic authority or from that dubious authority derived from experience in those fields (notably biomedical research) with a record of significant and high-profile ethical misconduct. In many countries, social scientists are being required to follow regulatory practices developed in disciplines with the worst record of ethical conduct. Ironically, ethical authority is not drawn from moral expertise. For some this will come as no surprise but, as I signalled at the beginning of this book, for those social scientists seeking ways to make research practice respectful, just and beneficial, it points to the need to look beyond day-to-day conduct and to negotiate even more vigorously with those who have already staked claims to ethical authority.

Various commentators and social science groups have argued that it is becoming increasingly important for social scientists to engage with research ethics. First, the apparent shift in ethical regulation in some countries from 'bottom-up', discipline- and institutionally sensitive approaches, to 'top-down', more centralized approaches may make it more likely that social scientists are subjected to regulations drawn up by bodies attuned more to issues of biomedical and institutional risk than they are to the ethical concerns of social science research participants. Second, these same issues of ethical domination are increasingly apparent where supranational and international approaches to ethical regulation are being developed. Enforcing universalism risks creating a bureaucratic ethics distanced from local ethical traditions to the detriment of research ethics governance, ethical research conduct and local ethical scholarship.

Note

1 This chapter can be read in its entirety to provide an unusual insight into global patterns of regulation of research ethics for social scientists. However, you may prefer to read selectively depending on the regions that most interest you. I would welcome hearing more about countries that are poorly represented here.

FIVE

Informed Consent

Most guidelines for ethical practice require participants to agree to research before it commences. They typically require consent be both informed and voluntary. Their approaches to informed consent depend on conventional Western notions of autonomy and the primacy of the individual (see Chapter 2) and are a response to a history of research practices – largely in biomedical research – that have come under intense criticism over the past 35 years.

The call for informed consent may seem relatively straightforward, but some researchers clearly do not understand what it would mean for participants to provide informed consent, while many have found it extremely difficult to gain informed consent in practice and argue that in some situations the need for such consent has damaged their research and has not been in the best interest of participants or the wider community. Social scientists have also launched deeper critiques, questioning whether an emphasis on informed consent has meant individual autonomy has trumped the principles of beneficence and justice, as well as more collective and evolving notions of community engagement, trust and reciprocity. Similarly, commentators point to the failure of researchers to engage with communities to build more meaningful understandings of how a process of informed consent might operate (Molyneux et al., 2005; Singer et al., 2008).

In this chapter, I look at some basic issues associated with informed consent – comprehension, coercion and deception – and examine situations where the question of how or whether to gain informed consent has proved problematic.

What constitutes informed consent?

Informed consent implies two related activities: participants need first to comprehend and second to agree voluntarily to the nature of the research and their role within it.

Informed

In a highly influential analysis of informed consent, bioethicists Ruth Faden and Tom Beauchamp (1986) argued research participants need to understand, first, that they are authorizing someone else to involve them in research and, second, what they are authorizing. Most commentators have concentrated on the second issue. In most circumstances, researchers need to provide potential participants with information about the purpose, methods, demands, risks, inconveniences, discomforts and possible outcomes of the research, including whether and how results might be disseminated, and data reused.

For Faden and Beauchamp, research participants can make an informed decision only if they have substantial understanding – an adequate apprehension of all information that, in their view, is material or important to their decision to grant consent (see Table 5.1). A piece of information may be material to a decision even though it might not alter the final decision. Researchers might be able to determine what they consider material as well as the kinds of things most research participants would want to know. However, it may be difficult to predict what a particular participant might want to know. Faden and Beauchamp concluded researchers must invite participants to engage actively in the exchange of information. Researchers should '... ask questions, elicit the concerns and interests of the ... subject. And establish a climate that encourages the ... subject to ask questions' (p. 307).

Table 5.1 *Terms developed in Faden and Beauchamp's* A History and Theory of Informed Consent *(1986)*

Term	Definition
Substantial understanding	Someone has substantial understanding of an action if he or she has an adequate apprehension of all information that is *material* or important to a decision
Autonomous action	Acts committed intentionally, with understanding and without *controlling influences*
Informed consent	Acts of informed authorizing of a professional to involve the participant in research
Controlling influences	Influences that stop independent or self-directed actions – may result from *coercion* or *manipulation* by others or from psychiatric disorders
Coercion	One person's *controlling influence* over another by presenting an irresistible and credible threat of unwanted and avoidable harm
Manipulation	Intentional *controlling influence* of someone by non-coercively altering the actual choices available or non-persuasively altering the person's perceptions of these choices

Term	Definition
Material information	All information that, according to the participant, is germane to his or her decision whether to consent, including the nature of the action and the foreseeable consequences and outcomes of consenting or not consenting
Effective communication	Communication that leads to both parties having justified beliefs about the other's statements and intentions

In some cases, this may take considerable time and effort, as both researchers and participants struggle to deal with complex risks, uncertainties and problems of cultural and linguistic divides. In other situations it may be sufficient to provide potential participants with a list of their entitlements and a range of information they can choose to request. In many codes of research ethics, the default position has been for participants' agreement to take part to be recorded, by asking them to sign a form, return a survey or give consent on audio- or video-tape, though the method adopted may change according to the research.

Standard approaches to informed consent often require participants to have high levels of literacy and linguistic ability. While some people may have the competence to make independent decisions about involvement in a research project, this can be diminished if written information is unclear or constructed without sensitivity. Written consent forms can be difficult to follow and may not be helpful in guiding queries. These problems can be overcome. For example, investigators engaged in participatory research have involved participants in both the construction of information sheets and the brokering of access to peers. Other researchers have attempted to check whether potential participants understand that they are authorizing research as well as what that research might be.

However, there are limits to the degree to which a researcher can respond to tensions between the assumptions behind a Western model of informed consent and specific cultural practices. This may be because research participants have no experience on which to base a particular decision. For example, Robinson (2010) grappled with how to explain to a remote, pre-literate community in the Philippines her intention to disseminate information on the internet. Alternatively, it may be because participants have little experience of exercising or indeed knowledge of their rights (Castro and Bronfman, 1997). Participants might also not wish to hear what researchers believe is relevant. For example, action researchers investigating health service provision for Aymara women farmers in highland Bolivia encountered local aversion to risk identification which Aymara saw as 'calling evil': 'In Aymara culture, the speaker who names possible adversity may be suspected of willing it to happen' (Mulder et al., 2000, p. 105).

Particular difficulties arise if researchers and participants do not share common languages or cultures. The Kenya Medical Research Institute is a collaborative multidisciplinary research programme aimed at tackling ill health. Informed consent for various research projects is sought in local languages. However, the programme's Consent and Communication Committee identified two significant problems with its consent forms (Boga et al., 2011). First, they were poorly written, failing to understand the concerns of the local audience and missing key information generally required by regulators. Second, they were written in English and then translated into local languages, a process that did not always remain faithful to the intent of the original document. The Institute established locally relevant templates for consent forms which were written directly into local languages and concepts, and then checked for accuracy by community facilitators. The templates were accompanied by standard operating procedures for the broader process of obtaining consent.

In many circumstances, researchers are expected to negotiate consent from all relevant people, for all relevant matters and, possibly, at all relevant times. For example, a study of deviance among school students might require the consent of an educational authority, school head, parents and students. A study of an online discussion board might require the approval of members, as well as the list-owner or administrator, based on knowledge of the norms of a specific site and internet community. Quinnell (2010) avoided the need to negotiate with a list-owner by creating her own discussion boards specifically as a research tool and explaining the purpose of the website as participants arrived online. Several commentators criticize researchers who lurk in chatrooms, reading and copying exchanges on the site. In the case of research on online sexual activity, Whitty (2003) condemned lurking as 'peering in online bedroom windows' (p. 209). Instead of lurking, Lawson (2004) pointed to the need to negotiate, through a fluid interaction with participants, a wide range of matters, including the ways in which communicative text would be used, and whether participants would be identified as authors by screen name or real name. In considering how material published on the web might be handled, Helen Nissenbaum (2010) introduced the concept of 'contextual integrity' to describe the idea of using data available on the web but keeping its use within the ambit intended by its author.

Many other researchers have also argued that consent should not be limited to the beginning of the research project but, rather, should be dynamic and continuous. This point has been made particularly forcefully by anthropologists and allows a far more nuanced and responsive approach than the default of show, tell and sign. For example, Carolyn Ellis (2007) urged researchers to 'practice "process consent," checking at each stage to make sure participants still want to be part of their projects' (p. 23). Mulder et al. (2000) pointed to the difficulty of obtaining informed consent through Andean logic in Bolivia where community members prefer an answer of 'maybe' to 'yes' or 'no' since it always leaves open a range of options and the possibility of reconciling opposing positions. Vivien Rooney (2013) argued that in the case of longitudinal qualitative research on intimacy and the use of communication technology in Ireland, formal consent should only be documented at the end of the data-gathering period once it becomes clear exactly to what participants might be agreeing. Shamim and Qureshi (2013) reported the problems they had faced in Pakistan when they had attempted to reveal too much too quickly to potential participants who had a poor understanding of research but a fair appreciation of their limited ability to resist institutional or state power. They found a more gradual approach to introducing themselves to teachers reduced anxieties. Shamim and Qureshi argued that while the require-ment they obtain informed consent might be a universal principle, it needed to put into operation in a way that made sense locally.

In some cases, changes may occur during the research that call into question the continuing capacity of the participant to give consent – a significant prob-lem for researchers working with people suffering from degenerative diseases. Other changes may occur between fieldwork and publication that require the researcher to renegotiate the nature of the consent. As part of work on counter-exile violence by the South African state, I interviewed political exiles in the United Kingdom in the early 1990s, providing assurances that the names of interviewees would remain confidential. By the time of publication (Israel, 1999), the government had changed in South Africa, removing the most impor-tant reasons for desiring anonymity. In addition, many of the exiles had related their stories in other fora, making it more difficult to preserve anonymity. As a result, I contacted interviewees and obtained consent to reveal their names. Of course, any threat of a return to a more repressive regime would have war-ranted a swift re-evaluation of this decision.

Voluntary

Faden and Beauchamp (1986) depicted informed consent as a kind of autono-mous action, an act committed intentionally, with understanding and without controlling influences resulting either from coercion or manipulation by others or from psychiatric disorders. The Nuremberg Code (1947) discussed this in terms of 'voluntariness'.

On the basis of the definitions proposed by Faden and Beauchamp, it is unlikely anyone could offer informed consent in the face of coercion or, in many cases, manipulation. For these authors, coercion occurred when someone forced another to act to avoid the threat of harm. For example, the American Anthropological Association was deeply concerned that anthropologists (among other social scientists) operating in war zones in Iraq and Afghanistan while embedded in United States military units could not possibly take consent proffered by participants at face value. As one Marine commander concluded: 'It's a combat zone, and when you're in uniform you have all the coercive force of the U.S. government' (quoted in American Anthropological Association Commission on the Engagement of Anthropology with the US Security and Intelligence Communities, 2009, p. 50). Sudhir Venkatesh (2008) was informed by a gang leader there would be no difficulty interviewing people about the illicit jobs within a Chicago housing project: 'I'll make sure they cooperate with you. Don't worry, they won't say no' (p. 190).

Of course, in other contexts, some threats and even some punishments may be so unimportant that the person subject to them is still substantially free of controlling influences. However, researchers may find it difficult to assess whether potential participants do have freedom of action. Young people may view researchers as part of government and believe they will be punished if they refuse to take part despite emphatic denials from researchers. In some societies, once community leaders have agreed to research, it may be difficult for community members to refuse to take part. In other settings, participants may be so desperate that they invest more hope than can possibly be warranted in the research and the researcher. Nyambedha (2008) was concerned that villages in Western Kenya were only prepared to talk to him because they hoped he might sponsor AIDS orphans.

Kamuya et al. (2011) pointed out that social norms in some settings, while not being coercive, were likely to constrain voluntariness. They offered the example of a Kenyan mother who might be expected to defer to her husband when it came to giving permission for a child to take part in research. Katyal (2011) argued teachers in the collectivist, hierarchical, Confucian-heritage culture of Hong Kong were happy for principals to determine whether staff would take part in a research project, and that asking participants to sign informed consent forms was therefore superfluous. Marzano (2007) pointed out doctors in Italy controlled social researchers' access to hospitals and the conditions under which they might act. While Marzano was eventually expected to declare his professional identity to patients in a palliative care unit, he was not allowed to explain that he was engaged in ethnographic research on those dying from cancer. Marzano recognized that British review boards would not have accepted the conditions under which he was required to operate in his home country of Italy.

The problem of assessing participants' freedom of action also arises in the context of research on or in institutions, revealing how formal hierarchically offered consent may be mixed with passive resistance. For example, Rowe (2007) engaged in ethnography of decision-making and discretion in a British police service. He received formal permission from the Chief Constable and was then allocated to particular officers by the shift sergeant. Officers generally knew who he was and why he was there, but not always, and he was occasionally mistaken for a police officer by police and civilians. While the organization had consented, individual officers could make it difficult for him to undertake his research, though given the nature of their institution it might be difficult for them to object openly.

For Faden and Beauchamp, manipulation takes place when the actual choices available to a person are altered non-coercively or, alternatively, perceived choices are altered non-persuasively, without appeal to reason. In some cases, research participants may be able to offer informed consent despite experiencing manipulation by researchers. However, the line may be difficult to draw, particularly when the manipulation comes in the form of an inducement – an offer of a reward to participate (Largent et al., 2012; Singer et al., 2008). Fontes (1998) described two Brazilian research projects that focused on street children in Porto Alegre. One group of researchers concluded that offering money to participants would compromise the ability of the children to reach an autonomous decision while a second research team decided that it would be exploitative *not* to pay the children. Dickert and Grady (1999) argued research participants might be offered a just and fair wage comparable to the amount that they would receive for similar work elsewhere, although there could be difficulties extending this argument to children. However, Molyneux et al. (2009) were concerned that even small gifts might 'introduce new social dynamics and unexpected outcomes' (p. 319) in their work with low income households in Africa, and chose in Kenya to offer a gift of food that would cover the basic needs for all members of the household for one day, and in South Africa to provide periodic food parcels to households depending on the needs of participants. Contentiously, Scott (2008) suggested multiple ways that offers of ten and twenty dollars to recruit intravenous drug users through respondent-driven sampling might have 'became part of the landscape of hustles in Chicago's most impoverished neighbourhoods' (p. 50). In response to these types of concerns, Hammett and Sporton (2012) maintained it might be better in some situations to provide funding for community projects but that many decisions might become fraught, problematic and contested.

In some cultural contexts, offering money to interviewees may be seen as insulting and undermining the value a community has placed on a research project. Alaska Native elders told Mohatt and his colleagues (Mohatt and Thomas, 2006, p. 269) that 'their story was not for sale ... They said that the reason they were agreeing to be interviewed was that they could give their story to the community, to help the community'. Conversely, Christie et al. (2010) observed that knowledge exchange was a significant part of Yolŋu economy in the Northern Territory of Australia and that it would be 'unethical for university researchers to receive significant knowledge without payment' (p. 70).

Faden and Beauchamp suggested the autonomy of an individual might be compromised by unwelcome offers that were difficult to resist. Although this is a subjective standard depending on the circumstances and inclinations of potential participants, Faden and Beauchamp counselled researchers to restrict offers to those that were likely to be welcomed, but could also be easily resisted by participants if they wished. As a result, it might be more sensible to regard the issue of autonomy as relational rather than absolute. In sub-Saharan health research, Tangwa (2009) described the test more colourfully as: 'You know very well when you are throwing corn to feed the chicken and when you are throwing it as a bait to catch it and cut its throat' (p. S19). Joanou (2009) wrestled with the ethics of offering cameras to street children in Lima, Peru to allow them to take photographs of their lives. She was concerned the young people might find it difficult to reject access to the technology even if they would otherwise have refused consent.

Participants' autonomy may vary over short periods of time. Oransky et al. (2009) interviewed 100 ethnically diverse, impoverished, illicit drug users in New York and Hartford, Connecticut. Respondents reported that recruiting research participants through financial incentives might be 'potentially coercive during periods of intense craving' (p. 1653). However, they also considered it to be 'patronizing, offensive and misguided' if researchers sought to substitute payment with more restrictive alternatives. Faced with such an apparent paradox, Oransky et al. suggested researchers seek advice from people with experience in the particular environment.

In some disciplines, particularly psychology, several researchers have claimed the integrity of research design might have been compromised if participants were not misled in some way. Two significant experiments, one by Milgram (1974) in the 1960s and another by Zimbardo in the 1970s, have been especially controversial. In 1971, psychologist Philip Zimbardo created a mock prison at Stanford University and recruited 24 male student volunteers as guards and prisoners. The volunteers had answered an advertisement in a local student newspaper and completed informed consent forms 'indicating that some of their basic civil rights would have to be violated if they were selected for the prisoner role and that only minimally adequate diet and health care would be provided' (Zimbardo in Zimbardo et al., 1999, p. 6). The research into the effects of institutional settings was abandoned after six days when the guards subjected prisoners to physical and psychological abuse and many prisoners started to behave in pathological ways (Zimbardo, 1973). One psychologist who visited the experiment and whose intervention led to the end of the project described 'feeling sick to my stomach by the sight of these sad boys so totally dehumanized' (Maslach, in Zimbardo et al., 1999, p. 18).

Zimbardo acknowledged that the research had been 'unethical because people suffered and others were allowed to inflict pain and humiliation' (Zimbardo, in Zimbardo et al., 1999, p. 14) well beyond the point at which the experiment should have been called off. However, he also argued there was no deception because there had been consent. While there may have been informed consent at the beginning of the experiment, it is not obvious this consent continued throughout. Although five student prisoners were released before the end of the experiment, this occurred only after one had had 'an emotional breakdown', three had 'acted crazy' and another had broken out in a full body rash (Zimbardo et al., 1999). Others may have wanted to leave but there is some evidence they believed they could not. At one point, one prisoner told the others they would not be allowed to quit the experiment. Zimbardo described this as untrue, yet recognized that 'shock waves' from the prisoner's claim 'reverberated through all the prisoners' and substantially altered their subsequent behaviour (Zimbardo, in Zimbardo et al., 1999). I shall return to the matter of deception later in this chapter.

The practices of informed consent

Most social scientists accept that the process of informed consent forms a worthwhile part of how they negotiate their relationship with participants. However, many scholars have had difficulty when a standardized process has been imposed on all research interactions.

Is formal consent really needed?

The principles of informed consent have been adopted slowly and unevenly by different parts of the social sciences. For example, the American Anthropology Association only included the matter in its statement on ethics in 1998 and Fluehr-Lobban (2000) argued two years' later that formal informed consent was still not commonly being sought by anthropologists. Part of the resistance has been directed towards the method of obtaining informed consent proscribed by institutional ethics committees. This, some qualitative researchers have claimed, has been biased towards quantitative research (Bosk and De Vries, 2004; van den Hoonaard, 2011). In contrast, researchers using open, inductive, methodologies may not have an interview schedule, nor will it be immediately apparent what the risks of such research might be.

In many countries, codes of ethics have required researchers to obtain the informed and voluntary consent of all participants except in specific, defined circumstances. Many social scientists have been concerned that the principle has been adopted mechanically by research ethics governance structures, creating an artificial, culturally inappropriate and occasionally dangerous bureaucratic process (Israel, 2004b; Schrag, 2010a).

In Canada, Will van den Hoonaard (2001) attacked the way anthropological fieldwork had been distorted by the 'hard architecture' of ethics forms imposed by ethics committees.

> One can imagine many instances where the insistence on a signed consent form may be unwise or tactless. In studies of street-corner men, poachers, prostitutes, fishers, drug users, professional thieves, the homeless and, in general, those with socially defined problems, this would simply elicit an angry response. (p. 28)

Researchers have argued against consent forms on several grounds. Any requirement that participants sign their name has the potential to remove the protection of anonymity from incriminating statements. But for the signed consent form, no identifying details would have been recorded. Instead of protecting participants, such a requirement places them at greater risk (Social and Behavioral Sciences Working Group on Human Research Protections, 2004). Although the previous and current versions of the Canadian Tri-Council Policy Statement allow for oral consent (Tri-Council, 2010, Article 3.1.2), the Social Sciences and Humanities Research Ethics Special Working Committee (2004) identified a case where a research ethics committee tried to insist that a researcher undertaking fieldwork outside Canada obtained signed forms from participants who might be killed if their government discovered they had cooperated with the researcher. Will van den Hoonaard (2001) also noted that some Canadian researchers felt consent forms were obtrusive, turning an exchange based on trust into one of formality and mistrust. Criminologists in Australia reported similar misgivings (Israel, 2004b).

The form itself may compromise informed consent if written information is unclear or constructed without sensitivity. In the United States, the Committee on Assessing the System for Protecting Human Research Participants claimed 'consent forms have been hijacked as "disclosure documents" for the risk management purposes of research organizations' (Federman et al., 2002, p. 92). The use of standardized wording can affect the quality of the research data by reducing response rates because participants believe they are being tricked or because the form encourages them to overestimate the risks of potential harms. The chances of participants taking consent forms seriously can be diminished if the forms direct questions and concerns to administrators located in distant cities or countries.

When researchers exercise excessive caution in negotiating informed consent, this can be interpreted as meaning that researchers distrust participants' capacity to make their own decisions. Norwegian ethnographers, engaged in a cross-disciplinary observational study of patients and therapists in a psychiatric hospital, were required by their Regional Committee on Medical Research Ethics to offer a careful explanation of their study and obtain signatures from patients on two different forms. One exasperated participant responded 'You know, I'm not stupid, I understand the purpose of the study' (Oeye et al., 2007, p. 2302).

In discussions with the Aboriginal Research Ethics Initiative in Canada (2008), Tester indicated situations where Indigenous communities wanted nothing to do with the paperwork demanded by the research ethics governance processes of Canadian universities. He was told that 'If we know you and trust you, we will work with you. Signing a lot of paper that talks about things we might not understand or care about, won't change that' (p. 38). The Aboriginal Research Ethics Initiative concluded that:

> Respecting other ways of doing things can often lead to conflicts between what is required by officialdom and what best suits others. This experience points to the tendency of bureaucracies to build and grow in attempts to deal with every possible aspect of what should be considered. Forms, rules and regulations proliferate accordingly. Then one encounters a community or individuals that, perhaps recognizing a cultural habit that is not theirs, in a simple statement such as the one above, dispense with all of it. (2008, pp. 38–39)

In New Zealand, Helen Moewaka Barnes and her colleagues (2009) also noted that Māori researchers and participants saw written consent forms as something required by the Pākehā (non-Māori) bureaucracy rather than for the protection of participants. They portrayed forms as '"something we fill in for Pakeha" independent of any expectation that the participant has about the acceptability of the research process' (p. 446). In the United States, Joan LaFrance and Cheryl Crazy Bull (2009) observed drily that in Indian Country:

> Signing a paper may not be perceived as a trustworthy practice, especially in communities with a history of broken treaties and 'paper'-based promises. (p. 145)

Similar comments have been made in relation to the legacies of colonialism in other environments, including indigenous peoples in Peru (Creed-Kanashiro et al., 2005) and Botswana (Ntseane, 2009), as well as in contemporary authoritarian states such as Uzbekistan (Wall and Overton, 2006). In Zimbabwe, Muzvidziwa (2006) noted the dangers of using the form mandated by his New Zealand university which employed the term research 'informant', a highly charged word in post-liberation Zimbabwe and indeed many other places where hostility towards the state is accompanied by violence towards those who provide information to authorities.

Many agencies have explicitly recognized that written informed consent may not always be appropriate. The European Research Council's draft guidance for social science researchers acknowledged:

certain groups may be more vulnerable to harm from having information they provided be linked to them (illegal immigrants, victims of home violence, prostitutes, HIV-positive employees, etc). In these cases, standard procedures for obtaining written informed consent may be harmful to the subjects instead of offering protection and therefore need to be replaced ... (European Research Council, 2010, p. 10)

In the United States, the National Science Foundation (2008) noted that 'in most ethnographic projects a request for written, formal consent would seem suspicious, inappropriate, rude and even threatening'. Unfortunately, there are many examples where institutional review boards in the United States have followed the more traditional medically inspired forms favoured by the Office for Human Research Protections, resulting in gaps in research on the vulnerable and the powerful. The National Research Council has called for the Common Rule to be rewritten to remove any language that might suggest written consent is the 'preferred norm' (2014, Recommendation 4.2). Similar problems were documented leading up to the introduction of the 2007 National Statement among Australian Human Research Ethics Committees reviewing research to be conducted in Australia, Cambodia, India and Papua New Guinea (Czymoniewicz-Klippel et al., 2010; Israel, 2004b).

One might hope that more research ethics committees will follow researchers and no longer view informed consent rigidly. Fluehr-Lobban (2000) argued that anthropologists should not see informed consent in terms of forms but as offering an opportunity to initiate discussion with participants about the research. Responding to strong criticism of the role played by a US anthropologist in research carried out since the 1960s on the Yanomami tribe of Venezuela and Brazil, the American Anthropological Association (AAA) commissioned a Task Force to review, among other things, how anthropologists had negotiated informed consent with indigenous peoples (El Dorado Task Force, 2002). As part of this review, Watkins (2002) called for anthropologists involved in work with indigenous peoples and related communities to move from research simply done with the consent of research subjects towards mutually beneficial collaborative and participatory practices. The Task Force supported this argument, though the Task Force's report was subsequently rejected for other reasons by the AAA membership (Dreger, 2011).

Whose consent should be obtained?

It may be necessary to obtain the consent of organizations, groups or community elders as well as the individuals concerned. Health researchers working with economically disadvantaged communities in rural sub-Saharan Africa have discussed the importance of seeking approval from formal community leaders. For example, Tindana et al. (2006) explored the understanding of paramount chiefs, divisional chiefs and community members in one district of Northern Ghana. They described paramount chiefs as gatekeepers: 'Consent from the chiefs in this community can therefore be a form of visa acquisition for researchers to conduct research' (p. 3). Doumbo (2005) reported that the Malaria Research Centre at Bamako in Mali used a stepped approach to gain approval from village elders, heads of extended families, groups of mothers and only then sought consent from individual families who might participate in the study. A similar approach has been advocated in Botswana by Ntseane (2009) and in China, where in the field of healthcare Zhai (2011) advocated 'informed consent with the support and aid of the family or community' in those contexts where 'family and community ties and traditional cultures are very strong' (p. 35).

Unfortunately, seeking approval from local leaders may either reinforce local patterns of exclusion, silencing particular voices, or, conversely, place pressure on members of the community to follow the decision of their leaders to take part. In a characteristically thoughtful piece, Sassy Molyneux and her colleagues (Molyneux et al., 2005) explored perceptions of consent in a rural Kenyan community. While there was widespread agreement that chiefs and elders could give permission for a research project to be conducted within an area, community members reserved the right for households and individuals to make their own decisions. However, there were differences in opinions on the basis of gender, age, status and educational attainment, particularly in relation to who should make decisions about research involving children: 'Simple comments on cultural differences between populations, or descriptions of community views as homogeneous, closed and static mask a far more complex reality.' (p. 452).

Joshua Rosenthal (2006) analysed attempts to achieve prior informed consent by anthropologists for two landmark bioprospecting projects involving the commercial exploitation of the traditional knowledge of indigenous peoples. While bioprospecting and research are distinct endeavours, with the former often entailing levels of resources and benefits inconceivable to most social science projects, Rosenthal's assessment of why one agreement with 55 Aguaruna communities in Peru succeeded while the other with the Maya people in Chiapas, Mexico, failed, is useful. Rosenthal argued that one of the most significant problems for outside researchers was the absence in many indigenous societies of a 'clearly delineated governance hierarchy' that 'formally establishes for the outside world what level of an indigenous community or nation has the authority to give consent' (p. 121). Traditional governance and authority structures may have been destroyed by colonization and contemporary governance structures may be fluid, overlap or be contested either within the relevant groups or by local or national formal political structures. In Peru, established, credible and preexisting community organizations, drawing on traditional local consensus-building assemblies, were able to represent authoritatively local indigenous groups. In Mexico, those geographically dispersed central highland villages that supported the bioprospecting agreements were unable to defend their position in the face of a concerted political campaign by a non-representative, metropolitan-based indigenous NGO. Rosenthal's analysis was contested by a series of commentators, including Simonelli (2006) who challenged the elitism of attempting to negotiate informed consent for a pre-existing project rather than giving 'agency to those to be studied as part of an equal partnership' (p. 136).

The United Nations Declaration on the Rights of Indigenous Peoples (United Nations, 2007) affirms the belief that 'control by indigenous peoples over developments affecting them ... will enable them to maintain and strengthen their institutions, cultures and traditions' (p. 2). So, research councils in various countries have sought to recognize and protect the collective interests of indigenous communities while still protecting the autonomy of individuals. Their attempts to incorporate matters relating to indigenous peoples within their codes and guidelines forms part of a broader shift of emphasis from research *on* and *about* Aboriginal peoples to research *with*, or *by* and *for* Aboriginal peoples (Smith, 2001). For example, the revised Tri-Council Policy Statement acknowledges Aboriginal entities in Canada have emphasized 'collective rights, interests and responsibilities' (2010, p. 106). It therefore requires researchers to plan for and 'seek engagement with the relevant community' where 'research is likely to affect the welfare of an Aboriginal community, or communities' (Article 9.1, p. 110). Such engagement might involve review and approval of a proposal by community leadership. However, it might also be part of a broader collaborative and participatory approach involving structures and processes that lead to the establishment of an indigenous advisory group, or a formal research agreement so that indigenous community organizations act as a research partner and share in the leadership of a project (p. 108). Of course, authority structures governing indigenous peoples may be complex and it may therefore be necessary to work with overlapping territorial interests, a diversity of views and interests, or gatekeepers whose authority rests on custom rather than election or appointment.

The 2012 Australian Institute of Aboriginal and Torres Strait Islander Studies' Guidelines for Ethical Research in Australian Indigenous Studies (GERAIS) called for research with and about Indigenous peoples to be 'founded on a process of meaningful engagement and reciprocity between the researcher and Indigenous people' (p. 4) involving: free, prior and informed consent (Principle 6) – a formulation derived from developments relating to biodiversity and genetic resources; ongoing consultation and negotiation (Principle 7); and mutual understanding about the proposed research (Principle 8). In New Zealand, Treaty of Waitangi principles requiring respect for and protection of Māori individual and collective rights have been interpreted as granting Māori *iwi* (tribe or nation) and *hapu* (group of families with a common ancestor) authority over their peoples' involvement in all stages of a research project (Hudson and Russell, 2009). Māori members of ethics committees (Hudson et al., 2010) have developed their own codes of ethics as have Canadian First Nations and Inuit organizations (Assembly of First Nations, n.d.; Nickels et al., 2007; van den Scott, 2012), and the San of Southern Africa (Working Group of Indigenous Minorities in Southern Africa, n.d.).

A report on homelessness in Canada (Tester, 2006) was used by the Aboriginal Research Ethics Initiative (2008) as a case study of community-initiated and directed research. The participatory action project was initiated by Inuit from a community in Nunavut, supported by advisors drawn from the community, and endorsed by the local mayor and council. It used a survey designed in and with the community, and administered by local youth trained by the project as researchers.

Many researchers have relied on consent from institutional gatekeepers, often senior management, and have not gone to the same lengths to obtain informed consent from other people present at the research site, whether the organization is a school or the police. The National Advisory Board on Research Ethics in Finland (2009) suggested participation should be informed but need not be voluntary in some hierarchical organizations, and offered the examples of participant observation of military conscripts or the observation of work processes where researchers have obtained management permission.

Nancy Plankey-Videla (2012) obtained formal consent from several levels of management and the management-aligned union president to study the work-force in a Mexican garment factory. While she introduced herself to the two teams to which she was assigned, practically it was impossible to request approval from the 1,000 workers on the factory floor. In addition, she was aware that many workers who had agreed to her research were unlikely to be in a position to refuse. Other workplace ethnographers have found it difficult to deploy the language of informed consent in negotiating the different levels of gatekeeping within complex hierarchical organizations. This has led to pre-dictions that we might be witnessing the extinction of workplace studies in Australia (Bamber and Sappey, 2007). In response, Cordner and Thomson (2007) noted the 2007 National Statement did not offer non-participants a veto over research even if research ethics committees might have interpreted the 1999 Statement in that manner. Instead, those members of an organization not participating in research are entitled to 'the respect and protection that is due to them':

So if research in industrial sociology were to carry a risk of adverse effects ('harm') on say an employer because of his or her unfairness to employees, protection from this harm may well not be 'due' to him or her ... (p. 45)

Special procedures are often adopted when attempting to obtain consent or assent from children. The United Nations Convention on the Rights of the Child (1989) requires that the best interests of the child must be the primary consideration in all actions concerning children (Article 3). Under Article 12, children capable of forming their own views should have the right to express those views freely in all matters affecting them, due weight being given to their age and maturity. For the British Educational Research Association (2011), this meant 'Children should be facilitated to give fully informed consent' (p. 6). However, some educational researchers have been deeply reluctant to work in this way and have used adults as proxies for children's consent. As a result, Hart (1992) identified a spectrum of children's roles in decision-making. The scale ranged from manipulation, decoration and tokenism through to 'child-initiated, shared decisions with adults' and reflected not only the 'increasingly evolved capacities of children' but also the 'corresponding capabilities of adults towards encouraging the participation of children' (UNICEF Evaluation Office, 2002, p. 3).

Any understanding of the nature of children's autonomy must recognize the broader political, social and economic contexts within which decisions might take place. For example, some teachers' 'requests' may really be requirements, and consent within the classroom may therefore 'shade into coercion' (David et al., 2001, p. 351), with participation in research becoming simply more schoolwork. Gallagher et al. (2010) identified various difficulties in complying with standard ethics codes and ensuring children understood the nature of the research project. Among other issues, adults and children often had very different views of the meaning of language, and children may well lack interest in discussing methods and findings.

Several commentators and organizations have argued researchers must obtain parental consent for research on their children (Schenk and Williamson, 2005; Society for Research in Child Development, 2007). However, some researchers have challenged the need to obtain parental consent if children have already given consent (David et al., 2001). The American Sociological Association (1999) requires its members to obtain consent from both children and their guardians except where: the research imposes minimal risk on participants; the research could not be conducted if consent were to be required; and the consent of a parent 'is not a reasonable requirement to protect the child' (s. 12.04b) as in, for example, cases where the child has been abused or neglected. A similar exception is outlined in the Economic and Social Research Council (ESRC)'s Framework for Research Ethics (2010, p. 30). However, some research ethics committees have been less flexible and it can prove difficult to meet their requirements (Israel, 2004b).

Article 15 of the United Nations Convention recognizes children's right to freedom of association. In a more general context of research, monitoring and evaluation, UNICEF (UNICEF Evaluation Office, 2002, p. 2) suggested managers of their programmes could seek children's perspectives through community, regional, national and global fora. This may fit within a wider move to augment individual informed consent for adults with community advisory boards, composed of people who may share a common identity, ethnicity, history, language or culture with participants (Kamuya et al., 2013a). Such boards can liaise between researchers and participants, helping to develop materials and providing advice for the process of informed consent. When constituted as partners rather than advisors, these boards may identify issues and concerns generated by the community for response by the board in a manner mutually beneficial to both researchers and the community. While boards have been criticized for masking lack of real community involvement, some successes have been claimed in health research in low-income settings in both developed and developing countries ranging through Kenya, Peru, South Africa, Tanzania, Thailand, Uganda, the United States and Zimbabwe (Newman et al., 2011; Shubis et al., 2009). They have also been used to good effect in research in the United States on intimate partner violence (Cerulli, 2011). On the other hand, community advisory boards comprised of vulnerable groups might veto research on the grounds that it might compromise the safety of group members (DePalma, 2010).

Should some research occur without consent?

Some social scientists have maintained research should occur without consent where the research takes place in public space or concerns public officials, or the harm caused by lack of consent might be outweighed by the public benefit obtained.

There is heated debate over the degree to which deliberate manipulation of information – deception by lying, withholding information or misleading exaggeration – might be warranted in research. Deception is difficult to justify on deontological and rule-utilitarian grounds (see Chapter 2). Does potential benefit to many justify infractions of the rights of an individual participant? Act-utilitarians might argue an act of deception could only be justified if the balance of expected benefits over expected harms were greater than would be achieved without deception. However, such a case is extremely difficult to achieve. Nevertheless, deception has been justified on the pragmatic grounds that it enables researchers to control stimuli, study low-frequency events and gain information that might otherwise be unobtainable. James Korn (1997) identified a long history of the use of deception in social psychology in the United States, and concluded that social psychologists had not seen their use of deception as a serious matter for research participants, but simply as part of the typical experiences of everyday life.

However, the use of deception has been criticized on the basis that it harms participants, researchers, research professions and society overall (Hegtvedt, 2007). Korn charged psychologists with institutionalizing and legitimating the deception that 'permeates our culture' (p. 10). Indeed, the practice has been entirely rejected by experimental economists because it contaminates the subject pool (Hertwig and Ortmann, 2001), and this has led to some tension between economists and psychologists working in adjacent areas (Cook and Yamagishi, 2008).

Korn traced a decline in the use of deception by social psychologists from the 1980s onwards. However, Hertwig and Ortmann (2008) still found 53 per cent of articles published in the *Journal of Experimental Social Psychology* in 2002 had employed deception, and its use in marketing research also seems to have risen since the 1970s. Over 80 per cent of papers involving human studies published in three consumer and marketing research journals (2006–7) used deceptive practices. Smith et al. (2009) identified mood induction and anxiety-arousing manipulations, and the provision of false feedback in relation to levels of participant empathy.

The American Sociological Association (1999) only authorizes the use of deception in research where it can be justified in terms of the value of the research, and there is no equally effective alternative that does not use deception (s. 12.05a). The National Statement (National Health and Medical Research Council, 2007b) in Australia refers to a need to ensure deception does not increase the risk of harm, participants will be debriefed (see Chapter 7) and there is 'no known or likely reason for thinking that participants would not have consented if they had been fully aware of what the research involved' (p. 24). The Canadian Sociological Association (2012) has continued to recognize that researchers may have to deploy deception 'to penetrate "official," "on-stage," or "on-the-record" presentations of reality' (s. 22). Similarly, Australia's National Statement (2007b) explicitly accepts that limited disclosure in order to reveal illegal activity might be justified on the basis of a harm–benefit analysis.

Often unhelpfully conflated with deception, covert research has several alternative rationales. First, it has been justified on the basis of utilitarianism in limited circumstances where it is necessary for the research to remain secret in order to maintain access to the research setting, perhaps in the face of the desire of 'powerful or secretive interests' (British Sociological Association, 2002; Socio-Legal Studies Association, 2009) to block external scrutiny. Drawing on archived discussion group material, Brotsky assumed the online persona of a 20-year-old woman with eating disorders in order to engage with 23 pro-anorexia groups on 12 websites (Brotsky and Giles, 2007). She took part in password-protected, user-driven discussion fora, chatrooms, e-mail groups, blogs and one-to-one e-mail exchanges, justifying her covert activity on the grounds that 'pro-ana' communities had proved hostile to researchers and that the study might deliver benefits to the eating disorders clinical field. Francine van den Borne (2007) justified the use of covert researchers posing as male 'mystery clients' in order to discover how Malawian women who bartered sex with men for money, goods or social capital, were able to negotiate condom use.

Without covert research, Pearson (2009) argued, some aspects of society, including harms and injustices will remain 'hidden or misunderstood' (p. 252) and the images that powerful groups wish to project may go unchallenged. During her research on the illegal trade in human organs, Nancy Scheper-Hughes (2004) travelled incognito in Argentina 'to enter a locked state facility for the profoundly mentally retarded ... to investigate and ultimately to document allegations of tissue, blood, kidney and child theft from the neglected, emaciated, socially abandoned and unknown, so-called "no-name" inmates' (p. 32). While researching police torture and murder in Brazil, Huggins chose to portray her work at the beginning of each interview as a 'comparative study about policemen's lives in times of conflict and crisis' (Huggins and Glebbeek, 2003, p. 375). Accurate, but clearly not the whole story. Various researchers have defended their use of covert methods to study right-wing groups in the United States (Blee, 1998), the United Kingdom (Fielding, 1982) and India (Sehgal, 2009). However, Macklin (1982) questioned whether researchers were in an appropriate position to decide which groups are bad enough to warrant covert research.

Second, covert studies have also been defended on the basis of non-maleficence, suggesting that it reduces disturbance of research participants. The argument of non-maleficence was dismissed by Herrera (1999) as failing to consider the need to protect research participants from having their interests infringed by paternalist researchers.

Third, researchers have defended partially covert research when they found it difficult to negotiate their presence as researchers because of the institutional, physical or virtual setting or the numbers of people that would be involved. For example, work on the night-time economy by a group of British criminologists (Winlow et al., 2001) involved one member of the team securing work as a bouncer without identifying himself as an academic researcher. Paweł Moczydłowski (1982/1992), later to become Director-General of prisons in post-Communist Poland, entered prisons to undertake his research by joining study groups of questionnaire-wielding students. Sallaz (2008) informed South African casino workers and their managers that he was examining working conditions for employees, but found it was not always possible to provide the same information to gamblers as this would have slowed down the games and compromised his role as croupier, without having any major impact on the risks faced by clients of the casino. In the light of this type of argument, the Swedish legislation relating to human research ethics (Swedish Research Council's Expert Group on Ethics, 2011) recognized it may not be necessary to obtain informed consent when an unreasonable amount of work might be required to achieve such an outcome, even if sensitive personal data is being collected.

Fourth, those who collect anonymized data as part of non-participant observation in public spaces have argued for a long time that informed consent is simply not required (Brewster Smith, 1979; Reiss, 1978). This argument has been extended to public areas online (Kitchin, under review) on the basis either that the data involved is publicly accessible or is perceived as public by participants. Despite these attempted distinctions, in practice it is not always clear whether or not particular internet sites should be treated as private, public (Buchanan, 2011; Markham and Buchanan, 2012) or, indeed, semi-public (Sveningsson Elm, 2009): 'what constitutes "person-based" research in cyberspace is much disputed – one person's "text-based" study is another's person-based study' (McKee, 2008, p. 106). Partly stemming from their interdisciplinary and transnational activity, internet researchers are more likely to be attracted towards situated rather than prescriptive ethics (see Chapter 2). So, Natasha Whiteman (2012) invited researchers to assess the environment, content and tacit and explicit markers of privacy when reaching a decision. She also argued that, as in the offline environment, decisions about the public nature of a site should be revisited throughout the research, as the status of sites may change:

> Websites are not homogeneous, and the activities of Internet users often suggest confusion and conflicting understandings of the privacy or openness of their actions. Both offline and online, the expectations of those we observe may be in conflict with more 'objective' definitions of the status of the environment. It is therefore important to emphasise the significance of paying attention to the local detail of our research contexts. (Whiteman, 2012, p. 76)

On the other hand, many codes are concerned to protect the dignity and privacy of people even in public space while allowing covert techniques to be used in particular circumstances. Drawing on a harm–benefit analysis (see Chapter 7), Petticrew et al. (2007) defended systematic observations of smoking in Scottish pubs following a ban on smoking in enclosed public areas in Scotland. The American Sociological Association (1999) accepted the legitimacy of this practice (s. 12.01c), as have the Canadian Tri-Council (2010, Article 2.3), and the National Health and Medical Research Council (2007b) in Australia. It would seem odd were covert research to be acceptable offline but unimaginable online, but these arguments have not always run smoothly.

The 'Tastes, Ties and Time' project harvested four years' worth of demographic, relational and cultural data from the Facebook profiles of the 2006 Harvard first-year cohort and connected the data to the University's housing records. The researchers did not seek informed consent on the basis that their work was akin to observation in a public space: 'We have not interviewed anyone, nor asked them for any information, nor made information about them public' (Kaufman, 2008). Zimmer (2010) was highly critical of the project, pointing out that the data was often only available to the researchers because they were in the same Facebook college network as the students and were therefore not subject to the blocks many students had placed on access to their pages from the outside world.

Finally, research may be covert, at least in the sense that it is undeclared, when social scientists engage in 'early musings' (van den Hoonaard, 2011, p. 252) or enter the research milieu without having formalized a research project. Spicker (2011) worked as an advisor, consultant and academic researcher, talking to officials, voluntary workers, politicians, activists and journalists:

> None of these discussions has been part of a formally constituted research project ... I do not do 'covert research' in the sense of deliberately constructing research that is intended to be concealed from view; but equally, there may be no point at which it would be opportune or appropriate to make an explicit disclosure. (pp. 131–132)

Rena Lederman's 'informal fieldwork on academic cultures' (2006, p. 487) drew on her ongoing collegial relations with colleagues. She never regarded her colleagues as human subjects and was only forced to reflect on how her work might be interpreted by United States regulations when she rejoined an institutional review board and began to consider her time on the board as fieldwork. One criminologist's interest in investigating taxi drivers' experiences of crime began while talking to a driver when stuck in rush hour traffic. It would have been absurd to have cautioned the taxi driver that his views on crime and criminal justice might trigger future enquiry: 'When the conversation took place, there was no research project, no planned research project, nor indeed any envisaged research project' (Denscombe et al., 2009, p. 304).

The value of covert studies has been accepted by British, Canadian, Australian, Norwegian and Swedish national codes and guidelines in exceptional circumstances. The American Sociological Association (1999) allows members to undertake covert activities only if the research involves no more than minimal risk to participants. Similar provisions are contained in other national and professional codes such as the National Statement in Australia and the ESRC's Framework for Research Ethics in the United Kingdom. It is unclear whether such provisions might exclude the possibility of using covert research in institutions to expose, for example, state violence or corporate misconduct. It depends on whether the institution is considered a research participant. In Canada, the Tri-Council Policy Statement (2010) suggests institutions should not be protected in this way. In the United Kingdom, the Framework for Research Ethics offers space for a similar argument to be made (Economic and Social Research Council, 2010, p. 29) and this is also how Cordner and Thomson (2007) interpret the National Statement in Australia. The Canadian Statement recognizes that 'social science research that critically probes the inner workings of publicly accountable institutions might never be conducted without limited recourse to partial disclosure' (p. 37). As a result, researchers are not required to obtain consent from those corporate or government organizations that they are researching, nor are such institutions entitled to veto projects, though private organizations may refuse researchers access to records or create rules governing the conduct of their employees that might make it difficult for those employees to cooperate with researchers. However, even in these situations, the research cannot involve more than minimal risk to participants (Article 3.7(a)), which might make it difficult for researchers to work with whistleblowers in some jurisdictions. The European Research Council's (2010) draft Guidance Note for social science researchers warned against allowing powerful figures or organizations the right to withdraw or withhold consent for fear of leaving social scientists 'without even the most basic rights to make enquiries by other social groups, such as investigative journalists, or even ordinary citizens who might confront such figures at public meetings' (p. 11).

Despite these moves by agencies to allow covert research under certain circumstances, the use of covert methodologies is in serious decline (van den Hoonaard, 2011). Indeed, some research ethics committees are even unwilling to allow researchers to analyse documents freely available under Freedom of Information legislation unless they have the consent of the authors (McKenzie et al., 2010).

Conclusion

Drawing on the principle of respect for persons (Chapter 3), a requirement that researchers should obtain informed consent from participants might seem relatively uncontroversial. Designed to combat a series of appalling abuses that had occurred in human experimentation, codes of research ethics (Chapter 2) generally require researchers first to explain to participants the nature of their research and the potential consequences of involvement. Then, before research can commence, participants need to agree to taking part in the research on the basis of a fully informed and voluntary decision. As part of the consent process, researchers have developed a range of tools for consulting and communicating with potential participants and for checking that participants understand the implications of the consent process.

However, in practice, the requirements of informed consent are anything but straightforward in the social sciences. First, the formal nature of the consent process that has been mandated by national codes or local committees can compromise both the possibility of gaining genuine consent and of providing assurances of anonymity. Second, some argue the assumption of individual autonomy within informed consent protocols fails to recognize the coercive nature of some institutional, community and family-based relationships. Conventional consent requirements also impose Western notions of autonomy on societies where communal decision-making structures have greater prominence. Finally, researchers claim requirements for informed consent are not always necessary or appropriate and that work in public spaces or involving public officials should occur without informed consent. In addition, and more controversially, some argue deceptive experiments and covert research might be justified in particular situations by reference to the balance of risk and public benefit. Although some national codes have ruled against covert research, recent Canadian, British and European regulations suggest a greater willingness on some occasions to sanction research that does not have the consent of all research participants.

In short, the regulation of informed consent could operate in such a way that it protects the interests of vulnerable groups from harmful research carried out by more powerful organizations such as government agencies. Alternatively, it could protect powerful agencies from scrutiny by independent researchers by robbing researchers of one of their most powerful methodologies, covert research. Various jurisdictions and institutions have continued to take different positions, and it is unclear in which direction future regulators will move.

SIX

Confidentiality

Introduction

Often, when people allow researchers to undertake research that involves them, they negotiate terms for the agreement. Participants in research may, for example, consent on the basis their names will not be disclosed and the information obtained about them will be used only by the researchers and only in particular ways. The participant regards the information as private and offers it voluntarily to the researcher in confidence.

The concept of confidentiality is frequently discussed in bioethics. In a medical context, patients typically approach a doctor and provide personal information in exchange for help. The research relationship in social science is generally very different. In the social sciences, it is the researcher who is more likely to approach a potential participant and ask for confidential information to be revealed in exchange for ... possibly not very much direct benefit. As two Canadian criminologists, John Lowman and Ted Palys, argued:

> Our research subjects divulge information in confidence about their own criminal activity ... and sexual activity to a person who has asked them to divulge the information, with the full knowledge they are offering us 'data' that will at some point be compiled, analyzed and published. The researcher usually initiates the interaction and, in our experience, the respondent divulges the information only on the condition that they are not named. Since the interaction would not have happened if we had not initiated it, a tremendous ethical burden is placed on us to ensure no adverse effects befall the participant because of our entry into their lives. (1999, p. 30)

While social science research participants might be hurt by insensitive data collection, a more significant danger may be posed by what happens to data after it has been collected during the process of analysis, publication and, indeed, archiving. In this chapter, I examine the difficulties associated with protecting the identities of research participants as well as the information they provide researchers in confidence.

Justifications for confidentiality

Justifications for confidentiality are often inadequately elaborated within social science. However, working in the field of bioethics, Tom Beauchamp and James Childress (2009) identified three different arguments – consequence-, rights- and fidelity-based – that might justify maintaining confidentiality.

Consequentialist arguments (see Chapter 2) examine the results of an ethical practice, consider what would happen if the practice did not exist and make a decision about what to do on the basis of the comparison. In social science, interviewees might be reluctant to reveal details about themselves if they think the information could be freely disseminated to third parties, despite assurances to the contrary (O'Neil, 1996; Van Maanen, 1983) and,

> Where there can be no trust between informant and researcher, there are few guarantees as to the validity and worth of information in an atmosphere where confidence is not respected. (Fitzgerald and Hamilton, 1997, p. 1102)

These claims seem to be particularly true where the research topic is sensitive and where dissemination of the information would have adverse consequences for the participant. Researchers who break confidences might not only make it more difficult for themselves to continue researching but, by damaging the possibility that potential participants will trust researchers, might also disrupt the work of other social scientists.

The second justification for confidentiality is rights-based. Allen (1997) maintained everyone has a right to limit access to his or her person. Such a right encompasses informational, physical and proprietary privacy. Beauchamp and Childress (2001) argued our right to privacy rests on the principle of respect for autonomy. On this basis, while some matters cannot or should not be concealed, people should have the right, as far as is possible, to make decisions about what will happen to them. In the context of research, they should be able to maintain secrets, deciding who knows what about them. This principle was accepted in the Nuremberg, Helsinki, UNESCO and Belmont documents.

Finally, fidelity-based arguments rest on the view that researchers owe loyalty to the bonds, and should honour the promises, associated with research – a deontological position. Researchers should be faithful to the obligations relating to respect for autonomy, justice and utility that are imposed by their relationship with participants. Researchers should, for example, meet those expectations that research participants might reasonably hold about investigators' behaviour. By offering a promise of secrecy, social scientists offer both to give and perform something. They offer to give allegiance and agree, at minimum, to keep silent or possibly even to do more to guard a confidence. As Sissela Bok (1983, p. 121) noted, 'Just what performance is promised, and at what cost it will be carried out, are questions that go to the heart of conflicts of confidentiality'.

Both Bok, and Beauchamp and Childress concluded that obligations of confidentiality are only *prima facie* binding. Indeed, Bok warned against the dangers of maintaining secrecy. This means that obligations of confidentiality cannot be considered absolute and in some situations we should contemplate disclosing to a particular person or group, information that we had received under an implied or explicit assurance of confidentiality. I shall return to this later in the chapter.

It is worth pointing out that not every research participant wants anonymity. Evans (2004) was troubled by the disappearance of people and communities, and their authority and voice, from qualitative research. During research on sexual abuse in Latin America, Lisa Fontes encountered shantytown leaders angered by inadequate recognition for their work

> the assurance of confidentiality seems to have contributed to participants' continued accurate perceptions that their labor and knowledge were being exploited by those in power, including academics like me. (1998, p. 56)

Similarly, Mohatt and Thomas (2006) reported the incredulity expressed by elders of Alaska Native communities when told that an Institutional Review Board had initially determined Indigenous people collaborating in a study of resilience in the face of alcohol could not be named in publications. The inappropriateness of such a blanket determination has been acknowledged by the American Anthropological Association (1998) and the Canadian Tri-Council Policy Statement (2010; see also Castleden et al., 2010; Ntseane, 2009; Szklut and Reed, 1991). So, in community-based and participatory action research, people who might have been once turned into anonymous participants are now being recognized as authors (see Chapter 8 on authorship).

In addition, not every participant should be offered confidentiality. Oral historians engaged in gathering personal narratives routinely do not offer anonymity or confidentiality, although restrictions on access may be negotiated (Boschma et al., 2003). Social scientists may feel it inappropriate to offer confidentiality to people in public office who are speaking about their public work (Sudnow, 1965; Rainwater and Pittman, 1967), a situation recognized in some national and professional codes and government regulations. In some contexts, researchers are expected to share data with other researchers, either to allow the research to be replicated, or to allow further analysis of the data. Indeed, the Swedish Research Council's Expert Group on Ethics (2011) goes so far as to suggest researchers owe it to the public to allow reuse of data collected with public money.

Negotiating confidentiality

Negotiations around confidentiality may be fairly straightforward. Some researchers are able to operate in relatively predictable contexts where standardized assurances may be included in a covering letter. However, other work takes place in informal and unpredictable environments, where agreements need to be negotiated with individuals and groups and renegotiated during the course of lengthy fieldwork.

Researchers can find it extremely difficult to keep secrets during fieldwork. Participants might discover the identity of other participants either by accident or as a necessary part of the methodology. For example, focus group members may be able to identify each other, and both snowball and respondent-driven sampling (at least in some forms) will mean that individuals cannot participate without at least one of their peers knowing. Some of the value of network analysis in management research, comes from allowing people to see the raw data identifying the connections between named participants. While these might be disguised for some purposes, participants within an organization may still be able to identify themselves, as well as other particular individuals and their known associates (Borgatti and Molina, 2003). Where photovoice is used to create and publish images of and by participants, it can be tough or even counterproductive to offer anonymity (Aldridge, 2012).

Researchers may also have to disguise material in any ensuing publications. Patricia Adler (1985) undertook a study of drug dealers and smugglers operating in California:

> Dealers occasionally revealed things about themselves or others that we had to pretend not to know when interacting with their close associates. This sometimes meant that we had to lie or build elaborate stories to cover for some people. Their fronts therefore became our fronts, and we had to weave our own web of deception to guard their performances. This became especially disturbing during the writing of the research report, as I was torn by conflicts between using details to enrich the data and glossing over description to guard confidences. (p. 26)

A further complication may arise if the participant has commercial interests to protect and the resources and expertise to ensure that these protections are stipulated in any agreement. For example:

> An agreement with a chemical company involved in an environmental clean-up or an insurance company involved in mass tort litigation may provide more rules governing confidential data and subpoenas than a short form of consent and confidentiality assurance that might be used in a study of mentally

ill homeless persons or elderly medical patients. Such an agreement might require notification if a subpoena is served or the use of best efforts by the researcher to resist production of confidential data; it might limit the 'except as required by law proviso' to a court order, not merely a subpoena; and it might provide for return or destruction of the data at the conclusion of the study. (Traynor, 1996, p. 122)

Table 6.1 Contractual procedures for protecting the confidentiality of individuals in research projects using administrative microdata files

Prohibition on re-disclosure or re-release
Specification of electronic data transmission (for example, encryption methods for network access)
Description of storage and/or handling of paper copies of confidential data
Description of storage and/or handling of electronic media such as tapes or cartridges
Description of network security
Requirement for notification of security incidents
Description of methods of statistical disclosure limitation
Description of disposition of data upon termination of contract
Penalties for breaches

Source: Brady et al., 2001, p. 255

Contracts with government may also specify a range of provisions to uphold confidentiality and security and could indicate the penalties that may be imposed if a breach of confidentiality occurs. In their review of confidentiality issues arising as a result of sharing administrative data gathered as part of United States welfare programmes, Brady and his colleagues (2001) generated a range of examples they thought should be specified in any written contract (see Table 6.1). Many national and professional codes contain provisions dealing with the long-term use of data, including considerations such as data storage and secondary use of data in hard-copy and various digital forms. These provisions often require researchers to conform to relevant data protection laws.

In some cases, researchers may face considerable pressure from government officials or courts to disclose data, thereby breaching assurances of confidentiality. Paluck (2009) had to evade a Rwandan government minister's request for information about how a particular community viewed local genocide trials. Adler (1985) was concerned about drawing police attention to her work on drug dealing in California and so avoided publicity by holding back on publications until she had finished her fieldwork. Fitzgerald and Hamilton (1996) were not so lucky. Their work on illicit drug use in Australia was compromised when one researcher was approached by a police officer working undercover:

The undercover police officer suggested that a trade of information could be done: the undercover officer would introduce the ethnographer to drug users to interview in exchange for information that the ethnographer could pass on to the police. (p. 1593)

Fearing police might seek access to their data by getting a warrant or by placing fieldworkers under surveillance, the researchers suspended their fieldwork while they clarified their legal position.

These extreme threats to the confidentiality of data may be rare but are not so uncommon that they can be ignored (Israel, 2004a). There are two kinds of measures that can be taken to preserve confidentiality. The first is methodological, the second legal.

Methodological precautions

Researchers have protected the confidentiality of research participants and their activities by using administrative, physical and technical safeguards. At their simplest, these may entail either not recording names and other data at all, removing names and identifying details from confidential data at the earliest possible stage, or ensuring the security of data storage. These precautions help to guard data against official interception, theft and accidental (Meth with Malaza, 2003) or improper disclosure by other members of a research team. For example, in quantitative research on child abuse and neglect, a North Carolina research team (Kotch, 2000) required participants to seal their answers to sensitive questions. These were then separated from other information that might have identified the respondent. Singer and his colleagues attempted to avoid videoing faces of illicit drug users in Connecticut and subsequently avoided screening images of those that they had filmed (Singer and Easton, 2006). Henderson et al. (2013) alerted researchers of social media to the need to strip identifying sensitive metadata from images subsequently submitted for publication in online journals. During qualitative research with property criminals, Kenneth Tunnell also took a range of methodological precautions. He:

never spoke participants' names during the recorded interviews, which were themselves quickly transcribed and the tapes erased. Although I kept an identifier list and assigned numbers to pertinent information obtained from individuals' case files, names were not connected to the information from the files or interviews. (1998, p. 208)

Other researchers have counselled participants not to give them specific information such as names or details of past criminal events for which they had not been arrested (Decker and van Winkle, 1996; Feenan, 2002; Sluka, 1995) or future crimes that they planned to commit (Cromwell et al., 1991).

Social scientists have gone to considerable lengths to safeguard their data. At various points in her research, Patricia Adler and her husband had to protect their data from suspicious and sometimes volatile drug dealers:

> We encountered several threats to our collection of taped interviews from people who had granted us these interviews. This made us anxious, since we had taken great pains to acquire these tapes and felt strongly about maintaining confidences entrusted to us by our informants. When threatened, we became extremely frightened and shifted the tapes between various hiding places. We even ventured forth one rainy night with our tapes packed in a suitcase to meet a person who was uninvolved in the research at a secret rendezvous so that he could guard the tapes for us. (Adler, 1985, p. 23)

Other researchers have sent files out of the jurisdiction, scanned consent forms and data and encrypted the digital copy, secured hard copies in the embassy of their home country, and avoided using mail or telephone systems so that data could not be intercepted or seized by police or intelligence agencies (Feenan, 2002; Fisher and Ragsdale, 2006; Loyle, 2011; Sluka, 1989). Any use by researchers of cloud computing in the form of remote data storage sites may have significant implications for the security of data, depending on the provider's terms of service, and the jurisdiction within which data is stored (Gellman, 2009; Buchanan et al., 2011).

Digital data may be increasingly susceptible to government interception. Researchers need to be aware of the degree to which internet traffic is monitored by the states within which they and their participants operate. Publicity following the enactment of the PATRIOT Act in the United States and leaks from Edward Snowden outlining some of the activities of the National Security Agency has alerted researchers to the difficulties of securing data in the United States. Indeed, some Canadian institutions have stopped their employees gathering sensitive data through American companies as a result (Palys and Atchison, 2012). It is not just the government that threatens data security. Most institutions have to counter daily attacks on their firewalls. In 2009, the University of North Carolina discovered spyware on a server holding records for 180,000 participants in a study analysing mammography results.

Using a commercial online web-based survey carries its own threats to anonymity including the possibilities that: staff from the commercial service may be able access confidential data; server defects might allow other customers to see research materials; or the server may be vulnerable to hacking (Buchanan and Hvizdak, 2009). Baker (2012) urged institutions to create their own in-house survey servers that allowed data to be de-identified before offline storage in encrypted form. This would include stripping data of identifiers such as IP addresses that are not to be analysed as research variables. However, there are multiple examples of university servers being hacked, and there is always a danger the host institution may not respect commitments made by a researcher (Palys and Lowman, 2012).

Identifiers such as real and online names, geographical clues and vernacular terms can be removed in the writing up stage (Hancock, 2001; Szklut and Reed, 1991), otherwise

> the interested reader can identify the revolutionary in the Santiago squatter settlement, the reformer among the Northern Ute, the Lebanese trader in central Ghana, or the patrón on the upper Rio Ucayuli. (Jorgensen, 1971, p. 331)

Some attempts to disguise location have been quite naive. The 'Tastes, Ties and Time' Facebook project discussed in the previous chapter sought to publish research on an 'anonymous, northeastern American university'. Sadly, the authors offered so many additional clues – that the institution was 'very elite', private, co-ed, had 1,640 students in its first-year cohort, and taught Near Eastern Languages and Civilizations, Sanskrit and Indian Studies – that it could only be their own institution, Harvard:

> the lesson learned here is how disparate pieces of seemingly benign information can be pieced together to make an otherwise presumed anonymous piece of data identifiable. I did it here by quickly analyzing the codebook, reading a press release, and watching a video presentation. (Zimmer, 2008).

While the Harvard example does suggest naïveté, large organizations such as Netflix, America OnLine (AOL) and the State of Massachusetts have also been forced to recognize their attempts to anonymize datasets prior to public release were woefully inadequate. In each case, the redacted data retained (surprisingly) unique combinations of variables (Ohm, 2010).

It may not be possible to quote directly from online interactions if the original source can be identified through a search engine and linked to other data (Battles, 2010). I once reviewed an article that had disguised the identity of an educational institution in the United States but had quoted directly from an online student blog. Researchers can also mask their own identity. Van der Geest (2003) initially published his work on witchcraft and abortion in a Ghanaian town under a pseudonym, disguising the names of the research location and residents, much to the eventual annoyance of the participants.

It can be difficult to hide the identity of some people from themselves, their peers, investigative journalists or officials. It may be impossible to anonymize institutions or even individuals from small, recognizable communities such as the island states of the Caribbean (Louisy, 1997), of the Indian Ocean (Moosa, 2013) or Macau (Morrison, 2006). When dealing with the possibility that members of a community might be able to identify information about each other, even if outsiders could not, Tolich (2004) recommended that researchers spend time learning from insiders what information might be damaging.

The process of rendering two people's accounts of the same interaction unidentifiable to each party while at the same time including enough detail to make the case study valuable may prove extremely difficult. Forbat and Henderson (2003) suggested members of paired interviews be allowed to read their transcripts and be asked if they were prepared to share data with the paired partner. In the case of focus groups, participants may be warned not to use personal identifiers, and may be assigned pseudonyms or numbers so that they can interact without breaching anonymity in any recording or transcript (Tolich, 2009). Of course, researchers cannot offer members of the focus group absolute confidentiality as they cannot guarantee confidences exchanged within the group will be respected.

Kaiser (2009) argued social scientists needed to provide participants with a larger number of options that went beyond the conventional offer of anonymity. Instead, she called for a negotiation between researcher and participant after data-collection which allowed respondents to select which pieces of information might warrant different levels of protection. At the request of participants, Hurdley (2010) agreed to pixelate parts of her images of mantelpieces to obscure faces in some photographs. Robson (2011) enabled all participants, including children as young as three years old, to view, comment on, and request alteration or deletion of video recordings that she had made of them.

In 2011, I interviewed Australian academics about their experiences of winning national teaching awards. After writing my report, I returned to interviewees and allowed them to choose whether and where they wanted their own voice to be heard, and whether, where and how they wanted their identity to be disguised. Given the pool of potential interviewees comprised around 100 publicly listed individuals and many were used to publishing or commenting in public on higher education, almost all chose to forego anonymity. However, at some points, generally where interviewees were critical of their institutions or described adverse reactions from colleagues, they elected to remain anonymous (Israel, 2011).

Of course, researchers' best attempts to disguise locations can be undermined if research participants reveal their involvement deliberately or inadvertently. The anonymity of two British families in Hall's (2009) ethnographic study of the ethics of consumption was threatened when they subsequently sought to befriend her on a social networking website. During work on a co-educational Roman Catholic state school in England, Robert Burgess (1989) had to handle a complaint from one of the teachers who claimed Burgess had broken assurances of confidentiality. Unfortunately, the teacher left his complaint with the secretary of Burgess' university department and, in so doing, revealed the identity of the school which, until then, Burgess had managed to conceal from his colleagues.

Several sociologists and anthropologists have found that attempts to maintain anonymity prove fruitless once they publish their findings (Scheper-Hughes, 2000; Ellis, 2007). Arlene Stein (2010), for example, wrote about a small Oregon town in the United States. Once her book was published, it was reviewed by the state newspaper. The paper identified the community as Cottage Grove which made it easier to unravel the pseudonyms. Stein found that 'A copy of the book, in which someone had crossed out the pseudonyms I had assigned to individuals, substituting real names, was making the rounds across town, and lots of people were upset' (2010, p. 558). As a result, one woman who had spoken about her sexuality to Stein was 'outed'. Stein felt she had let the community down, discovering she had compromised 'privacy in the interest of telling a good story' (p. 562). Like Scheper-Hughes, Stein concluded that it would have been better not to have offered the community or individuals an anonymity that fooled so few. Academia, Scheper-Hughes argued, would be better off with 'less poignant, more circumspect ethnographies' (2000, p. 128).

One response to this challenge has been the practice of 'storying', creating composite and fictional accounts that correspond to participants' narratives but avoid presenting specific events that might be identifiable. Piper and Sikes (2010) used this technique in their analysis of the experiences of teachers who had been wrongly accused of sexually abusing secondary school students: 'We chose to story as an ethical strategy both to protect our informants and to guard against the sort of scandalizing that tends to go on in media reporting of teacher–pupil sex.' (p. 572). Markham (2012) reported one publisher had blocked the creation of composite, fictional but representative blogs on the basis the authors in Sweden had 'fabricated' the data, a term Markham embraced as both epistemologically sound and 'a sensible and ethically grounded solution for protecting privacy in arenas of shifting public/private contexts' (p. 341)!

In quantitative research, practices of stripping data of individual identifiers may be compromised by improved capacities to manipulate multiple, linked datasets. While a survey might not include individual names or other unique identifiers, it may include sufficient identifying attributes to allow a person's identity and/or various sensitive attributes to be inferred. Bluntly, there may be only one 80-year-old, tertiary-educated, Canadian-born Buddhist female in a particular neighbourhood, and if linked datasets then reveal that unnamed individual's income or number of sexual partners, then confidentiality would be compromised. Indeed, Sweeney (2000, cited in Albright, 2011) suggested it might be possible to predict a person's identity in the United States with 87 per cent accuracy on the basis of just the date of birth, gender and zip code.

There are various statistical methods that can disguise or conceal the identities of individuals whose attributes are reported in datasets (Duncan et al., 2011). Disclosure:

can be limited by making sure that the amount of information about any particular person never exceeds some threshold that is adjusted upward as the sensitivity of the information increases. (Brady et al., 2001, p. 229)

Two major methods may be used to limit disclosure of sensitive information. The first involves altering the data and the second requires restricting access to the data (Duncan et al., 2011). As the United States National Research Council (Mackie and Bradburn, 2000) recognizes, each method offers advantages and disadvantages. Alteration may allow data to be disseminated more broadly, but may affect the confidence that people can place in particular aspects of the data. Conversely, 'Restricting access may create inconveniences and limit the pool of researchers that can use the data, but generally permits access to greater data detail.' (Mackie and Bradburn, 2000, p. 29). The United States Census Bureau has limited the use of some data to a secure environment, known as an enclave or 'cold room', though researchers have complained about the cost and utility of these facilities (VanWey et al., 2005).

Brady et al. (2001) and Albright (2011) list various forms of data alteration (see Table 6.2).

Table 6.2 Methods for data alteration

Cross-tabulations	Presenting aggregate data in the form of tables
Aggregation	Creating rules for minimum number of units before information is reported
Suppression	Not providing any estimate where cells are below a certain size
Random rounding	Rounding cells to a certain level, rounding up or down on the basis of probability not proximity
Controlled rounding	Adjusting rounding so that published totals equal actual totals
Confidentiality edit	Selecting a small sample of firms and swapping or altering values
Tables of magnitude data	Suppressing sensitive cells to ensure that information about dominant contributors of data (such as near monopoly firms) cannot be inferred

Source: Brady et al., 2001, pp. 259–260

We can mask data in various ways: by sampling; eliminating obvious identifiers; limiting geographical detail; limiting the number of data elements presented; simulating and coarsening data through microaggregation (synthetic average persons are described from aggregated data); adding top and bottom coding on continuous data which would allow, for example, all people over 75 years old to be treated as one group; recoding into intervals and rounding (so that, for example, date of birth is transformed into an age group); adding random noise; swapping, blanking and imputing, and blurring data in ways that do not significantly change the statistical properties of the database, and including error inoculation (contaminating statistical data in random ways so that it is impossible to determine whether the responses recorded from an individual were those that he or she gave) (Kimmel, 1988). Given the possibility that external information might be used to compromise the anonymity of material in a database, absolute privacy can never be achieved. Currently, studies in statistical disclosure control are developing mechanisms for estimating risks of disclosure and minimizing these risks while also balancing the preservation of the usefulness of collected data with the protection of privacy. Nevertheless, Stiles et al. (2011) warned the advance of technology 'allowing merging, reuse, and exchange of data outpaces establishment of policies and processes to do it ethically' (p. 183). The pace of change in technologies relating to capturing, storing, integrating and disseminating personal data is likely to accelerate (Duncan et al., 2011).

Anonymity can be compromised when personal data can be linked with spatial or social network data. As the researchers using material derived from Facebook at Harvard University eventually were forced to concede, even when researchers believe that they have stripped away or encoded all individual identifiers, it can be relatively simple for remaining information to be pieced together to reidentify particular people (Zimmer, 2010). Anonymity can also be difficult to maintain when still or moving images are released that might reveal clothing, mannerisms or facial features. Even when efforts are made to obscure identifiers by cropping, blurring or editing, this may not be able to block identification through readily available image-matching technology.

Legal protections

A range of legal protections are also available in some jurisdictions. Some researchers may receive statutory protection for their data. In the United States, the Department of Health and Human Services and the Department of Justice have issued confidentiality certificates to individual projects or classes of research in the areas of health and justice. Statistics Canada researchers guarantee confidentiality to research participants under the protection of the Statistics Act 1985, although this protection might not be absolute if challenged on the basis of the Canadian Charter of Rights and Freedoms or, possibly, provincial mandatory reporting laws. In some Australian jurisdictions, there is a statutory duty to maintain confidentiality of any information concerning the affairs of another person, where that information was gathered as part of a 'prescribed study'. However, the Commonwealth legislation necessitates a cumbersome and time-consuming approval process that can only cover prescribed epidemiological projects conducted by or on behalf of the Commonwealth government (Chalmers and Israel, 2005). Social scientists have attempted to reach agreements with criminal justice agencies. In St Louis in the United States, Wright and Decker (1997) negotiated a written agreement with the police that allowed the researchers to be taken to the site of armed robberies by offenders without any intervention from the police. Criminal justice agencies are not always this accommodating.

Even when there has been no statutory protection, researchers have refused to reveal information to government investigators or to courts. As the examples in Table 6.3 illustrate, the reasons for their decisions and the point at which they decided they could no longer co-operate with the legal system vary considerably. For example, Steven Picou, a professor of sociology in Alabama, undertook a longitudinal study between 1989 and 1992 of the social impact on small coastal villages in Alaska of the Exxon Valdez oil tanker disaster. Picou had guaranteed confidentiality, telling respondents that 'immediately following the receipt of their final interview, all personal identifiers, including names, addresses, and phone numbers, would be eliminated from the master data file and all hard copies would be discarded' (Picou, 1996, p. 151). In 1992, Exxon subpoenaed Picou's files. Picou was able to persuade the court to allow access only to data used for published papers while blocking access to unpublished and incomplete material from later research. He also ensured the earlier information would be released solely to an expert sociologist retained by Exxon who was to use the data for statistical analysis only.

Table 6.3 Attempts to obtain confidential research data through the legal system

Case	
Welfare cheats	In the 1970s, records of participants in the New Jersey Negative Income Tax Experiment were sought by a grand jury and a congressional investigating committee. A New Jersey prosecutor issued 14 subpoenas calling for the names of welfare families who might be cheating the system (Kershaw and Fair, 1976). The researchers persuaded the prosecution to drop their demands.
Police violence	In 1974, a Californian graduate student observing police patrols witnessed a police assault on a civilian (Van Maanen, 1983). Although Van Maanen gave police internal investigators a sworn statement about the incident, the patrol officers were exonerated. The police officers sued a newspaper that covered the assault. When the paper subpoenaed Van Maanen's field notes, he refused to show them.
Environmental decision-making	In 1976 Marc Roberts, a Harvard professor of public health, refused to produce documents for a Californian civil court about interviews that had been conducted with a gas and electricity utility company about their environmental decision-making (*Richards of Rockford v. Pacific Gas and Electric*, 1976).

Case	
Long Island arson	In the 1980s, a New York student engaged in an ethnography of Long Island restaurants was subpoenaed together with his field notes by prosecutors investigating arson in a restaurant (Brajuha and Hallowell, 1986). Brajuha negotiated with prosecutors to remove the names of informants from sensitive material, but not before a lengthy and expensive court battle which resulted in Brajuha losing his money, his family and his desire to work in sociology.
Microsoft and Netscape	As part of its defence to an antitrust action, Microsoft unsuccessfully sought access to notes and interview tapes compiled by two American business and management professors as part of their book on Netscape Communications (McCollum, 1999).
Medill Innocence Project	In 2009, the Cook County State Attorney in Illinois obtained a subpoena demanding that David Protess, a Northwestern University professor, hand over material relating to interviews by investigative journalism students in connection to a claimed miscarriage of justice. Despite Protess' denials, the court found he himself had already made much of the material available to the convicted murderer's lawyers. Northwestern University later accused the professor of misleading the institution (*Chicago Tribune* Editorial, 2011).
Provisional Irish Republican Army	In 2011, the British government sought a federal court order in the United States requiring Boston College to surrender oral history interview data relating to the 1972 murder in Belfast of a suspected police informant by the Provisional IRA (Schmidt, 2012). The researchers obtained political and media support and sought to protect the data that they had deposited with the College. However, the College initially turned over some material. It later attempted to hold on to data provided by an interviewee who was still alive (Palys and Lowman, 2012). In April 2013, the First Circuit Court of Appeals reduced the amount of material to be handed over from 85 interviews (roughly half of the archive) to segments of 11 interviews. Apparently, on the basis of this information, Sinn Féin leader Gerry Adams was arrested in Belfast in 2014 (Israel, 2014). Following Adams' release, the Police Service of Northern Ireland indicated its intention to obtain further data from Boston College.
Ottawa murder suspect	In 2014, two Ottawa criminologists successfully petitioned the Quebec Superior Court to block the execution of a search warrant by police (Fine, 2014). The police sought data from an interview the researchers had allegedly conducted with a Montreal sex worker in 2007. The researchers had published the data but had not revealed the interviewee's identity. The male sex worker was later charged with the murder and dismemberment of a female student.
Urban explorers	Bradley Garrett, an urban ethnographer, took part in exploration of British urban space that involved trespass onto land owned by the public transport authority. Garrett and eight participants were charged with conspiracy to commit criminal damage and the prosecution based its case on research notes seized from Garrett. The case ended with Garrett (2014) receiving a conditional discharge.

Although potential liability will vary between jurisdictions, researchers may be vulnerable to legal action in several ways. If they refuse to disclose information where ordered by a court, researchers may be found guilty of obstructing the police in execution of a warrant or even of contempt of court. In 1972, a Harvard political scientist, Samuel Popkin, failed to disclose to an American grand jury the names of, and the data provided by, Vietnamese villagers and government officials who had discussed a classified American Defense Department project with him. Popkin spent eight days in jail. In 1993, an American sociology graduate student spent 159 days in jail in Washington State for contempt of court. Rik Scarce had failed to comply with a demand from a grand jury that he disclose information gathered during research concerning radical animal rights activism.

In the only case where a Canadian social scientist has been charged with contempt for failing to disclose confidential information relating to the identities of research participants, a Masters' student investigating the deaths of AIDS patients by suicide was subpoenaed by the Vancouver Coroner to appear at an inquest – the first of three subpoenas served on him over ten years. In his interviews with people who had assisted in the suicides, Russel Ogden had offered absolute confidentiality following a procedure approved by his university's ethics committee. Ogden agreed to discuss his research findings with the court but refused to divulge the names of research participants. Ogden won his case on the basis that the information had been obtained in confidence, confidentiality was essential to the research relationship, that the research was socially valuable and that the harm of breaching confidentiality outweighed the benefit to be gained by disclosure (Palys and Lowman, 2010). Two academic staff at Simon Fraser University argued that not only had the student acted ethically, but that their university – in disassociating itself from Ogden – had not. Ogden ran into further trouble when, as an independent researcher, he received a subpoena to appear as a prosecution witness in the preliminary hearing of a British Columbian woman charged with counselling, aiding and abetting suicide. Ogden's decision has received indirect endorsement in the 2010 Canadian Tri-Council Policy Statement which now requires researchers to 'safeguard information entrusted to them and not misuse or wrongfully disclose it' (Article 5.1).

One way researchers have responded to demands by third parties to see their research data has been to offer redacted material, information where the identity of study participants has been removed. In some cases, such as those involving short questionnaires, redacting data may be quite easy. Even digital audio recordings may be redacted before being provided to data archives (Southall, 2009). In other cases, it may place an enormous burden on researchers. For example, difficulties in de-identifying material may arise in long-term, in-depth, studies such as ethnographies:

Anthropologists' data are less easily 'cleaned', disguised, separated or aggre-gated than are, for example, quantitative data gathered by more formal means for which various methodological safeguards have been devised. (Ellen, 1984, pp. 148–149)

As one anthropologist acknowledged, 'The prospect of having to refuse to respond to a subpoena or to testify clearly chills the depth of researchers' inquiries' (McLaughlin, 1999, p. 934). As a result, some American and Canadian researchers have argued that research data should be privileged, shielded from court discovery (Social Sciences and Humanities Research Ethics Special Working Committee, 2008). Bernhard and Young (2009), for example, argued in favour of such a shield, having concluded that they could not protect 'the confidentiality and security of people living with precarious immigration status' (p.189) in the face of demands for information from the Canadian Border Services Agency. Palys and Lowman urged social scientists to consider the value of their work and act accordingly:

If the research enterprise is important and confidentiality integral to gather-ing valid data on controversial and/or sensitive topics, then researchers should vigorously defend their research and the rights and interests of their research participants. (2010, p. 275)

Disclosing confidential information

Earlier, I noted obligations of confidentiality were only *prima facie* binding. Confidentiality should not be seen as axiomatic or as a given. So, while many researchers have sought to avoid releasing confidential information, there are some situations where it might be appropriate to do so.

In some circumstances, in law, it might be permissible for researchers to disclose information they hold in confidence. As Palys and Lowman (2000) have argued, this does not mean that it might be ethically acceptable for a researcher to disclose such information. However, it does mean the research participant would be unable to take legal action for damages arising from breaches of con-fidence. In some instances, legislation or the courts may require information to be disclosed. For example, various jurisdictions have mandatory reporting requirements, requiring particular professionals to report specific activities such as child abuse or elder abuse. As we have seen, courts may also order documents to be disclosed during criminal investigations or civil litigation. Of course, these are legal and not ethical obligations, and researchers and courts may reach different conclusions as to what the right course of action might be (Allen, 2009). Some researchers have raised the matter of what Palys and

Lowman (2001) call the problem of 'heinous discovery' – what should research-ers do if they discover that participants intend to harm either themselves or someone else? What should they do if they uncover a miscarriage of justice and are in a position to prevent the wrongful conviction of a third party for a serious offence? British criminologists, Elaine Genders and Elaine Player warned:

> in our experience, the unpredictable nature of fieldwork ensures that unwel-come and unsolicited materials can be generated as instantaneously and as inexplicably as a rabbit from a magician's hat. (1995, p. 42)

Rony Duncan's work as a research psychologist entailed interviewing young Australians with chronic health conditions (Duncan et al., 2009). She also spoke to their parents. She offered interviewees confidentiality and specifically told Toby, a 15-year-old, that his mother would not discover what he said. Toby subsequently revealed he was not taking his prescribed medication daily, in order to avoid unpleasant side-effects. Duncan's response offers a good exam-ple of identifying and assessing options and acting on the basis of that reflec-tion. Following the interview and without disclosing Toby's identity, Duncan sought medical advice from her research team and found Toby's pattern of adherence was likely to significantly reduce the benefit of the medication without having an impact on the side-effects. She concluded she had four options: do nothing; attempt to persuade the interviewee to disclose his non-compliance; breach confidentiality by disclosing the non-compliance to either his parents or doctor; or offer to help the 15-year-old discuss the matter with his parents or doctor. The team decided to contact Toby to urge he discuss his decision with his parents or doctor. In doing so, they sought to respect the young man's autonomy and keep their promise of confidentiality. However, by sharing their concerns with him they hoped that might led to an improvement in his health – indeed, the team thought it possible this might have been Toby's reason for disclosing his actions. Of course, the decision to contact Toby again did pose risks, as the attempt might have both angered the young man and alerted his parents to the possibility that something was wrong.

Indian anthropologists explored the work of auxiliary nurse midwives in Surat (Coutinho et al., 2000). They found some health professionals were halv-ing the dose of a DPT vaccine administered to children in order to reduce the risk of fevers and ensure mothers returned with their children to the clinic. Unfortunately, the lower dose put the children at risk of not gaining immunity. The researchers had to balance the promise of confidentiality to the nursing staff and the harm to their professional standing that might flow from disclo-sure, against the risk to the children posed by non-disclosure. The team chose to warn those staff who admitted to the practice that children were being placed at risk, and in reporting the research identified the district but not the health centres nor the staff.

In contrast, Scott Atran found it a fairly easy decision to inform United States Senate Foreign Affairs staff in September 2005 that a rogue South-East Asian suicide squad linked to Jemaah Islamiyah had vague plans to attack western targets, possibly tourist spots in Bali. When he sought to continue his interviews with suicide bombers, he was floored to find his university's ethics committee at Michigan thought such a decision 'ethically remiss by disrespect-fully violating the bombers' wishes in helping to save their lives and the lives of their intended victims' (Atran, 2007).

While many ethical codes make rather unsophisticated general statements about the need to reveal criminal activity, there are some interesting exceptions. The National Advisory Board on Research Ethics (2009) in Finland argued that the task of research does carry responsibility for not revealing sensitive infor-mation about individual participants to authorities. The Board resiled from this position only when breaching confidentiality might allow an immanent and serious crime to be avoided. The same obligation exists for every citizen under the Finnish Penal Code. So, 'A researcher does not have an obligation to reveal information regarding crimes that have already been committed, unless reveal-ing information helps to prevent an imminent serious crime' (p. 12).

Offering limited confidentiality

In some situations, researchers may offer only *extended confidentiality*. Information disclosed to the researcher may be shared within a research team. In other cases, social scientists may agree to or even be required to deposit data in archives determined by funders, employers, governments or host communi-ties (Caplan, 2010; Ruusalepp, 2008). Subject to privacy legislation, archives can allow data to become a community resource. Different disciplines have varying attitudes towards the archiving and subsequent reuse of quantitative and qualitative data. Archivists have pointed to the ethical concerns caused by reuse of even redacted data, given that participants may not be available to offer consent tailored to specific further use (Van den Eynden, 2008). However, where the Finnish Data Archive contacted a variety of qualitative research participants seeking permission for data to be deposited with them, they found 89 per cent agreed and only two per cent were opposed (Kuula, 2010/11). Archiving of qualitative data may become more attractive to stakeholders when linked to a tiered access system that offers the choice for datasets to be made public, restricted to particular categories of registered users, released on a case-by-case basis or embargoed (Bishop, 2009; Neale and Bishop, 2012).

Some researchers offer *limited assurances of confidentiality* because they believe they have an obligation to a third party. For example Ivan Zinger, a

Canadian psychologist, told prisoners who participated in his doctoral research on administrative segregation that:

> he had an obligation to disclose any information you may provide if it's in regards to your safety or that of the institution. Those areas include suicide plans, plans of escape, injury to others and the general security of the institution. (Zinger 1999, quoted in Lowman and Palys, 2001)

Zinger's decision to offer only limited confidentiality contrasts sharply with the decision made by Kenneth Tunnell in work with Tennessee property offenders. Tunnell discovered that an offender that he had interviewed in prison had assumed a false identity before his arrest, an identity that allowed him to qualify for early release from prison to a halfway house. This information was leaked by a member of the research team and Tunnell was confronted by the director of the halfway house. Tunnell was concerned about the reaction of correctional authorities when they realized that the entire department 'had been duped by a three-time loser' (Tunnell, 1998, p. 209):

> I denied it was true and claimed he was misinformed. I lied. I lied and was glad that I did. I lied and today remain happy that I did. (p. 209)

Palys and Lowman (2001) argued Zinger's approach privileged institutional loyalties over the interests of research participants. They also claimed that as areas excluded from confidentiality were central to the research study, the limited assurance compromised the research to the point of rendering data obtained invalid. They suggested the researchers should either have made an unlimited guarantee of confidentiality and stuck to that or not undertaken the research (Lowman and Palys, 2001).

Recognizing full confidentiality may not be assured, some codes and ethics committees instruct researchers to offer only limited assurances of confidentiality. For example, the Economic and Social Research Council's Framework for Research Ethics (2010) requires that when working with 'children, families and vulnerable populations', British researchers ought to make clear any limits of confidentiality. One commentary suggested that indicating to participants that researchers might be forced to hand data over to courts might have a 'chilling effect' on research:

> It cannot help but exacerbate the reluctance of respondents who worry that their revelations might be used against them or their friends, colleagues, or family members. (Adler and Adler, 2002, p. 518)

When Lowman and Palys opposed mandatory inclusion of limited confidentiality clauses on the basis that they might be willing to violate a court order, the university ethics committee at Simon Fraser University refused to approve their research on the Vancouver sex industry, a decision that led to the intervention of the University President. However, some researchers are happy to comply with the inclusion of limited confidentiality clauses, and several British and American researchers have warned they would breach confidentiality in order to protect children from abuse (Barter and Renold, 2003; Tisdall, 2003). In his research on the illicit economy in the United States, Sudhir Venkatesh told potential informants he would report any information he had about future crimes to law enforcement agencies:

> Obviously this is not the most optimal way to initiate a relationship with someone from whom you are going to seek information! Indeed, several perceptive informants have then queried me, 'Would you tell the police my name? Would you give them your field notes, or would you go to jail and protect me?' After some proffered estimation of the odds that this might occur (which I say are relatively low if the past is any indication), I say that I will not compromise my position by disclosing names and other identities. (1999, p. 990)

At the Seattle Homeless Research Project in the 1990s, researchers adopted an interventionist stance towards the runaway, homeless and street youth during their evaluation of a new intensive care management programme. Participants' reports of suicidal intent were routinely shared with caseworkers and 'several dozen calls' were made reporting previous child abuse to protective services:

> In one case, when an interview took place during the evening and the adolescent appeared quite agitated, she was walked over to the closest emergency room where she was evaluated and held overnight. (Cauce and Nobles, 2006, p. 207)

These examples largely relate to the need to breach or offer limited confidentiality in order to prevent immediate and specific harm. However, Benjamin Baez (2002) argued we ought to think more broadly. He suggested automatic conventions of confidentiality served to further oppressive power relations, thwarting transformative research by silencing stories of abuse on the basis that this was necessary to protect the abused. Baez argued we should be wary of always privileging secrecy at the expense of resisting oppression. We might often choose to maintain confidentiality but need to continue to ask 'what are the possibilities and foreclosures of open-ness and secrecy in given contexts?' (p. 53).

Conclusion

While not every research participant may want to be offered or even warrant receiving assurances of confidentiality, it seems most do, and social scientists regularly assure them confidentiality will be maintained. While public attitudes towards sharing personal information may well be changing, researchers expect and are expected to keep their promises to participants. Researchers generally respect the privacy and autonomy of participants and if researchers did not, who would talk to them in the future?

Nevertheless, researchers are not always in control of their environment. Other people, organizations and agencies motivated by 'cyberterrorism, commercial espionage, governmental intrusion, and identity theft' (Duncan et al., 2011, p. 147) may be keen to see what information researchers have gathered. As a result, social scientists have developed a range of methodological precautions in relation to collecting, analysing and storing data as well as strategies to respond to legal challenges.

Researchers find out about all kinds of things and there are occasions when they have argued confidentiality should be breached. The question of whether to break a promise of confidentiality can be particularly difficult when researchers consider there is some possibility of someone else being harmed if they keep silent. Recognizing there may be times when they will have to reveal information that they had promised to protect, some researchers have attempted to identify to potential participants the situations in which they will not protect material. Indeed, such an approach has been required by some research ethics committees. Other researchers have argued that the point at which their colleagues are willing to breach confidentiality might destroy the credibility of the research enterprise in general and in some cases has so compromised their methodology as to render particular findings utterly worthless.

SEVEN

Avoiding Harm, Doing Good and Seeking Justice

We might expect that researchers would be very careful to protect participants from at least physical harm caused by their research programmes. After all, most moral systems require people to refrain from hurting anyone else intentionally unless there is good reason. However, as I discussed in Chapter 3, research ethics grew as a result of the need to protect participants from the considerable harms that had been done to them in biomedical research. The appalling impact of medical experimentation on vulnerable groups, it was argued, made it imperative that researchers not be allowed to regulate themselves. As a result, early ethical codes sought to protect research participants from various forms of harm.

Contemporary researchers are normally expected to minimize risks of harm or discomfort to participants (the principle of non-maleficence). In some circumstances, they may also be expected to promote the well-being of participants or maximize the benefits to society as a whole (the principle of beneficence). In this chapter, I examine the ways in which social scientists have grappled with the concepts of harm and benefit and how they have sought to balance the two. Researchers have not always been successful. We know some of our colleagues still leave participants feeling exploited, 'seething with rage and determined to skin alive the next aspiring researcher who seeks access' (Punch, 1986, p. 47; see also Ellis, 1986; Darou et al., 1993; Scheper-Hughes, 2000).

Avoiding harm

The meaning of harm itself is debatable. Joel Feinberg (1984) defined it as the 'defeating of an interest', where the interests of an individual are defined as 'the range of things in which that individual has a stake'. Although the influence of bioethics means harm is most often understood in physical terms, it also includes psychological, social, economic, legal and environmental damage. Indeed, in social science research, harm is generally more likely to involve psychological distress, discomfort, social disadvantage, invasion of privacy or infringement of rights than physical injury.

Just one research study may cause a range of harms. Consider three examples, the first hypothetical, the second and third real. The first involves a study of sexual practices among employees of a particular organization. Perhaps in an effort to assess the existence of discrimination or unsafe sexual practices, employees are asked whether they are sexually active, what types of sexual activities they have engaged in and the gender(s) of their partners. Various harms may flow from this research if, for example, confidentiality were to be breached and answers given by individual respondents revealed to current or prospective employers and fellow employees. As a result, one employee may be refused promotion or a new job because of his sexuality, another may be physically abused by colleagues because she is HIV-positive, a third might fear a break-up of his relationship with his partner after revelations of his sexual history, and so on.

The second case concerns social scientists in Iraq and Afghanistan operating within the United States Army's Human Terrain System. The American Anthropological Association Commission on the Engagement of Anthropology with the US Security and Intelligence Communities (CEAUSSIC) found that the programme might be engaged in research while also gathering intelligence, albeit inadvertently. They might also be 'performing a tactical function in which the military mission of combating an insurgency is the primary objective of data collection' (2009, p. 53). The Commission concluded Human Terrain Teams were unable to control the use of data they collected and therefore could not ensure participants received adequate protection. Indeed, as the AAA Executive Board had concluded two years earlier, there was a risk such data 'could be used to make decisions about identifying and selecting specific populations as targets of U.S. military operations ...' (CEAUSSIC, 2007). The 2009 AAA Code required researchers 'ensure' no harm came to research subjects. The 2012 Code took a more realistic view of anthropologists' capacities and simply required they sought to avoid causing harm. The activities of the Teams also threatened the future of anthropology by encouraging the military, local populations in Iraq and Afghanistan, and social scientists working for the army, to equate counterinsurgency with ethnography. Reuse of data for military or terrorist ends has been termed 'dual use'. It has become a matter of concern in health and scientific research (Miller and Selgelid, 2007), but has also troubled anthropologists, geographers, sociologists, political scientists and international relations experts in the face of a long history of covert and overt funding of social science research by American military and intelligence organizations (Horowitz, 1967; Social Science Research Council, 2008; Engerman, 2009; Bryan, 2010).

In the third example, Sudhir Venkatesh (2008) was studying the illicit economy in a Chicago housing project. Having interviewed tenants, he was invited to discuss his findings by two key informants, JT and Ms Bailey, who had brokered his access to other residents. He provided 'breakdowns on each hustler's earnings'. When he next returned to the project, he was told the key informants had used this information to 'tax' various tenants, and that JT 'beat the shit out of Parnell and his brother because he thought they were hiding what they were doing' (p. 203). Venkatesh's naïveté had triggered a small wave of violence and extortion, led to rumours that he was spying for the local gangs and receiving kickbacks, and consequently made it difficult for him – or possibly anyone else – to complete research there. As Venkatesh (p. 204) acknowledged to C-Note, one of his interviewees, '... I fucked up. I told them things, and I had no idea that they would use that information.' C-Note responded bluntly: 'That has to be one of the stupidest things I *ever* heard you say'.

Usually, researchers should try to avoid imposing even the *risk* of harm on others. Of course, most research involves some risk, generally at a level greater in magnitude than the minimal risk we tend to encounter in our everyday lives. The extent to which researchers must avoid risks may depend on the degree of the risk (prevalence) as well as the weight of the consequences that may flow from it (magnitude): 'It is commonly said that benefits and risks must be "balanced" and shown to be "in a favourable ratio"' (National Commission for the Protection of Human Subjects of Biomedical and Behavioral Research, 1979). Or, put another way, 'Grave risks require commensurately momentous goals for their justification' (Beauchamp and Childress, 2001, p. 118).

Ellsberg and Heise (2002) offered an example based on research on violence against women in developing countries. For them, the major danger when working with abused women:

> is the potential to inadvertently cause harm or distress. Respondents might be vulnerable to physical harm if a partner finds out that she has been talking to others about their relationship. Additionally, there is the potential for respondents to become distressed by an insensitive interview, or from having to recall painful or frightening experiences. (pp. 1599–1600)

So, domestic violence victims in Mexico have been revictimized by partners because they participated in a survey that explored their experiences (Health and Development Policy Project, 1995), and refugee women who discuss their experiences of sexual assault have faced violence and social exclusion from their own communities in refugee camps in Kenya and Thailand (Zwi et al., 2006).

While interviewing people who have experienced violence, investigators might help participants reduce isolation and support their recovery or, alternatively, they may end up retraumatizing them (Sikweyiya and Jewkes, 2012). In their discussion of prison research, Bosworth and her colleagues (2005, p. 258) identified a 'collective failure' among researchers 'to acknowledge the pain their questions may evoke in their participants'. On the other hand, Griffin and his collaborators concluded that trauma survivors 'are not too fragile to participate in trauma research even in the acute aftermath of a traumatic experience' (Griffin et al., 2003, p. 221). However, little empirical evidence exists for researchers and regulators seeking to make informed decisions.

There are some exceptions, and these may form the basis for a move towards evidence-based informed decisions by researchers and regulators. For example, Kuyper and her collaborators (2012) found 899 self-selected young people in the Netherlands were not distressed by answering survey questions about sexual behaviours. Another team investigated the perceptions of adult women who had participated in their research on experiences of childhood sexual maltreatment (Newman et al., 1999). Although some underestimated the upset they thought they would experience, most reported their participation in the interview- and questionnaire-based study had been a positive experience despite the sensitive nature of the questions. Hlavka and colleagues (2007) interviewed 142 women incarcerated in Minnesota and asked about their involvement in both violent offending and victimization. Whether and how people agreed to complete the interview were related to the nature and extent of the violence they had experienced. Some women did not wish to talk about their victimization, some talked around their experiences, while others were only willing to talk outside the formal interview:

> participants want to talk with interviewers about a range of traumatic experiences, but for some (and particularly those who have been revictimized) it needs to be on their own time and on their own terms ... (p. 914)

Management researchers often agree to brief corporations on their findings in return for access to the organization. In such situations, the boundaries between consultancy and research may become blurred, producing some unpleasant outcomes for participants. When data is collected for network analysis, Borgatti and Molina (2003) claimed employees are rarely offered sufficient information about what management will see, how results might be used and what the consequences could be for the participant. And yet, briefings by researchers to management might lead to participants being dismissed from their job. Management researchers might not be able to promise not to do any harm, but they could at least avoid harming innocent employees by allowing non-participation and making clear what the consequences of the study might be.

Programme evaluators face similar issues. As Leviton (2011) noted, the only inherent justification for an evaluation is that it may be of value to funders, administrators, staff, beneficiaries or other stakeholders. Evaluations may have a direct or indirect impact on whether a programme continues. To the extent they might influence funding decisions, flawed evaluations might damage a successful programme or support the wasting of resources on an unsuccessful programme. Other forms of research may also have an impact on policy formation. For example, in the Sahel, representing particular communities as nomadic pastoralists or arable farmers may be used to support or deny the claims to land of specific ethnic groups (Nyamnjoh, 2006).

Researchers are normally expected to adopt risk minimization strategies which might involve monitoring participants, maintaining a safety net of professionals who can provide support in emergencies, excluding vulnerable individuals or groups from participation where justifiable, considering whether lower-risk alternatives might be available, and anticipating and counteracting any distortion or misuse of research results that might act to the detriment of research participants.

In randomized experiments and quasi-experiments in field settings, some participants may find the conditions to which they are assigned leave them at a disadvantage, either relative to other participants or to non-participants. For example, it is typical to compare a new programme or intervention with a condition that is thought to be relatively ineffective. As a way of reducing risks or mitigating harm, Mark and Lenz-Watson (2011) suggested researchers might compare a new programme with current 'best practice' rather than 'practice as usual', unless there was little prospect of the best practice option ever being adopted across the study population. Participants might also be offered the more effective practice once the study has been completed. In other field experiments, participants may be placed in real situations and required to make decisions that impact on their well-being. For example, where economists seek to test a policy by introducing incentives in a real market to see if it produces a desired change in behaviour, they may also have to provide a safety net so participants cannot lose more than a certain amount.

Martacan Humphreys (2011) considered the ethics of embedded experimentation in political science, pointing to the possibility that researchers might be involved in projects of the kind that blocked access to political information in some areas or led to the use of water cannon in others. In each case, Humphreys noted such experimentation rode on the back of existing government initiatives and occurred without the informed consent of citizens.

Humphreys pointed out social scientists might evade their ethical responsibilities by distinguishing between their roles as consultants or activists on the one hand and researchers on the other. He also acknowledged these government initiatives were likely to be pursued with or without the involvement of academics. As a result, Humphreys described the ethics of such situations as largely 'unanswered and unanswerable' (p. 23) but attempted to develop an argument based on separate 'spheres of ethics'. He sought to distinguish between those parts of the experiment that might be the ethical responsibility of the host agency and subject to the standards associated with its sphere of activity and those that might fall within the domain of the researcher:

> if the intervention may be implemented ethically by the implementer, and if the intervention with a research component is at least as good as the intervention without, then the implementation with the research component is ethical also, even if, when undertaken by researchers alone, it violates ethical standards of the research community. (p. 23)

Humphreys argued researchers would only be justified in taking part if: the implementing partner were acting with legitimacy and independently of the researchers; where possible, experimental conditions involved variations that decreased risks; potential benefits justified risks; and the researcher were free of conflicts of interest, including financial remuneration for the work being undertaken.

Several methodological practices might also limit harm caused within randomized and other experiments. Power analysis can identify the minimum number of participants required to test a hypothesis, thereby avoiding either putting too many participants at risk or leaving the study at too small a scale to provide useful information. Some studies can be designed to incorporate a 'stop rule' which ensures data gathering stops once a significant effect has been observed (Maxwell and Kelley, 2011). Mark and Lenz-Watson (2011) also advocated the use of adaptive randomization which biases the allocation of new participants towards more effective conditions as these are determined through the study, and regression-discontinuity design (Imbens and Lemieux, 2008) which could enable participants to be assigned non-randomly to different conditions on the basis of need, circumstance or merit.

It may be difficult to assess whether non-statistical methods developed to minimize risks are adequate. Debriefing has been used extensively within deception-based experimental research as a risk-minimization strategy. Once data have been collected, the researcher explains to participants the true nature and purpose of the research. Critics of the value of debriefing have caricatured the process as meeting the needs of the researchers rather than of the participants by allowing the former to imagine that they have achieved a 'magical undoing ... an eraser for emotional and behavioural residues' (Tesch, 1977, p. 218) thereby allowing researchers to maintain their self-image as virtuous seekers of truth.

However, the process of debriefing may also suffer from several defects depending perhaps on how it is conducted and whether it is part of a respectful dialogue or a didactic lecture designed as 'cooling the mark off' (Tesch, 1977). Rather than wiping away the impact of manipulation, Ortmann and Hertwig (2002) concluded effects may extend well beyond a debriefing. Indeed, the debriefing itself may exacerbate or even constitute the only source of harm. For example, Finn and Jakobsson (2007) ran experiments in which they subjected students and eBay users to a fake phishing attack – an attempt to obtain by deception private information via the internet that might subsequently be used for fraud. The researchers were concerned that participants who were unaware that they had been scammed (without actual harm being caused) might become angry, upset or anxious only when discovering the scam during debriefing and that, because the experiment was being conducted outside the lab, researchers might have little opportunity to respond to these feelings. Several psychologists have also found participants may not place great value on the information they received during debriefings (Smith and Richardson, 1983), sometimes even believing it was an additional part of the deception.

In a systematic review of the ethics of debriefing, Miller et al. (2008) cautioned that the *prima facie* wrong of deception may at best be ameliorated rather than erased by debriefing. While accepting deception might be justifiable in some situations, they called for the researchers responsible for deceiving participants to demonstrate respect by offering a sincere apology to those who had been deceived, and asking participants to consent to the use of data obtained through deception. They hoped that such requirements might act as a check on 'cavalier' use of deception. Finally, in an effort to build an empirical base around the use of deception and debriefing, they urged researchers to report on participants' 'approval or disapproval of deceptive methods, trust in science, willingness to participate in future research, appraisal of the debriefing process, and the number of participants electing to withdraw their data' (2008, p. 248).

The argument of Miller and his colleagues has not been universally accepted. Bryan Benham (2008), for example, cautioned against placing a moral obligation on researchers to provide an apology. Benham was concerned that turning an apology into part of the protocol risked rendering the expression of regret void of meaning but full of 'insincerity and condescending paternalism' (p. 264) and might also place too much moral significance on minor ethical transgressions. Instead, he called for an enhanced debriefing process that offered enhanced benefits for participants (Benham, 2007). Oczak and Niedźwieńska (2007) found participants – in their case a small sample of Polish university students – were more likely to value a debriefing that, while revealing the nature and rationale for the deception, also provided strategies for identifying and resisting manipulation. This offered the possibility of improving how participants felt about involvement in the experiments and, indeed, in psychology as a discipline, and provided a direct benefit for those who participated in the experiments, the result advocated by Benham.

Another way of responding to the possibility of harm is by incorporating in the planning and running of the research members of those communities who form the focus of the work. For example, Patricia Lundy and Mark McGovern (2006) joined the committee of the Ardoyne Commemoration Project which was gathering grassroots-based testimonies to the 99 deaths that had occurred within that North Belfast Republican working-class neighbourhood during almost 30 years of conflict. Community members 'collaboratively controlled the decision-making process and worked with the academics on an equal basis to identify action strategies' (p. 55). Transcripts were returned to interviewees to edit and subsequent drafts were then circulated among all interviewees connected to a particular case study so that differences of opinion and disputes might be negotiated before documents were published. Researchers also brokered access to community-based counselling groups for victims and survivors. Interviews with participants at the end of the project revealed members of the community had found the need to recount traumatic experiences to be difficult but also important and necessary so that their stories might be told with their own voices. The relative of one victim described the interview as not offering 'any healing in it whatsoever ... I found it more upsetting but worthwhile' (p. 59).

One criticism of traditional views of risk minimization has emerged within anthropology. Graves and Shields (1991) argued codes of ethics overstated the knowledge of, and autonomy of action available to, social scientists:

> in biomedical experimentation the research paradigm gives researchers both maximum control over subjects and maximum potential to harm them irreversibly ... (p. 135)

> In contrast ... it is not at all clear in most forms of social science research who we are protecting, how we are protecting them, what we are protecting them from, or what constitutes the limits of our capacity to protect ... (p. 136)

While Teela Sanders (2005) was conducting fieldwork on sex industry workers in Birmingham, in the United Kingdom, her participants were sexually and physically assaulted, imprisoned or separated from their children by child protection agencies. She concluded 'I was not a social worker but a researcher, and although awful to witness, I was relatively powerless in making any difference to individual situations' (p. 36). Similarly, Christopher Kovats-Bernat (2002), an American anthropologist engaged in fieldwork with street children in Haiti, has criticized those who assume anthropologists are powerful enough to control or negotiate danger on behalf of those with whom they are working. Kovats-Bernat suggested such a belief was part of his discipline's 'colonial legacy' (p. 214):

the ability to protect against harm or to offer aegis is not the exclusive domain
of the anthropologist but, rather must be regarded as power shared among
actors in the field toward the well-being of everyone concerned. (p. 214)

Kovats-Bernat is pointing towards a far more sophisticated understanding that
draws on Foucauldian notions of power relations which are contingent and
multiple rather than fixed.

Another challenge to the idea that researchers should 'do no harm' derives
from covert ethnography. During covert work on violence in the nighttime
economy, a British criminologist worked as a bouncer (Winlow et al., 2001). In
this role, he had to deal with violence, witness violence and sometimes do
violence. The research team argued it would be naive and dangerous to imagine such research could be done without engaging in violence and that
'Complying with formal academic codes when we seek to understand the
complex interaction of social worlds that do not acknowledge such bourgeois
conceits is an unrealistic tactic, particularly for ethnographers' (p. 546). The
team suggested the value of the work justified the legal harm that might be
caused by, and indeed to, the researcher. Other criminologists have gone further and have maintained it was necessary to commit criminal offences in
order to be accepted in a covert role as a soccer 'hooligan' as 'a refusal to commit crimes on a regular basis would have aroused suspicions and reduced
research opportunities. As a result, I committed "minor" offences' (Pearson,
2009, p. 246). The offences included participating in pitch invasions, smuggling alcohol onto football trains and threatening other supporters. Although
Pearson acknowledged his main motivation was to gather data for his thesis
without disturbing the field, he thought his decisions might be justifiable in
order to reveal harm and injustice in the longer term.

Independent evaluators employed to produce reports by government have
been particularly concerned by their inability to protect participants. For
example, Williams et al. (2011) pointed to the difficulties they and their colleagues had encountered working with remote Indigenous communities: commissioners of the project might provide inadequate time or funding for an
appropriate relationship to be negotiated; parameters of the work were often
pre-set by contract; funders might refuse to allow results to be shared with
participating communities. Finally, results might be used to defund a programme or initiative valued by a community.

> This can be particularly frustrating if the evaluator has put in a positive report on
> a program, which is then de-funded, and the evaluator is required not to explain
> to the program personnel that the evaluation findings were positive. (p. 6)

Williams and her colleagues were troubled that evaluation was treated as a
subset of research and the differences between evaluation and research

inadequately understood by the ethics literature and research ethics governance processes.

Doing good

Researchers and research ethics governance structures have tended to concentrate on the need to avoid harming others, but some ethicists have argued researchers' obligations extend well beyond this. On the basis of the principle of beneficence, some have claimed that, in certain situations, we should also act to benefit others. For example, Beauchamp and Childress (2009) argued that because we all obtain benefits from being members of a society, we all might be under an obligation of *general beneficence* – to everyone else – under certain limited circumstances. Paraphrasing Beauchamp and Childress, a researcher might have to act if he or she knew: other people were at risk of significant loss or damage to a major interest; the researcher's action were needed to prevent loss or damage; the researcher's action had a high probability of preventing it; the action would not entail significant risks, costs or burdens to the researcher; and the benefit that others could be expected to gain outweighed any harms, costs or burdens the researcher was likely to incur.

Researchers might therefore be expected to owe a duty of beneficence to people even if they are not directly affected by the study. For example, the National Committees for Research Ethics in Norway (2006) argued researchers had a responsibility to disseminate the results of their research in a way that was socially relevant, informed the formation of public opinion and contributed to the maintenance or development of cultural traditions (p. 33). This meant researchers from small linguistic communities should publish in their native language as a way of contributing to the flourishing of their own culture (p. 8). However, although some ethicists have suggested that perhaps we should try to help as many other people as much as possible (Singer, 1999), the obligations of beneficence are normally limited in some way. For some commentators, there needs to be a special relationship between the person who is under an obligation and the person or class of people to whom he or she has an obligation. So, an obligation of *specific beneficence* might flow from family or friendship bonds, or from a legal contract. It might also be the product of a formal relationship created by a negotiated research agreement. In short, undertaking research may impose duties and obligations on the researcher to act to the benefit of participants.

One example of this occurs when commercial biomedical research takes place in developing countries. Here, the Council for International Organizations of Medical Sciences (CIOMS) (2002) has acted to stop research undertaken on behalf of multinational pharmaceutical companies exploiting research subjects.

Instead, CIOMS required researchers to be responsive to the health conditions and needs of vulnerable participants. The 2013 Declaration of Helsinki adopted similar language. CIOMS and the UNESCO (2005) Declaration, however, were more specific when it comes to implementation. So, this might involve: supplementing health services where the government is unable to meet local needs (CIOMS Guidelines 10 and 21); or 'enabling developing countries to build up their capacity to participate in generating and sharing scientific knowledge, the related know-how and the benefits thereof', thereby helping build the local research base by contributing to the host country's 'sustainable capacity for independent scientific and ethical review and biomedical research' (Commentary on Guideline 12). There has been some debate about the extent of the obligation that might flow from such concerns, and the degree to which it might transcend the questions of distributive justice, how benefits from the research should be fairly distributed. Emanuel (2008) argued biomedical researchers could not be expected to 'address underlying background global injustice' (p. 727). In contrast, London (2005) claimed Western countries had contributed to the existence of these underlying conditions and that all citizens of those countries therefore had a humanitarian duty to act to rectify injustice faced in low-income countries.

Facing criticism for failing to remove Kenyan sex industry workers from the sex trade during a 25-year observational study, Lavery et al. (2010) reflected on their decisions and sought to delineate the duty of biomedical researchers on the basis of 'relief of oppression', a term borrowed from public health. They called for researchers to work with research participants to generate the kinds of benefits – and distribute them in such a way – that might 'ameliorate some of the effects of the background conditions that limit fundamental freedoms of research participants'. Molyneux et al. (2009) noted a household study in Limpopo Province in South Africa had set up a community office to link local residents to social workers and social grants, and to allow researchers to donate second-hand clothes.

In social science, scholars often claim that by contributing to a general body of knowledge, the class of people who make up the participants might eventually benefit from the research. For example, in the field of research on HIV and intravenous drug users, medical anthropologist, Merrill Singer and his colleagues pointed to several benefits that have flowed from their anthropological studies, including:

> documenting the rapid diffusion of HIV among injection drug users ...; identifying little known routes of HIV transmission in drug-using population; determining the important role of crack cocaine in the sexual transmission of HIV ...; monitoring the emergence of new drug use and HIV risk patterns ...; documenting the effectiveness of outreach approaches to the recruitment of hidden populations of drug users into intervention ... (Singer et al., 2000, p. 390)

This may be of limited utility to research participants. While working in a camp for internally displaced people in northern Uganda, Ross (2009) offered to send a camp leader a copy of the resultant article:

> He laughed and said: 'Sure send your paper. When we get it (here he made a gesture of rolling a set of papers into a log) we can put it into the fire and maybe have a hot dinner, if there is any food. Send a book! Ha ha'. (p. 184)

As a result, Lisa Fontes (1998) took issue with approaches that stopped at the point of data gathering and analysis and argued for

> increasing use of research designs that benefit the participants directly … Here I am not referring to some theoretical benefit down the road, but rather to the extent to which these specific participants benefit from their participation. (p. 58)

In fact, Singer et al. (2000) were sympathetic to arguments such as these. Indeed, they made an even stronger assertion:

> in working with high-risk populations, researchers should also be concerned with using their research findings and interactions with vulnerable individuals to help protect participants from harm that might befall them outside of the research context. (2000, p. 391)

In short, Singer (1993) maintained researchers need to take an active stance to combat social suffering. Although Singer's team had used research money to fund a range of services for drug users in Hartford, Connecticut (including outreach educators, HIV testing and counsellors), had referred research participants to treatment and other health and social services, and had supported the development of a number of new service providers, following the death of one of their participants team members still wrestled with the possibility that they – and researchers like them – were just not doing enough (Singer et al., 2000; VanderStaay, 2005).

When working in countries controlled by more-authoritarian regimes, researchers may become involved with pro-democracy groups. Smeltzer (2012) preferred providing back office support for Malaysian non-government and community-based organizations and social movements rather than entering a front-line struggle she thought might endanger her, her students and the activist groups. She wrote grants, proofread documents, conducted background research, coordinated internship placements and, as a communications specialist, provided assistance with new media campaigns.

Guidelines produced by indigenous groups have called on researchers to maximize the benefits of research to indigenous peoples:

Research in Indigenous studies should benefit Indigenous peoples at a local level, and more generally ... A reciprocal benefit should accrue for allowing researchers access (often intimate) to personal and community knowledge. (Australian Institute of Aboriginal and Torres Strait Islander Studies, 2012, Principle 11)

This might occur by 'training, local hiring, recognition of contributors, return of results' (Tri-Council Policy Statement, 2010, Article 9.13), by providing broader education and training to Indigenous researchers, communities and organizations so that they can conduct partnered or autonomous research, or by helping a community to develop evidence-based policy and social interventions (Aboriginal Research Ethics Initiative, 2008; van den Scott, 2012).

In domestic violence research, Ellsberg and Heise (2002) maintained that interviews could provide an important opportunity for victims who might 'welcome the opportunity to share their experiences with someone who will not judge or condemn them' (p. 1600). However, Fontes (2004) warned that how women who had been the victims of violence weighed up the consequences of participating in research might vary with the culture of the participant. Most research that considered the impact of participation is not longitudinal and is unlikely therefore to detect psychological harm over time: 'Clearly, there is a disincentive for researchers to ask these questions' (Fontes, 2004, p. 166). Many studies do try to provide emotional and practical support for victims, offering information about, and organizing access to, formal and informal services, offering feedback to the study community and relevant agencies, and supporting or engaging in advocacy on behalf of abused women (Usdin et al., 2000; World Health Organization, 2001).

Rebecca Campbell and her colleagues (2010) identified those elements of feminist research methodologies – reducing hierarchy, providing information and communicating warmth – that might play a role in reducing harm and offering benefits for survivors of sexual violence. The research team acted as a doorway to information and brokered referrals to support agencies. They found victims of trauma generally saw participation in research as helpful rather than harmful. Their project offered participants an opportunity to talk to a supportive and engaged listener, and control what was revealed and how. Survivors remarked that they gained new insights into their experiences and the recovery process. However, not all feminist researchers have found their political agendas matched those of their research participants. Drawing on experiences studying prostitution in Lima, Lorraine Nencel (2001) was concerned an assumption by feminist anthropologists that research must provide direct benefits to participants 'could ultimately lead to a process of exclusion of a large group of women whose unwillingness to cooperate is, for example, attributable to their desire to avoid confrontation with their pain' (p. 82).

Many social scientists have been troubled by their position as data collectors who offer little more than the illusion of change to the subjects of their research. In disability studies, traditional research practices have also been vulnerable to attack from a politicized disability movement that described studies of disability as the exploitation and victimization of people with disabilities at the hands of traditional, non-disabled researchers who seemed more concerned with developing their own careers than in changing the position of disabled people. In the 1990s, some social scientists shifted away from notions of participatory research towards what they termed emancipatory research (Barnes, 2009; Zarb, 1992). For Oliver (1992), it was exploitative to engage in research that simply captured the perspectives of disabled people. Instead researchers had a responsibility to work with people with disabilities and use their research to develop ways of empowering people with disability, by influencing policy-making and practice. Lloyd et al. (1996) argued that researchers should share knowledge, skills and experience with people with disabilities and offer them greater opportunities. Following such an agenda, Stevenson (2010) collaborated on a research project with young people with Down Syndrome in Australia, ensuring her co-researchers were paid and their voices were 'continually in earshot, their presence felt, and their influence brought to bear at most stages of the research journey' (p. 48).

Researchers engaged in action research aim to generate knowledge that would be of value to 'the well-being of individuals, communities, and for the promotion of large-scale democratic social change' (Brydon-Miller et al., 2003, p. 11). Building on an action research framework, Hugman et al. (2011) described the possibilities of reciprocal research in social work where 'research participants are actively involved in all stages and it is they who determine what is to count as a "gain".' (p. 1279):

> the way that this research began was through establishing relationships that demonstrate actual benefits for the participants (in this case, prior provision of a valued service). It then progressed through the direct involvement of participants in all stages of the research, including establishing the agenda and the questions to be asked. Then, following initial stages, the participants continue to be involved in taking action, review and further questioning. (p. 1280)

The 1998 Code of the American Anthropological Association maintained that its members 'should recognize their debt to the societies in which they work and their obligation to reciprocate with people studied in appropriate ways' (1998, Section IIIA, point 6). Debates in anthropology, however, suggest that we should be cautious. For example, it may not always be easy to know how best we might support vulnerable populations. In 1995 American anthropologist, Nancy Scheper-Hughes, called on her colleagues to engage in militant anthropology, taking an activist stance as comrades in the face of oppression, 'colluding with the powerless to identify their needs against the interests of the bourgeois institution' (1995, p. 420). Scheper-Hughes' more recent work on the international trade in human organs led to her deciding to avoid remaining complicit in the behaviours she was studying which constituted international crimes against vulnerable populations (Scheper-Hughes, 2009). Instead, she established a university-based documentation centre to research human rights abuses in this field, alerted local law enforcement agencies to abuses, and sought 'to challenge and to change':

> the international transplant profession. I wanted them to acknowledge what was happening within their field, how it was being transformed by organs markets. And I think that that I have accomplished that. (quoted in Bartoszko, 2011)

Rylko-Bauer et al. (2006) argued anthropologists should not reject the obligations of reciprocity, finding it

> ironic, and more than a little self-serving, to legitimize advocacy for the compendium of knowledge or promotion of anthropology while questioning its appropriateness for the very groups who give of their time, knowledge, and other resources so that we in our individual careers and as a discipline might benefit. (p. 184)

Maiter et al. (2008) explored how the nature of reciprocal relationships might shift over time as the flows involved in exchanging knowledge, skills and support changed in nature and extent.

However, Scheper-Hughes' calls for a more activist discipline drew sharp comment from some respondents. D'Andrade (1995), Kuper (1995) and Gledhill (1999) pointed out it was 'not always obvious that the oppressed constitute a clearly defined class with an unambiguous shared interest' (Kuper, 1995, p. 425). Other ethnographers have found it painful to contemplate how and when to intervene in complex and dangerous situations. Despite his conclusion that ethnographers could not walk away from a family's self-destruction, Steven VanderStaay (2005) believed his attempt to pay the electricity bill of the great-grandmother of a teenage research participant in the United States may have played a small part in precipitating 'a horrific sequence of events that included several drug deals, a murder, the arrest and imprisonment of my subject, and the ruin of his mother ... wreaking havoc in several lives, including my own' (p. 372). Indeed, as Philippe Bourgois (1995) found in his study of the crack scene in Spanish Harlem, the attempts of a researcher to contribute to the host community can be met with utter derision from research participants and may jeopardize the research project:

> they thought I was crazy ... On several occasions my insistence that there should be a tangible political benefit for the community from my research project spawned humiliating responses.
>
> Caesar: Felipe, you just talking an immense amount of shit. (pp. 46–47)

The requirement of reciprocity was dropped in the AAA's (2012) Statement in favour of a call to 'weigh competing ethical obligations due collaborators and affected parties' (Principle 4).

Much of the literature that has urged researchers to provide greater benefits to research participants has been based on work with disadvantaged, powerless communities apparently in need of help. However, there has been little discussion of what scholars might owe powerful or dangerous groups – should researchers be required to provide benefits to corporations or government departments who are not paying for their services, to racist political groups or to men who engage in sexual violence? Gallaher (2009) regretted appearing with members of an American militia on a television show run by the movement, fearing the militia had derived legitimacy through attachment with a university researcher. Sehgal (2009) considered her position compromised when she was filmed sitting on the podium at a meeting of a Hindu right-wing movement. In those cases, would it really be inappropriate for researchers who might otherwise have a commitment to emancipatory or activist research to undertake work on, but not for or with, these groups? Of course, attitudes may change to host institutions during fieldwork. Given that the nature of many social science research projects may evolve during the course of the research, even researchers who enter the field intending to provide benefits may find that they reach conclusions that are quite critical of participatory institutions – conclusions that may not always be welcomed by host organizations.

In isolation, the principles of non-maleficence and beneficence might justify a researcher acting against the wishes of others on the basis that he or she knows what is best. For example, a researcher might decide not to tell participants about all the risks they might face if they take part in a study. She might say the risk is small and she does not want to worry participants. Alternatively, she might claim that even though the risk might be significant, many other people would suffer if the participants refused to take part in the research. These are paternalist arguments and could be criticized on a range of grounds. Antipaternalists such as Ronald Dworkin (1978), James Childress (1982) and Joel Feinberg (1986) would argue that such a decision by the researcher displayed disrespect to autonomous people, failing to treat them as moral equals. On the other hand, Beauchamp and Childress (2009) would accept people might be able to weigh autonomy against paternalism, and conclude that where very minor impositions on an individual's autonomy prevented significant harm or provided major benefits, there might be some justification for overriding an individual's wishes. However, their discussion of the possibility of justifying paternalism has been limited to significant preventable harms associated with medicine and it may be difficult to extend that argument to social science.

A more likely argument in social science is whether vulnerable populations (Santi, 2013), such as victims of violence (Becker-Blease and Freyd, 2006; Newman and Kaloupek, 2009), should be excluded from the opportunity to participate in research, and have their voices heard, on the basis that the project may place them at risk. Writing about research ethics in general, Miller and Wertheimer (2007) suggested outright antipaternalism obscured distinctions between decisions made with respect to non-autonomous and autonomous individuals. They described decisions made in relation to the former 'soft' and those in relation to the latter 'hard' paternalism. In addition, they pointed out that 'policies justified by paternalism were typically targeted at groups of individuals, not all of whom have impaired judgment' (p. 28). They termed this *group soft paternalism* and claimed regimes of research ethics governance largely justified regulation of work involving vulnerable groups on the basis of group soft paternalism, 'the unfortunate and unavoidable by product of a policy designed for the sake of those who are not capable of acting autonomously' (p. 28).

Returning to the victims and survivors of interpersonal violence, one consequence of making decisions for this group could be that research codes block scholarly investigations and as a result there is insufficient information available to allow that group to be helped. However, there may be an argument that we ought to curtail activities involving victims of violence that are likely to result in exploitative and extractive encounters but yield little benefit to victims directly. So, while fostering students' capacities as researchers may generally be seen as a good, Mitchell (2013) warned against the commodification of the experiences of the powerless in the developing world merely in order to create marketable fieldwork experiences for students from developed nations.

Balancing costs, risks, benefits and opportunities

Even research that yields obvious benefits may have costs. It is likely to consume the time and salary of the researcher, or the time of participants. It may also have negative consequences, causing various harms. In general, obligations to do no harm override obligations to do good. However, this may not be always the case, such as on those occasions where we might produce a major benefit while only inflicting a minor harm (Beauchamp and Childress, 2009). In such a situation, the decision whether or not to proceed with research might draw, in part, on utilitarian principles (Chapter 2). In the following four examples, Canadian, American and British scholars had to assess whether risks of harm to participants might outweigh the possible benefits.

Buchanan and his colleagues (Buchanan et al., 2002) investigated the use of syringes by intravenous drug users in Connecticut and Massachusetts. As part of the research, ethnographers followed informants and, with their consent, watched where they obtained their syringes. However, African-American and Puerto Rican informants who hung out with white ethnographers in particular neighbourhoods were more likely to be picked up by the police who appeared to assume that any minority person found in the company of a white person was likely to be purchasing drugs for them. The researchers, and indeed the informants, had to weigh the benefits of identifying which sources might be distributing contaminated needles against the increased possibility that participants might be arrested.

In the second case, a Canadian postgraduate student analysed discussions relating to the human papillomavirus vaccine among adolescent girls and young women on a public internet message board (Battles, 2010). Some dangers were obvious. The researcher, a participant in the discussions, might have intruded into private and sensitive conversations among young people who had no wish to take part in the research, triggering a 'rippling sense of resentment and betrayal' (online respondent quoted in Eysenbach and Till, 2001). These messages might also be reported in such a way that the online or offline identities of the senders become identifiable. As a result, the research might have posed a threat to the continued existence of the community that used the message board. Battles gained informed consent from the administrators of the website (who had also been involved in moderating the postings), and from participants who had contributed to the relevant threads. She ensured that the research was anonymous by de-identifying data and avoiding quotes that might be entered into a search engine, and concluded that she had minimized risks of harm.

In the third example, Merlinda Weinberg (2002) investigated the use of a particular planning document by a maternity home that helped young single mothers in Ontario. Use of this document was a mandatory requirement for homes licensed under provincial legislation. Weinberg found that, although the executive director believed the home was complying with regulations, front-line staff had bypassed the legislative requirements. At the request of the research participants, the researcher had agreed to provide some benefit to residents by naming those who had helped her with her work. However, if she allowed the licensing authority to identify the home, the home might lose its funding. Weinberg was reluctant to harm an institution that, for all its faults, 'ultimately supported and protected the very young women whom I was concerned about serving' (p. 91) and concluded the potential harm caused by the threat to the home outweighed the minor benefit offered through acknowledging those who participated in the research:

> There is no simple, pat hierarchy of ethical principles … in evaluating the conflicting needs of different participants, the researcher should assign very high priority to the needs of the most disadvantaged in determining which route to take. However, doing no harm also maintains prominence as an ethical principle. Additionally, a researcher must weigh potential costs and benefits, which he or she can determine only situationally. (Weinberg, 2002, pp. 93–94)

Finally, members of a research team investigating inequalities hoped their work might challenge homophobia in English primary schools and promote equality through exploration of a 'crucial and under-explored area of social justice' (DePalma, 2010, p. 224). However, they had to weigh such possible benefits against a broad array of risks whose magnitude rose in the face of 'disgust and outrage' (p. 217) expressed by media determined to portray the project in a sensationalist manner. The potential harms included discomfort for and/or media exposure of Lesbian, Gay, Bisexual and Transgender (LGBT) teachers, parents and children in LGBT-headed families. The team found it 'impossible to predict the long-term repercussions on people whose "controversial" family or personal characteristics are now public knowledge' (p. 222). The project also prompted: physical threats to researchers and participants; and the possibility that participating teachers might lose their jobs, and schools their funding if parents transferred their children to another institution.

The Belmont Report (National Commission for the Protection of Human Subjects of Biomedical and Behavioral Research, NCPHSBBR, 1979) called for a 'systematic, non-arbitrary analysis' (para 1. 9–1. 10) of the risks that research may pose to participants and the benefits the work may produce for participants and the wider society. Attempts have been made to reduce the relationship between benefits and costs into financial terms. Cost–benefit analysis allows research programmes with different goals to be compared. Although, in principle, any form of measurement could be used, in practice most measurements are expressed in financial terms. Any attempt to reduce relationships into such terms has its problems, partly because the process of reduction often displaces key non-financial values. While cost–benefit analysis has gained some purchase within biomedical and other forms of experimental research, Cassell (1982) and MacIntyre (1982) questioned its value in supporting ethical decision-making by most social scientists. MacIntyre argued that even in more predictable, quantifiable and definable experimental and quasi-experimental research projects, cost–benefit analysis could never by itself determine the appropriate course of action as it took no account of matters of distributive justice – who received the benefits and who bore the costs – and placed no constraints on what costs might be morally intolerable. In the less predictable realm of ethnography,

> cataloguing potential harms and weighing them against benefits before research is carried out becomes primarily an exercise in creativity, with little applicability to the real ethical difficulties that may emerge during the conduct of research. (Cassell, 1982, p. 150)

MacIntyre also warned that cost–benefit analysis was neither culturally nor morally neutral. In order to decide what counts as a cost and what counts as a benefit, 'we must first decide who is to have a voice in deciding what is to count as a cost or a benefit' (1982, p. 183). This is a concern that can be raised for all harms and benefits. Freedman (1987) argued any assessment of the value of research required an investigation not only of the views of academic peers but also the opinions of the community as a whole, including, one would imagine, the many different views that may be found among research participants. Some studies have started to examine how participants might view costs and benefits. When Milgram (1977) conducted a 12-month follow-up of participants in his obedience study, he found fewer than one per cent regretted they had participated in the research. In follow-up interviews with participants in his simulated prison study, Zimbardo (1973) also found no persistent negative effects (see Chapter 5). However, Warwick (1982) criticized the methodology used in these follow-up studies, claiming the researchers had adopted exactly those forms of instruments they had discarded in favour of the simulations in the first place. Gina Perry's interviews over 40 years later with American and Australian participants in Milgram's own and replicated studies also reveal a more complex picture (Perry, 2012). As I have already discussed, there may be more sophisticated ways of engaging with the views of research participants.

Researchers working with active drug users in Hartford, Connecticut sought to develop an evidentiary base for assessing the harms and benefits associated with research conducted with potentially vulnerable populations. Using focus groups of Hispanic illicit drug users, Singer et al. (2008) found participants were 'prepared to accept significant risk in the pursuit of valued benefit' (p. 366), weighing the risks that damaging personal information about their HIV-status or drug use might find its way to their families and communities against financial incentives, and access to health information and services. This assessment of costs and benefits was a continuing part of their lives as drug addicts.

It may be difficult to assess how costs, benefits and risks might be distributed across a population both socially and spatially (Smith, 1998). In one situation, the same person may face all the risks and stand to receive all the benefits. However, in another case, one person may bear all the risks while another is likely to receive all the benefits. Alternatively, several people may bear the risks but only a few obtain the benefits or, conversely, all may reap the benefits but only a few share the risks. For example, according to Fontes (1998), one Indian researcher decided not to investigate what had happened to women who had been burned by their husbands as a result of disputes about dowries. She was unwilling to place the women at further risk. However, Fontes drew attention to the costs of this decision: it also removed any possibility that the women interviewed – and women like them – might benefit from an end to their isolation and vulnerability. In this case, the researcher had to balance the potential harm to participants against the possible benefits to a larger group of women.

It may be tempting to over-generalize obligations of beneficence, non-maleficence and justice on the basis of principles developed to meet the needs of biomedical research. Indeed, I suggested in Chapters 3 and 4 that several ethical codes do. However, as DePalma discovered in her participatory action research on sexuality-based equalities in English schools, 'whether, when and whom to protect ... are complex issues and difficult to separate from the contexts in which they arise' (2010, p. 216). Research undertaken in the social sciences may quite legitimately and deliberately work to the detriment of research participants by revealing and critiquing their role in causing 'fundamental economic, political or cultural disadvantage or exploitation' (Economic and Social Research Council, 2010). For example, I have explored the violent counter-exile activities of South African intelligence agencies in the 1960s (Israel, 1998). I had little interest in minimizing harm to those agencies. Similarly, researchers uncovering corruption, violence or pollution need not work to minimize harm to the corporate or institutional entities responsible for the damage, though, as far as the Economic and Social Research Council (2010) is concerned, they might be expected to minimize any personal harm. Canadian and Finnish guidelines also acknowledge the issue by recognizing that research 'should not be blocked through the use of harms/benefits analysis' (Tri-Council Policy Statement, 2010, Article 3.6) and 'research concerning the use of power and the functioning of social institutions must not be restricted on the grounds that results can have negative effects for subjects' (National Advisory Board on Research Ethics, 2009, p. 9). The Finnish guidelines explicitly rejected a utilitarian cost–benefit analysis on the basis that assessing value and risks was 'a question of normative evaluation of values that are in themselves incommensurable' (p. 14).

Early ethical codes were concerned primarily with the welfare of individuals. For Emanuel and Weijer, for example, Belmont 'was written under the grip of an individualist vision' (2005, p. 181). Ethicists have also become interested in how communities might be protected in research on the basis that people perceive their identity and values in relation to broader groupings, and the nature of the relationship between individuals and communities varies in different societies. Charles Weijer and his colleagues (Weijer et al., 1999) identified 23 specific requirements for the protection of communities that had been adopted by national or international research ethics documents. Of course, there may be considerable difficulty in defining a community or identifying what steps might be justified in order to protect one. In Chapter 5, I discussed attempts to negotiate with indigenous communities. Indigenous communities may have shared histories and cultural traditions, can be geographically bounded and may elect their own political representatives. It may be more difficult to negotiate with other collectivities based on ethnic, political, sexual, professional or other commonalities.

Seek justice

While explorations of research ethics may have concentrated on harms and risks, more recent interest has focused on two elements of distributive justice – fair access to participation in, and to the results of, research – on the basis that:

> no persons should receive social benefits on the basis of undeserved advanta-geous properties ... and that no persons should be denied social benefits on the basis of undeserved disadvantageous properties ... (Beauchamp and Childress, 2009, p. 248)

The Belmont Report endorsed the relevance of justice to bioethics arguing that 'research should not unduly involve persons from groups unlikely to be among the beneficiaries of subsequent applications of the research' (NCPHSBBR, 1979, p. 10). It is easy to identify matters of justice in a tradition of biomedical research in the United States that has harmed prisoners and delivered benefits to those who can pay for private health insurance. Researchers in the United States initially responded to Belmont by barring vulnerable groups from participating in research. However, even if better protected from exploitation, such groups remained firmly excluded from the benefits of research. For example, Weijer (1999a) highlighted the adverse consequences for health provision of excluding women from clinical trials. A similar argument might be made for research that influences social policy on the basis of a sample that excludes ethnic minorities, women, children or the elderly, or people from developing countries (Morrow and Richards, 1996; Nama and Swartz, 2002). As a result, since 2001 the National Institutes of Health (NIH) in the United States have required women and ethnic minorities be included within clinical research so research results may be generalized across the population. While not specifically aimed at social sciences, the NIH definition of clinical research included patient-oriented outcomes and health services research. The Canadian Tri-Council Policy Statement (2010) also required researchers not to restrict their sample population by means of culture, language, religion, race, disability, sexual orientation, ethnicity, linguistic proficiency, gender or age without a 'valid reason' (p. 48) connected to the scope and objectives of the project. So, children and the elderly cannot be excluded from a general population pool simply on the grounds of administrative convenience. Researchers requiring people to have access to particular technologies to allow them to participate need to take care not to exclude already marginalized groups.

There are various suggestions that the principle of justice has long been neglected within the research and bioethics literature (Jonsen, 1998). In addition, there are claims that justice has been conceived inadequately by research ethicists and that much is lost by reducing justice to questions of distribution of the benefits and risks associated with research. For example, in the field of social work research, Hugman et al. (2011) argued obligations of non-maleficence and beneficence had to be integrated with concepts of respect and justice so researchers and participants shared understandings of the nature and distribution of benefits. Hugman's concerns take us beyond the questions of distributive justice considered by Belmont and into matters more closely related to procedural justice. King (2005) also called for researchers to take compensatory justice seriously by providing redress for those harmed through their participation in research activities.

One difficulty with the research ethics literature has been its concern with small-scale issues related to individual research projects. In contrast, the Uppsala Code developed by Swedish researchers in the 1980s called on researchers to avoid undertaking research that might result in ecological harm or the development of weapons, or that might be in conflict with human rights (Gustafsson, 1984). Fontes (2004) spoke for many social scientists when she pointed out that 'Research that is truly just will illuminate relevant issues of social injustice' (p. 161).

A significant challenge to traditional formulations of justice has come from Alex London. For London, reducing issues of justice to questions relating to fair access both to participation in, and to the results of research was based on a minimalist and 'particularly anemic theory of justice' (2005, p. 25). In the context of clinical trials in developing countries, he pointed out that the minimalist position enabled research to be justified if it improved the lives of the desperately poor who might be participating in the trial. Given their situation, such help could be offered at small cost when compared to the profits from a clinical trial or even from taking advantage of the difference in cost between conducting research in a poor rather than a wealthy country. London argued a minimalist theory thereby allowed researchers, their funders and sponsors both to absolve themselves of any responsibility for international inequalities and to exploit their bargaining position in relation to poor communities (London and Zollman, 2010). Even if researchers themselves were unhappy with operating in this way, they faced pressure from their funders to limit the benefits that they might offer a host community. In contrast, London sought to enable researchers to engage with broader questions of justice and 'consider whether the interests that are frustrated or defeated by less-than-decent social structures are so fundamental as to generate a duty on the part of others to assist them' (2005, pp. 31–32), because justice is not about working around unjust social structures, but rather is about building basic social structures 'that guarantee to community members the fair value of their most basic human capacities' (p. 32). Aware that many international clinical trials would fall short of this requirement, London wanted discussion around justice to occur at a higher level as decisions are made 'about what scientific questions should be explored, which research initiatives should be funded, where research should be carried out, and how research can benefit those who most need aid' (p. 34).

Conclusion

In most contexts, researchers are expected to minimize the risks of causing physical, psychological, social or economic harm to research participants. Our strategies include debriefing after an experiment in psychology as well as the participatory and emancipatory methodologies adopted by feminist, indigenous and activist scholars.

In addition, many researchers seek to provide benefits to participants either as individuals or as collectivities. Researchers in those parts of social science such as disability studies or Indigenous anthropology who work regularly with disadvantaged groups are particularly keen to improve conditions for their research groups. Nevertheless, some of their colleagues have been concerned these goals overstate the ability and resources of researchers to achieve meaningful change in the lives of the groups they study. Others have noted that attempts by researchers to help may be judged paternalist, misguided, partisan or simply incredibly stupid. In many regulatory environments, those researchers who investigate more powerful parts of society may have to justify not only their failure to promote the interests of elite groups but also the possibility that their findings might be intended to undermine the privileged positions of such groups.

Many research projects in the social sciences do provide some benefit, but at some cost. As a result, researchers may have to assess the relative weight of a diverse array of potential harms and benefits. They may also discover that these harms and benefits have different impacts on, and different meanings to, various parts of a community. Assigning financial values to each element may be attractive in some situations but, in others, such an exercise runs the risk of ignoring key non-financial matters and imposing the researchers' values on participants. It is not surprising, therefore, that many researchers have found it particularly difficult to use rule-based approaches in the field and have adopted other situated responses, and have also chosen to challenge limited understanding of harms, benefits and justice.

EIGHT

Integrity and Misconduct

Introduction

Researchers owe a professional obligation to their colleagues to handle themselves honestly and with integrity. They need to maintain intellectual honesty in proposing, performing and reporting research, accuracy in representing contributions to research proposals and reports, fairness in peer review, and collegiality in scientific interactions, including communications and sharing of resources. Such matters may not appear in codes or guidelines relating to research ethics, as many national and institutional governance arrangements distinguish between research ethics and research integrity. The former invites scrutiny before research takes place, the latter after. The former concerns relationships with research participants, the latter with the host institution, sponsors and other stakeholders. The regulators, investigatory powers and penalties for breach of ethics and integrity may also be quite different. So, the United States has separate Federal legislation (42CFR93), Australia has the Australian Code for integrity, and Canada has the Tri-Agency Statement. Work by the Global Science Forum of the Office of Economic Cooperation and Development, the European Science Forum and the World Conferences on Research Integrity has stimulated greater international and interdisciplinary consideration of research integrity and misconduct. It has also spurred the creation of further international codes and guidelines as well as national structures that remain separate to the research ethics sector.

And yet, the distinctions are often more apparent than real. In some languages, the same word covers both ethics and integrity. From the point of view of a researcher, both ethics and integrity involve working through a series of possible actions and reaching a conclusion about what might or might not be defensible. For a researcher, determining whether or not to deceive a participant, accept credit as an author or declare an interest in a decision, all look like questions that relate to the appropriate conduct of research. Conceptually, research ethics does not stop once a proposal has been reviewed and matters of integrity may arise well before data is collected. In practice, conflicts of interest appear in both kinds of codes and some statements on integrity regard breaches of research ethics as constituting a breach of integrity.

Research integrity

Some codes and guidelines such as the Canadian statements issued by the Research Councils United Kingdom (2011), the Canadian Tri-Council (2011), the National Health and Medical Research Council, Australia (NHMRC) (2007a), the Association of Universities in the Netherlands (2004/2012) and the German Office of Ombudsperson describe their remit in positive tones and emphasize integrity and the concepts of honesty, carefulness, independence and fair recognition. However, the dominant position in many other jurisdictions dwells on misconduct. In 2000, the United States Office of Science and Technology Policy published the Federal Policy on Research Misconduct. The policy applied to all research funded by Federal agencies, including work in the social sciences. The policy defined research misconduct in the fairly tight terms of fabrication, falsification and plagiarism. *Fabrication* is 'making up data or results and recording or reporting them'. *Falsification* is 'manipulating research materials, equipment, or processes, or changing or omitting data or results such that the research is not accurately represented in the research record'. *Plagiarism* is the 'appropriation of another person's ideas, processes, results, or words without giving appropriate credit'.

The threefold definition of misconduct as fabrication, falsification and plagiarism (or 'ffp') has become part (albeit in varying forms) of research codes for Australia, China, Denmark, Estonia, Finland, Germany, Hungary, India, Japan, Norway, the United Kingdom, The Singapore Statement on Research Integrity (Wager and Kleinert, 2011) and the European Science Foundation. However, the definition of integrity varies over time and space, or in Cossette's terms, is a 'spatio-temporal intersubjective construct' (2004, p. 214), depending in part on the role played by the definition. Where the definition has legal status and is meant to hold researchers and institutions accountable, the acts and degree of intention associated with misconduct may be tightly demarcated. Where definitions are intended to promote broader research or social values, the field may be conceived more broadly (Fanelli, 2011).

So, several codes extended their definition to include other matters (as did the original Office of Science and Technology Policy code). These are sometimes known collectively as 'questionable research practices'. In the case of the Australian Code for the Responsible Conduct of Research (NHMRC, 2007a), for example, research misconduct also includes conflict of interest and 'deception in proposing, carrying out or reporting the results of research' (s. 10.1). The remit used by the Research Councils in the UK encompasses: undisclosed duplicate publication; misrepresentation of data, interests, qualifications, experiences, and involvement; mismanagement of data; and breach of duty of care (including improper conduct in peer review) (Research Councils United Kingdom, 2011, pp. 7–8). The Canadian Tri-Agency Framework (2011) also covered destruction of records, redundant publication, invalid authorship, inadequate acknowledgement and mismanagement of conflict of interest. The Norwegian Research Ethics Act of 2007 defined academic dishonesty as including 'other serious violations of good scientific practice that is committed willfully or with gross negligence in the planning, implementation, or reporting of research' a definition also adopted in Danish legislation (Danish Committees on Scientific Dishonesty, 2009). Behaviours addressed by the Chinese Association for Science and Technology (Xinhuanet, 2008, cited in Zeng and Resnik, 2010) included: duplicate publication; 'unethically interfering with other people's research'; 'conspiring with other people's misconduct or retaliating against whistle-blowers and giving unfair review due to a conflict of interest'.

A review of international practice for the Canadian Research Integrity Committee (Hickling Arthurs Low, 2009) distinguished between three kinds of national regulatory systems. The first type, typified by the United States, Norway and Denmark, had a narrow legal definition of integrity and a central regulatory agency with powers of investigation. In Norway, the legislation was administered by the National Commission for the Investigation of Scientific Misconduct and encompassed all research institutions, including the private sector.

The second type – which would include Australia, Canada, Germany, the Netherlands, the United Kingdom and Sweden – had no national legislation, but research councils had created model guidelines and devolved responsibility to research institutions to develop their own policies as a condition of funding, and advice or investigation is provided by an independent body. In the United Kingdom, the United Kingdom Research Integrity Office had no statutory powers, could not investigate independently. It is no longer funded by Universities UK, but it does still maintain an advisory service supported by voluntary contributions. Instead, funding agencies switched their attention in 2012 to a Concordat to Support Research Integrity to which institutions had to subscribe if they wanted grant funding. Having rejected an earlier draft, the Academy of Social Sciences (2013) eventually supported the Concordat, though the Academy remained wary the agreement might turn into a cumbersome, risk-averse, bureaucratic exercise that did little to encourage scholars to grapple with issues of professional integrity. In China, Croatia and Poland, the state established an independent commission to investigate misconduct.

The third group, comprising countries such as Japan, Eire, France, Spain and Portugal, as well as most middle- and low-income countries had neither national legislation nor independent oversight, and responsibility was at best diffuse and at worst ambiguous (Ana et al., 2013). It may have rested with individual institutions or was left to peer review. In Eire, guidelines developed by research funders were applied by institutions, although the closure of the Irish Council for Bioethics in 2010 probably hindered further policy development. In the case of Japan (Masui, 2011) and France (Alix, 2011), systems were still being developed.

At a supranational level, several organizations have drafted their own statements on research integrity. The European Commission funded a European Network of Research Integrity Offices, and the European Science Foundation set up a Member Organisation Forum on Research Integrity. The Forum supported the establishment of national institutions in its member countries. It drafted a European Code of Conduct for Research Integrity in association with the European Federation of National Academies of Science and Humanities – ALL European Academies (ALLEA) (European Science Foundation, 2011). In 2010, the Second World Conference on Research Integrity completed The Singapore Statement on Research Integrity (Wager and Kleinert, 2011) as a guide for future regulations. The authors of the Statement argued that it contained fundamental principles relating to honesty, accountability, professional courtesy and fairness, and good stewardship of research, as well as 14 professional responsibilities that together ought to transcend legitimate national and disciplinary differences. The Statement was augmented in 2013 by the Montreal Statement on Research Integrity in Cross-Boundary Research Collaborations.

Commentators have been divided on the extent of research misconduct. In defending the withdrawal of funding from the United Kingdom Research Integrity Office, the Chair of the Higher Education Funding Council for England (HEFCE) pointed to the very small number of cases of significant, proven research misconduct. In reply, the editor-in-chief of the *British Medical Journal* and the Chair of the Committee on Publication Ethics (COPE) suggested the lack of examples had 'more to do with a closed, competitive, and fearful academic culture than with Britain's researchers being uniquely honest' (Godlee and Wager, 2012). Godlee's survey of 2,700 British-based scientists and doctors found that over ten per cent had witnessed colleagues altering or fabricating data.

Closer to social science, Cossette (2004) received 136 responses to a survey of administrative science researchers in Quebec. Researchers reported that fragmented publication, plagiarism and self-plagiarism, guest authorship and poor citation practices were all moderately frequent. Bedeian and his colleagues (2010) asked faculty based in 104 management departments in United States business schools whether they had observed or heard about colleagues engaging in various forms of research misconduct in the previous academic year. Among 438 usable responses, over 70 per cent reported knowledge of colleagues who had 'withheld methodological details or results' (79.2%), 'selected only those data that support a hypothesis' (77.6%) or plagiarized (72.1%), all matters that fell within the United States Federal Policy on Research Misconduct. In addition, over three-quarters reported knowledge of faculty who had engaged in post-facto hypothesizing (91.9%), duplicate publication (86.2%), or had accepted or assigned ghost or gift authorship (78.9%).

Several factors that might encourage misconduct are likely to pose an even greater threat in the future. Many academics are under increasing pressure to publish (and to do so in English irrespective of their competence in that language) as their nation or institution seeks to establish or defend its placing in international research rankings. So, individuals are forced to meet publication targets in order to obtain jobs and grants. In other cases, such as the United Kingdom, Australia, New Zealand and Hong Kong, research infrastructure is funded according to the results of a national research performance evaluation. A fear these pressures will corrode research integrity has been voiced in many countries including Brazil (Vasconcelos et al., 2009), Canada (Hickling Arthurs Low, 2009), China (Postiglione, 2007; Zeng and Resnik, 2010), Hungary (Hungarian Academy of Sciences, 2010), Iran (Ardalan et al., 2009) and Malaysia (Poon and Ainuddin, 2011).

One factor propelling plagiarism in particular into the public eye is the tension between norms that govern academic conduct and those that appear to have been operating in other spheres. There is, for example, a tendency within government and corporate bureaucracies to adopt authorship practices that would constitute misconduct in an academic setting. In 2011, several German politicians were found either to have plagiarized their doctorates or to have relied rather heavily on work undertaken by parliamentary researchers. By May 2012, the website VroniPlag had used crowd sourcing to identify misconduct in the case of 23 research higher degrees, and had triggered the proceedings that had led to many being rescinded (Schuetze, 2011; Vogel, 2012). Similar websites have been established in Russia, Romania and Spain. In some countries, a university undergraduate or postgraduate degree is either required or highly desired among those seeking public office, and politicians and bureaucrats have taken short cuts in order to overcome this hurdle. Scandals relating to higher degree theses have brought down cabinet ministers in Germany, the president of Hungary and a vice-president of the European Parliament, and have troubled the Prime Minister of Romania. Vladimir Putin was undisturbed by claims that a part of his economics thesis was lifted from a 20-year-old American management text. Nevertheless, in 2013 when the Russian Prime Minister announced a campaign against plagiarism by school students, a news website dared him to open investigations into Putin, the Ministers of Defence and Culture, and the leader of Chechnya.

Within most countries, there are some clear gaps in the domains covered by regulatory regimes. Institutions funded by some research councils may be covered by national codes but, in Australia and Canada for example, not all government departments or research agencies, private research organizations, corporations or independent professional practitioners have been subject to the national codes (Hickling Arthurs Low, 2009). As a result, researchers have faced an uneven mix of policies and practices. This has caused difficulties when research or researchers operate across disciplinary, sectoral or national borders (European Science Foundation, 2011).

Fabrication and falsification

In the United States, the Office of Research Integrity has considered allegations of misconduct, although its remit extended only to publicly funded biomedical research. In 2011, 240 allegations were reported and research misconduct was found to have occurred in 13 of the 29 closed cases (Office of Research Integrity, 2011). In each case, the matter involved falsification and/or fabrication. The National Natural Sciences Foundation of China investigated 542 allegations of misconduct involving government-funded scientists between 1998 and 2005. It found misconduct in 60 cases – 40 per cent involved falsification, seven per cent fabrication or theft and 34 per cent plagiarism (Gong, 2005). Following this, the Ministry of Science and Technology established the Office of Scientific Research Integrity Construction to investigate misconduct.

Working within psychology, Sterba (2006) classified misconduct in data analysis and reporting, distinguishing between overt and covert forms of activity and providing examples of each (see Table 8.1). The different forms reflected various distortions of the scientific data. As a Chicago statistician observed, 'The more you torture your data, the more likely they are to confess, but confessions obtained under duress may not be admissible in the court of scientific opinion' (Stigler, 1987, p. 148, cited in Bedeian et al., 2010).

Table 8.1 Overt and covert misconduct

Overt misconduct	
Dichotomizing continuous data	reduces variability and can create significant results
Cross validating exploratory data procedures with confirmatory data procedures on the same dataset	capitalizes on chance variation in the dataset

Overt misconduct	
Not testing alternative models that equivalently fit the data but imply different theoretical conclusions	prematurely thwarts the consideration of competing theories
Covert misconduct	
Trimming data in a systematic way	omits outlier data points to sway the significance level in the direction of stated hypotheses
Capitalization on chance variations in datasets	predictors reported as if theoretically conceived a priori, with no mention of other predictors tried and eliminated
Selective reporting	of background literature to inflate the importance of a proposed project; of model fit criteria on the basis of a skim for acceptable values; of the parameters of the model that was fit to the data

Source: Sterba, 2006

For example, Leung (2011) criticized the practice within management research of presenting post hoc hypotheses as if they were a priori (capitalization on chance variations in datasets). Leung found none of the 47 quantitative studies published in the *Academy of Management Journal* in 2009 had rejected more than half of their hypotheses. Over the year, only 16.4 per cent of 251 reported hypotheses were not supported. Although this may reflect 'impressive foresight' on the part of researchers or, indeed, bias in the peer review process towards suppressing 'loser hypotheses' in favour of positive results, Leung concluded some degree of shift away from the formal hypothetico-deductive model may have contributed. While Kerr (1998) rejected all forms of what he termed 'HARKing' (Hypothesizing After the Results are Known), Leung was prepared to accept there might be reasons not to publish hypotheses that detracted from the coherence of a study. Equally, Leung accepted a researcher, inspired by empirical findings, might modify hypotheses 'to provide an insightful, coherent theoretical basis for the research, but not to artificially inflate the positive findings' (p. 475).

Although investigations of falsification and fabrication have progressed further in biomedicine, there is some recognition these practices may be rife in other disciplines, such as management and economics, areas that have otherwise not developed much of a literature on research ethics or integrity. In a study by Bedeian et al. (2010), over one-quarter of respondents in departments of management reported knowledge of colleagues falsifying data. Bailey et al. (2001) undertook a self-report study of American academics using a randomized response technique and concluded about 3.7 per cent of articles in the top accounting journals and four per cent of articles in leading economics periodicals were seriously tainted by falsification. List et al. (2001) surveyed 20 per cent of attendees of the 1998 meetings of the American Economic Association. From a 23 per cent response rate, they estimated more than four per cent of respondents had falsified data at least once, though not necessarily for publication. While some might argue falsification of data in disciplines such as economics may have a less harmful impact than in biomedicine, List and his colleagues noted such practices could lead to the adoption of harmful economic policies.

There are documented examples of falsification or fabrication in history, management and psychology. The language of the American Historical Association's Statement on Standards of Professional Conduct (2011) has been particularly scathing when it comes to forgery and fraud as an 'undetected counterfeit undermines not just the historical arguments of the forger, but all subsequent scholarship that relies on the forger's work' (p. 3). Yet, in 2002, Michael Bellesiles was forced to resign as professor of history at Emory University in the United States after an investigating committee questioned his scholarly integrity and veracity, finding evidence of falsification and misrepresentation of historical evidence or the sources of that evidence in his book on the origins of American gun culture (Katz et al., 2002). Cramer (2006) meticulously detailed Bellesiles' falsification and misrepresentation of original sources, finding serious errors 'on almost any page, picked at random' (p. 168).

In 2006, an internal investigation by the University of Colorado found lack of integrity in the research of Ward Churchill, a professor of ethnic studies, and subsequently fired him. The investigative committee determined he had published an article under another professor's name and then cited that article to support his subsequent claims, misrepresented two pieces of legislation relating to Native Americans, and falsified and fabricated claims the military deliberately infected Indians with smallpox at Fort Clark in 1837. Having reviewed three pages of data drawn from seven published versions of Churchill's smallpox tale, Thomas Brown concluded: 'Churchill has fabricated incidents that never occurred and individuals who never existed. Churchill falsified the sources that he cited in support of his tale, and repeatedly concealed evidence in his possession that disconfirms his version of events' (2006, p. 100). The University's findings were rejected by the Colorado Conference of the American Association of University Professors (2011).

Ulrich Lichtenthaler, a management professor at the University of Mannheim in Germany, had 13 papers retracted by eight different journals, after readers noticed irregularities in his statistical analysis in 2012. Dubbed a 'serial salami slicer' (West, 2013), Lichtenhaler submitted similar papers to different journals without declaring the overlap and, bizarrely, offered diverging interpretation of the same dataset in different publications.

In 2011, Marc Hauser resigned his position in the psychology department at Harvard University, after an internal investigation found him solely responsible for eight counts of scientific misconduct. With a background as an evolutionary biologist, he was working in cognitive neuroscience on the issues of cognition and morality in research comparing monkeys, tamarins and human babies. Hauser had, among other things, fabricated data relating to control experiments. Hauser's Dean later identified that Hauser's experiments had problems involving data acquisition, data analysis, data retention as well as the reporting of research methodologies and results (Smith, 2010). In 2012, the Federal Office of Research Integrity concluded Hauser had engaged in six cases of research misconduct in work supported by the National Institutes of Health.

The reputation of social psychology in the Netherlands took a battering when, in three separate cases, academics were found to have fabricated data. Erasmus University Rotterdam (2012) withdrew three articles published by Dirk Smeesters, professor of consumer behaviour and society, and accepted his resignation. Smeesters' 'massaging' of data was uncovered by Uri Simonsohn, an academic at the University of Pennsylvania, who found the data too good to be true (Enserink, 2012a). A more serious case concerned Diederik Stapel, a social psychologist working at Tilburg University. In 2011, he was found to have fabricated the data for 55 peer-reviewed journal articles and ten PhD theses that he supervised. Other work contained serious methodological flaws. For some of the articles, Stapel took responsibility for gathering data and then provided his co-researchers with a fictitious dataset that fit their hypotheses. An investigation (Universiteit van Tilburg, 2011) into Stapel's work concluded that 'effects were large; missing data and outliers were rare; and hypotheses were rarely refuted' (translated from the original Dutch in Callaway, 2011). Stapel (2012) finally admitted 'The truth would have been better off without me' (translated from the original Dutch in Enserink, 2012b). Finally, in 2014 an internal investigation by the University of Amsterdam called for the retraction of an article co-authored by Jens Förster, one of its experimental psychologists (van Kolfschooten, 2014). The Dutch psychologists' fabrications might have been more easily spotted if they had documented their work in such a way that others might quickly check their findings. However, as Wicherts and his colleagues discovered (Wicherts et al., 2006), 73 per cent of researchers who had published in one of four high-impact American Psychological Association journals failed to share their data (in breach of APA Ethical Principles): 'Several data sets, authors said, had been misplaced, whereas others were kept secret because they were part of ongoing work, or because of ethical rules meant to protect participants' privacy' (Wicherts, 2011). These results were particularly disturbing as Bakker and Wicherts (2011) found a high incidence of reporting errors in relation to null-hypothesis significance testing among a representative sample of 281 published papers in psychology journals (around half had reporting errors and 15 per cent contained at least one result that was erroneously presented as statistically significant) and that some errors were predictive of researchers' unwillingness to share data (Wicherts et al., 2011).

Some of the most serious allegations in psychology involved Cyril Burt, a prominent British psychologist. After his death in 1971, he was accused of fabricating data obtained when studying pairs of twins for his work on the inheritance of intelligence. Hearnshaw (1979) argued Burt added to his original data by inventing results from new sets of twins. Even now, the argument has not been settled. Hearnshaw's claims were initially accepted by the British Psychological Society. However, the Society later withdrew its statement and no longer has a position on the matter (British Psychological Society, 1992). Unfortunately, many of Burt's papers were destroyed after his death and, because of inadequate description of his methodology, it proved impossible to replicate his work. Joynson (2003) suggested: 'Either Burt had committed the most serious scientific fraud since Piltdown man, or he was guilty of no more than carelessness and muddle' (p. 410). One reason for the sloppiness in Burt's research and writing was that he seems to have had few scruples about how he promoted his own work. For example, he was the founding editor of the *British Journal of Statistical Psychology*, in which he published 63 of his own articles. Apart from taking short-cuts in reviewing his own work, he altered the work of others without their permission, often to his own advantage, and attacked colleagues under pseudonyms.

Unfortunately, the Dutch scandals were not limited to social psychology. Mart Bax, a retired professor of political anthropology from the Free University of Amsterdam, was found by his former institution to have engaged in 'serious scientific misconduct', 'deception' and 'unethical scientific behaviour'. He padded his curriculum vitae by adding 64 non-existent papers, inventing awards and roles at prestigious universities, and may well have fabricated his fieldwork in both Brabant and Bosnia (Baud et al., 2013). In 2014, the first of his papers was retracted by *Ethnic and Racial Studies*.

Plagiarism

Plagiarism is one of the more prevalent forms of academic misconduct outside the biomedical field, particularly in qualitative social science research. The Office of Research Integrity (1994, p. 5) in the United States defined it as:

> both the theft or misappropriation of intellectual property and the substantial ... unattributed verbatim or nearly verbatim copying of sentences and paragraphs which materially mislead the ordinary reader regarding the contributions of the author.

Working within their own discipline, two American economists surveyed 127 journal editors (Enders and Hoover, 2004) and 1,208 economists (Enders and Hoover, 2006) around the world. The editors reported that collectively they encountered at least 42 instances of plagiarism each year, while 24.4 per cent of the researchers reported they had been plagiarized – 87 by having their original idea or methodology used without attribution, 42 their model, proof or derivation, and 15 their privately collected dataset. The rest involved infringement of copyright as chunks of text (up to and including 90 pages) were reproduced as if original. Levin (2011) noted that, over one year in the mid-2000s, editors of 20 major primary research journals connected to the American Psychological Association on average reported one case of plagiarism, mostly relating to incidents of self-plagiarism.

Plagiarism is one of the more difficult forms of academic misconduct to prove. In his detailed examination of the process of detecting, analysing, assessing, reporting and preventing plagiarism, Decoo (2002, p. 120) identified various ways people who have been accused of plagiarism have attempted to neutralize the accusation:

> The wording is quite different from that of the alleged source. The overlap is minimal and accidental. The sources used were properly cited, but in a different place. Every competent reader would know what the obvious source was. The sentence is a truism that many people would write the same way. The copying of that part was inadvertent.

Accusations of plagiarism have been levelled against senior researchers on every continent, including in Australia, Brazil, China, Croatia, Egypt, India, Iran, Korea, Latvia, Pakistan, Peru, Serbia, South Africa, Vietnam, the United Kingdom and the United States (several incidents were discussed in Heitman and Litewka, 2011). Academics whose native language is not English may find it more difficult to express their findings in English in ways that are accepted as original and, as a result, scientists in both Brazil (Vasconcelos et al., 2009) and Turkey (Yilmaz, 2007) have reported seeing either a lack of understanding of the nature of plagiarism or a lack of appreciation that it breaches acceptable conduct.

Findings against academics in social science are rarer. In 2002, David Robinson, the vice-chancellor (president) of Australia's largest university, Monash University, was forced to resign after the university discovered he had been found guilty of plagiarism on at least two separate occasions while working as a sociologist in the United Kingdom. Robinson had not told Monash of his misconduct when the university appointed him vice-chancellor. One of Robinson's critics commented: 'Having a plagiarist as head of a university is like having an embezzler running an accounting firm' (Bigelow, quoted in Madden, 2002).

Abebe Zegeye, a professor of sociology, was dismissed from his research directorship at the University of the Witwatersrand in 2010 and then forced to resign from the University of South Australia early the following year. The South African university initiated an inquiry as a result of complaints from three senior international academics, Kwame Appiah, Stuart Hall and David Goldberg, that Zegeye had 'blatantly, repeatedly and extensively misrepresented published work of a range of authors [including themselves] as his own' (from the report of the arbitrator, quoted in Maslen, 2011). The institution appointed an arbitrator who reportedly uncovered 140 instances of plagiarism in nine publications for work that was undertaken over eight years, with material being recycled from 30 scholars (MacFarlane, 2011).

The head of the Beijing University Anthropology and Folklore Centre, Cai Hua, was accused of plagiarizing and misrepresenting the work of earlier Chinese anthropologists after his work on the Na received strong reviews from Western anthropologists of the calibre of Clifford Geertz and Claude Lévi-Strauss. Xiaoxing Liu criticized Cai: 'He plagiarizes his data, ideas and other sources from his predecessors, Chinese researchers of the 1960s, selects only data that support his arguments, and maligns these researchers to cover up his misconduct' (2008, p. 298). Cai published his doctorate in French in 1997 and it was only after it was republished in English in 2001 that Norwegian and Chinese anthropologists began to question its integrity. Cai was able to take credit for the work of his compatriots by translating their material at a time when few works by Chinese scholars had been translated into Western languages and few Western anthropologists had studied Chinese. Cai was the second plagiarism case at Beijing University in a short period of time. In 2002 another director of the Folklore Centre, anthropology professor Wang Mingming, was demoted after plagiarizing almost 100,000 words of William A. Haviland's book *Cultural Anthropology* (Xueqin, 2002).

There have been cases elsewhere. A professor of psychology and education at Columbia University's Teachers College in New York was dismissed for 'two dozen instances of plagiarism' (Bartlett, 2008). A political scientist and former head of the Middle East Center at the University of Utah was sacked in 2011 for engaging in a 'pattern of plagiarism' that included his doctoral thesis and five book chapters (Maffly, 2011). In 2008 and 2009, the director of the Centre for the Study of Ethnicity and Culture at the University of Birmingham in the United Kingdom, was found guilty on multiple counts of plagiarism in relation to a book, an edited collection and an article (Newman, 2009). Ten per cent of English-language articles in Serbian social science journals by Serbian authors published between 2000 and 2009 involved plagiarism, according to a study by the Centre for Evaluation in Education and Science in Belgrade (Šipka, 2010).

When a group of Russian academics reviewed 25 history postgraduate theses written by public officials graduating from Moscow Pedagogical State

University, they discovered 24 relied on plagiarism for at least half their contents and that the same number had fabricated references (Shuster, 2013; Sonin, 2013). Vroniplag found three authors from the University of Münster had plagiarized large parts of their book on legal writing. It is hard to resist reproducing Wikipedia's comment: 'even the chapter on plagiarism was plagiarized. And although the book told students not to use Wikipedia, the book itself contained 18 fragments taken from the German Wikipedia' (Wikipedia, 2012).

An Indonesian professor in international relations at the Parahyangan Catholic University resigned after publishing an opinion piece in *The Jakarta Post* that reproduced material from an Australian academic (Fitzpatrick, 2010). In 2011, the vice-chancellor of the University of Peshawar was found by a committee of Pakistan's Higher Education Commission to have plagiarized work on Afghan–Pakistani relations (Aftab, 2011). A more complex set of affairs emerged in Vietnam when a professor at the University of Economics Ho Chi Minh City, whose textbook had been copied by another, was in turn found to have translated and published under his own name a book by an American author on international financial management (*Vietnam News Brief Service*, 2010).

Authorship

Leaders of research teams may also be in a position to exploit the labour of their colleagues. Researchers face enormous pressures to publish or, at least, look like they are publishing as they struggle to obtain grants or jobs. Quantity may take precedence over quality in publication. Different disciplines maintain incompatible conventions and different countries face distinct pressures to determine authorship in particular ways. An inevitable consequence has been that tensions have arisen over the attribution of authorship.

Some were the result of blatant research misconduct. In 1990, Carolyn Phinney, a psychologist at the University of Michigan, was awarded US$1.67 million in damages after a court found another psychologist, Marion Perlmutter, had stolen her research. Perlmutter had falsely claimed the work belonged to her, had sacked Phinney from the laboratory, and then stolen the data from Phinney's office (Charatan, 1997). However, most researchers engaged in misconduct are less brazen. Health researchers have had long-standing concerns (Mowatt et al., 2002; Sheikh, 2000) that the names that appear at the top of an article in their field do not reflect the true authorship, either because someone who has insignificant involvement has been added – gift, honorary or prestige authorship – or because junior staff who made significant contributions have been omitted – ghost authorship. Maruši et al. (2011) conducted a meta-analysis of 14 studies in various disciplines that surveyed researchers' own experiences or knowledge of others' problems with authorship. On average, 29 per cent of respondents had encountered such difficulties. For example, Martinson et al.'s (2005) study of 3,000 scientists funded by the United States National Institutes of Health found ten per cent of respondents admitted to 'inappropriately assigning authorship credit'. Indeed, drug companies have cross-bred research with marketing by using the names of senior academics to launder the source of the data and legitimate the process (Grassley, 2010):

> In extreme cases, drug companies pay for trials by contract research organizations (CROs), analyze the data in-house, have professionals write manuscripts, ask academics to serve as authors of those manuscripts, and pay communication companies to shepherd them through publication in the best journals. (Sismondo, 2007, p. 1429)

In one of the few investigations of authorship decisions adjacent to the social sciences, Geelhoed et al. (2007) surveyed 109 authors who had published in major clinical psychology journals in 2001. Twenty-seven per cent reported having encountered ethical violations in relation to assignation of credit with respect to their 2001 article, 18 per cent in relation to gift and nine per cent in relation to ghost authors. In work I undertook with colleagues in health sciences, we argued:

> The implications of ghost and gift authorship can be serious. First, concerns about authorship may bring the integrity of the research into question. Quite simply, the people who are putting their names to the research might not be able to attest to a lack of fabrication or falsification of results. If these forms of misconduct were rife, such misrepresentation might be sufficiently high to bias the evidence base ... Second, it is difficult to respect academic work that is based on a falsehood or the exploitation of more junior members of a research team. Finally, any failure to tackle dubious practices may entrench a culture that rewards with funding, promotion and prestige those researchers who, at best, make questionable decisions about attributing authorship ... (Street et al., 2010, pp. 1458–1459)

Other conflicts arise from varying disciplinary traditions and national priorities. Roger Jeffery explored how difficulties in international collaboration involving researchers from both developing and developed countries could emerge from 'differences in capacity and ability to engage with the requirements of international peer-reviewed journals or book chapters; varying and temporary engagements with the project; and different priorities for academic and research careers' (2013, p. 16). These could cause tensions between approaches that build capacity in the global South and enhanced collaboration and those likely to yield an output valued by research assessment exercises conducted in the global North.

In the Singapore Statement for authors, Wager and Kleinert (2011) stated what should be blindingly obvious: 'authorship of research publications should ... accurately reflect individuals' contributions to the work and its reporting' (s.6.1). The International Committee of Medical Journal Editors (ICMJE) released Recommendations for the Conduct, Reporting, Editing, and Publication of Scholarly Work in Medical Journals in 2013. This recommended four conditions be met before someone be included as an author (s.II.2):

1. Substantial contributions to the conception or design of the work; or the acquisition, analysis, or interpretation of data for the work; AND
2. Drafting the work or revising it critically for important intellectual content; AND
3. Final approval of the version to be published; AND
4. Agreement to be accountable for all aspects of the work in ensuring that questions related to the accuracy or integrity of any part of the work are appropriately investigated and resolved.

The Australian Code for the Responsible Conduct of Research drew on the earlier Vancouver Protocol which only included the first three conditions. Consequently, elements from this standard are applied to all social science researchers in that country. However, the Australian Code has not required all authors to meet all conditions. This more inclusive position mirrored the codes adopted by professional associations associated with psychology, sociology and education in the United States (Bebeau and Monson, 2011).

The British-based Committee on Publication Ethics (COPE) is a voluntary body for scientific journal editors. Its *Guidelines on Good Publication Practice* (2003), no longer available on its website, acknowledged 'there is no universally agreed definition of authorship' but required 'as a minimum, authors should take responsibility for a particular section of the study' (section 3). Where authors could only take responsibility for specialist disciplinary contributions, this could be indicated in the article. COPE required the names of any professional writers be disclosed and urged researchers to be 'vigilant' in ensuring their names were not added to a paper simply to 'add credibility' (section 3(6)). COPE also counselled researchers to reach early agreement on what was expected of each contributor and collaborator and how this would be reflected in decisions about authorship.

Outside the biomedical field, academics have been found putting their name to the work of others. In 1996 Julius Kirshner, a history professor from the University of Chicago, was found guilty of plagiarism by his own institution. A book review written by Kirshner's research assistant had been published under Kirshner's name in a journal he co-edited. Kirshner claimed, implausibly, he believed he owned the ideas in the review because the research assistant was employed by him (Cage, 1996). Somewhat bizarrely, one research assistant appropriated the name of an academic psychologist, Mitchell J. Prinstein, albeit in a slightly disguised form. The junior researcher sought to create a fictional co-author in the hope the real academic's standing in the field might improve the chances journals would accept his manuscripts. A bemused Prinstein (2011) reported how he first came across a manuscript bearing the name Mitch Prinstein and ultimately discovered a graduate with a history of felony arrests had been appointed to a job on the basis of a fraudulently inflated curriculum vitae. Once in post, he was laundering money through the lab and running a 'fraudulent practice using the lab resources' (p. 180).

Even in the unlikely event that the issues of guest, gift and ghost authorship do not arise regularly in social science journals, social scientists collaborating with colleagues from medical backgrounds may have to confront such practices. In the medical field, Albert and Wager (2003) urged researchers being pushed towards actions they regarded as unethical to do two things. First, they should explain calmly to their collaborators that they thought the action might constitute academic misconduct and that an editor might decline to publish if he or she found out. Second, they should document the discussion. Many social scientists may be pleasantly surprised to find that, despite its origin in medical science, ICMJE's work might support their own views of what does not constitute authorship.

Indeed, if interpreted in the way favoured by the Australian Code, the Vancouver Protocol would recognize the roles played by indigenous communities in community-based participatory research and scholars from the global South engaged in multinational projects (Jeffery, 2013). Castleden and her colleagues (Castleden et al., 2010) surveyed Canadian scholars engaged in collaborative work with Indigenous groups. They found a variety of views on what constituted authorship. Some researchers required Indigenous community members to contribute to the writing process itself, others saw authorship as requiring broader intellectual input into a project. The latter position reflected a collaborative process negotiated throughout the research relationship (see Chapter 5) and aimed at maximizing benefits for the community (see Chapter 7). Unfortunately, the 2013 ICMJE recommendations have closed down this possibility for medical journals.

Duplicate and redundant publication

Other difficulties arise when researchers engage in duplicate or redundant publication, publishing papers that share exactly the same data, discussion and conclusions, or present little or no new material and test what Doherty (1998) described as the '"minimal publishable unit" to achieve the maximum number of publications'. In his discussion of 'the dirty dozen habits of highly masochistic authors' (2005, p. 326) Daniel Feldman, the editor of the *Journal of Management*, railed against submissions 'Skating on thin ice in terms of idioplagiarism, simultaneous submissions, slicing the salami too thinly on data sets, and not providing full disclosure to the editor of potential manuscript overlaps' (p. 327).

Wager et al. (2009) investigated the views and practices of 231 editors-in-chief of the academic journals published by Wiley-Blackwell (three per cent of whom were editors of social science journals). Editors were particularly concerned about duplicate and piecemeal publication. In their role as associate editors of the *Academy of Management Journal* and the *Journal of Applied Psychology*, Kirkman and Chen (2011) recalled receiving submissions that used, without acknowledgement, the same data-set as another paper that they had encountered: 'While we cannot ascertain the intent of authors who did this, the attribution made by such behavior is almost always negative and can really hurt the reputation of authors' (p. 442). Similar stories were repeated to Schminke (2009) by editors of other management journals, and by Eden (2010), the editor-in-chief of the *Journal of International Business Studies*. Bretag and Carapiet (2007) used electronic text comparison software to uncover unattributed textual reuse among ten, randomly selected and high-publishing, Australian scholars working in the social sciences, arts and humanities. Having examined 269 digitally available articles published between 2003 and 2006, Bretag and Carapiet found evidence of substantial self-plagiarism among four academics and lesser self-plagiarism among two more. In one case, two articles published virtually simultaneously contained a 55 per cent overlap of text.

It may be appropriate to publish similar articles in different journals in order to ask different research questions, link to different literatures or reach new and different audiences. However, many editors expect authors to identify and justify such a strategy, declaring whether they had published or were preparing to publish papers closely related to the manuscript that had been submitted, thereby warning later researchers that sought to develop a meta-analysis (ICMJE Recommendations, 2013, s.III.D). Without such transparency, it is easy to interpret overlapping publication as poor academic practice and an attempt to pad a researcher's curriculum vitae. Nevertheless, sometimes it is a difficult line to draw and editors may be reluctant to be punitive: 'It can be difficult to know how finely to slice and dice the ideas in a given research program and still maintain some originality of publishable importance in each further morsel that is produced' (Rosser, 2010, p. 15).

On the other hand, some cases are more obvious. In Korea, a professor of education asked for his appointment as presidential senior secretary for education, science and culture to be withheld, in the face of allegations of duplicate publication (*The Hankyoreh*, 2008). In 2011, Bruno Frey, an economics professor at the University of Zürich was censured by the *Journal of Economic Perspectives* and blacklisted by the *Journal of Economic Behavior and Organization*. Working with two Australian-based co-authors, Frey had published four papers about passenger behaviour during the sinking of the *RMS Titanic*. The four papers presented the same research without citing each other and were described by one editor as 'substantively identical' (Autor, 2011, p. 239). Frey took full responsibility and promised the journal it would never happen again. Unfortunately, the blogging community quickly identified Frey had a long history of publishing closely related pairs of papers (Storbeck, 2011b). In addition, Autor recognized 'considerable overlap' between the papers and an article published by another Queensland academic in 1986 (Storbeck, 2011a).

Editorial ethics

How editors allocate limited space in their journals has been a source of debate. Very little has been written about editorial misconduct, and what little exists has been about medical research. However, two examples offer some indication of possible problems within the social sciences. In 2004, Donald Light and Rebecca Warburton, an economic sociologist and a health economist respectively, submitted a paper to the *Journal of Health Economics*. This led to what the former editor of the *British Medical Journal*, described as a 'ripping yarn of editorial misconduct' (Smith, 2008). Light and Warburton were critical of an analysis by academics from the Tufts Center for the Study of Drug Development in Boston of expenditure on research and development by big pharmaceutical companies, a paper that had appeared in 2003 also in the *Journal of Health Economics*. Among other things, the two social scientists were concerned the Tufts authors had inflated the amount spent on research, used data that remained confidential and so could not be independently verified, and had failed to declare to journal readers that the Center at which the work was done had received funding from the drugs industry. The editors, all professors in health economics at Harvard, accepted the critique for publication but demanded major changes and retractions of information about industry funding. In addition, the editors allowed the authors of the 2003 article several months to write a rejoinder that was longer than the original critique. Light and Warburton were allowed two weeks to deliver a brief reply. The editors then pulled all papers out of production. Following threats of legal action by Light and Warburton, the editors reinstated the papers but subjected the reply to heavy editing and published it in 2005 together with a second rejoinder from the Tufts team. Light and Warburton (2008) wrote an account of the episode for a health policy journal edited by Harvard students in which they detailed authoritarian, unethical and unaccountable practices employed by the editorial team.

Teixeira and da Costa, two Portuguese economists, submitted work to a special issue of a journal specializing in 'innovation studies'. Their paper was accepted by the guest editor and proofs were sent out, corrected and returned.

The authors were surprised to discover their paper was to appear in a different journal, albeit one with the same editor-in-chief and publisher. According to Teixeira and da Costa (2010), the shift in journals occurred at the behest of the editor-in-chief and without the agreement of the authors nor the approval of the guest editor. When challenged, the editor-in-chief told the authors that they were attempting to apply pressure on the publisher to accept a paper that did not meet the requirements of the first journal.

Peer review is used by editors of journals and books to seek advice from experts on the quality of manuscripts submitted for publication. The majority of English-language social science journals use a double-blind process where the identity of the reviewer and author are withheld from the other party (British Academy, 2007). The process confers legitimacy on both the publication and authors. In 2013, COPE published guidelines for peer review. Most editors believe reviewer misconduct is not a serious issue for their journal (Wager et al., 2009). Yet, there has been some evidence in the biomedical field that it fails to operate as a reliable mechanism for quality control. Stung by criticism of their discipline in the wake of the Smeesters and Stapel retractions, social psychologists pointed to a bias against uncovering fraud unless there were already reasons to suspect it:

> There are several reasons for such reviewer blindness. Because fraud is relatively rare, its possibility is not generally contemplated. Science is based on trust, and scientists find it difficult even to consider that members of the club might be cheating ... There is a rich social psychological literature on biases in human reasoning and decision-making, including both the 'hindsight bias' – explaining why people are always cleverer after the fact – and the confirmatory bias in hypothesis testing, whereby researchers seek information that confirms their hypothesis and ignore data that contradict it. (Stroebe and Hewstone, 2013, p. 34)

Indeed, the peer review process may be open to bias on grounds that include the author or the reviewer's nationality, language, specialism and gender (House of Commons Science and Technology Committee, 2011). Richard Smith described peer review as 'slow, expensive, ineffective, something of a lottery, prone to bias and abuse, and hopeless at spotting errors and fraud' (2006, p. 116).

In smaller research communities defined by geography, language or academic specialism, or where authors' self-citation cannot be excised, it can be difficult to secure anonymity for authors or reviewers. As a result, the 'temptation to find fault with a rival's efforts must sometimes be irresistible' (Goodstein, 2002, p. 31). Some researchers have used their position as peer reviewers to block publication of an article that might threaten their own interests (World Association of Medical Editors, 2002). Evidence of bias in the peer review process has been less obvious in social science. Indeed, in the British Academy (2007) review of the practices of 96 journals in the humanities and the social sciences, only six per cent of respondents required referees to complete a conflict of interest declaration.

Instead, in the social sciences, conflicts of interest in peer review are more often conceived as political than ethical. There have been criticisms of the long-term cumulative effect of editorial decisions and editorial appointments. Joe Feagin (1999), as president of the American Sociological Association, noted mainstream editors of journals such as his own Association's *American Sociological Review* rarely published qualitative or theoretical pieces. He was particularly troubled when his Association's Council rejected its own publications committee's first two choices for editor of the *Review* and instead chose two other candidates. The Council's rejection of the committee's recommendations was unprecedented and was condemned by members at the Association's annual conference and by the executive committee of the Association of Black Sociologists.

It is also possible that the peer review process can be unkind to interdisciplinary scholarship. A professor of healthcare organization warned the House of Commons Science and Technology Committee in the United Kingdom that 'a paper which seeks to bring disciplines or ideas together ... can be sent to academics who work in narrow silos who will reject work as wrong, inappropriate or not relevant ...' (Mark, 2011). On the other hand, there have been suggestions that authors have attempted to subvert peer review. Xiao-Ping Chen (2011), editor of *Organizational Behavior and Human Decision Processes*, indicated authors might send out manuscripts to potential reviewers, note the names of any that were critical in their acknowledgements, and thereby ensure journals excluded these academics from the list they consulted. And yet, despite these failings, most journals still use peer review because, in the words of a *Times Higher Education* Editorial it 'remains the worst system we have, except for all the others' (Gill, 2013).

There are also examples of 'coercive citation practices' where editors have required authors to add citations from their own journals into submitted articles without any indication why the addition might improve the quality of the papers. Wilhite and Fong (2012) analysed responses from 6,672 researchers and 832 journals in business, economics, sociology and psychology and concluded such 'coercion is uncomfortably common' (p. 542). In its most extreme form, some editors have produced review articles that, by excessively citing their own journals, inflate a journal's impact factor. This can be relatively easily identified when authors or journals self-cite, and Thomson Reuters has suppressed metrics for some journals as a result. However, it could be tough to spot if a cartel of journals engaged in such practices (Davis, 2012). In 2012, 88 journal editors mostly working in the areas of psychology and management endorsed a code of conduct that condemned 'tactics more focused on engorging impact factors than the advancement of science' (Ethical Practices of Journal Editors, 2012).

Conclusion

This chapter has reviewed issues relating to integrity that rarely find a place in social science research commentary. In the biomedical field, many of these matters – such as the issues of fabrication, falsification and plagiarism – are considered in terms of research integrity and scientific misconduct, and important work has been completed on defining, describing, assessing and preventing misconduct. The United States Office of Research Integrity has identified problems in relation to research integrity in the biomedical research in that country. There are, of course, examples of misconduct in other countries and in other disciplines. However, the extent of the problem is largely uncharted, and there are reasons to believe that the underlying causes of research misconduct might be intensifying as scholars and institutions cut corners in efforts to chase greater output. On the other hand, crowdsourcing the monitoring of plagiarism offers a very promising avenue for curtailing the freedom past plagiarists have enjoyed, by overcoming physical or linguistic barriers to accessing source or copied material.

Few jurisdictions have bothered to investigate the nature and extent of research misconduct in the social sciences even if they have adopted national guidelines. The evidence from surveys and from a few high-profile investigations indicates we cannot be complacent. Those disciplines and jurisdictions that have been slow to attend to research ethics need to respond more quickly to threats to research integrity. Some will inevitably follow the narrower 'fabrication, falsification and plagiarism' definition and more punitive approach of the United States. However, other questionable research practices may offer an equally important challenge to research integrity, and these may be better tackled by placing integrity within the broader and more constructive discourses of honesty and fairness favoured by Australian, British, Canadian, Dutch and German documents. After all, the lines between acceptable and unacceptable academic conduct are not always easy to draw.

NINE

Relationships

Introduction

As we have seen in the previous four chapters, much of the literature on research ethics in the social sciences is concerned with relationships. Indeed, Kellehear (1989) suggested ethical conduct is at root 'a way of seeing and interpreting relationships' (p. 71). However, the relationship on which attention is conventionally focused is the one between researcher and participant. Should a researcher preserve the confidentiality of the information that he or she has been given by a participant? How might a researcher obtain informed consent from a participant? How might a researcher minimize the risk of causing harm to a participant? and so on. Yet, researchers have relationships with their peers as well as with a range of other individuals and organizations, many of which raise significant matters of ethics and integrity.

In this chapter, I consider the ethical dilemmas and responsibilities associated with conflicts of interest, researcher safety, membership of a research team, taking your own family into the field, and relationships with employers and sponsors.

Conflicts of interest

Research agendas and projects are vulnerable to pressure from financial, political, social, cultural or religious interests. These can influence the kinds of topics, methodologies, researchers and institutions likely to be funded, and the way research might be reported. Not surprisingly, the National Committees for Research Ethics in Norway (2006) called for institutions and agencies to facilitate 'free and independent research' even where the 'intrinsic need of research for originality, transparency and the verification of prevalent opinions can come into conflict with some parties' desire to prevent topics from being explored' (p. 10).

Conflicts of interests occur when various personal, financial, political and academic concerns coexist and the *potential* exists for one interest to be illegitimately favoured over another that has equal or even greater legitimacy, in a way that might make other reasonable people feel misled or deceived. So, conflicts of interest may arise even when there has not been research misconduct: 'Conflicts of interest reside in a situation itself, not in any behaviour of members of a research team' (Committee on Assessing Integrity in Research Environments, 2002, p. 38). Researchers caught in a conflict of interest risk appearing negligent, incompetent or deceptive.

Such conflicts have been best explored in biomedical literature where academics who obtain financial benefit from industry through research funding, consultancies, royalties or by holding shares in companies have been found to be more likely to reach conclusions in their research that favour their corporate sponsor (Lexchin et al., 2003). On some occasions, they have conducted research of lower quality and less open to peer review, at times because researchers were barred from publishing by commercial-in-confidence clauses. Put bluntly, researchers sponsored by tobacco companies have been less likely to conclude that passive smoking is a health hazard than those researchers funded by non-profit organizations (Barnes and Bero, 1998). The incidence of financial conflicts of interest appears to be very high in biomedicine. Krimsky et al. (1996) found one-third of the articles they examined in 14 leading biomedical journals had a first author who held a financial interest in a company whose business was directly related to the area within which he or she had published. In 1995, the United States required researchers receiving grants from the National Science Foundation or the Public Health Service and its National Institutes of Health to disclose to their institution any 'significant financial interests ... that would reasonably appear to be affected by [their] research' (National Science Foundation, 1995). Most American research universities have adopted policies in line with this requirement. However, Slaughter and Rhoades (2004) argued such policies were symptomatic not of better ethics but of an erosion in understandings of scholarship as being performed for the public good, by disinterested and sceptical researchers. Now,

> discovery is valued because of its commercial properties and economic rewards, broad scientific questions are couched so they are relevant to commercial possibilities..., knowledge is regarded as a commodity rather than a free good... (p. 107)

Although the chances that social scientists may have a financial stake in the area they are studying may be less likely than in health and the sciences, many issues are still relevant (Israel, 2000; Ziman, 1991):

- What sort of financial arrangements should academics have with corporations, domestic or foreign government agencies?
- Should there be a limit on how much money an academic might receive from a private company or government agency?
- Should academics let companies or government agencies pay for their trips?
- Should academics disclose corporate or government affiliations when giving advice to the public or publishing research (Geis et al., 1999)?
- Should academics with consultancies be able to act as reviewers for grant-awarding bodies if the research being funded may provide other academics with the expertise to act as a commercial competitor, or if the research might be critical of the reviewer's client?
- How should researchers distinguish between intellectual property that belongs to a client and that which belongs to the university
- How is an academic society to deal with 'huckstering' by members who 'tart up or adulterate the goods in their shop windows' (Ziman, 1991, p. 54) to secure funds or support their sponsors?

Ziman also noted the problems that might arise when research specialists consulted in drawing up the specifications for tenders use this to gain insider advantages in the subsequent competitive tendering process.

Following the Global Financial Crisis, the failure of economists to predict the financial meltdown led to claims that senior academics were hopelessly compromised by their connections to the financial industries responsible for the crisis. In 2006 for example, Frederic Mishkin, a professor at Columbia University, had coauthored a report extoling the stability of Iceland's financial institutions and ignoring the risky nature of their investments that prompted the country's economic meltdown two years later. At the time, Mishkin failed to disclose he had received US$120,000 from the Iceland Chamber of Commerce, only revealing this when he was subsequently appointed to the US Federal Reserve Board (Nelson, 2012). Mishkin's behaviour was certainly not unique. Carrick-Hagenbarth and Epstein (2012) analysed the curricula vitae of 19 prominent academic financial economists. Fifteen worked with private financial institutions. Eight served on the boards of directors of private financial firms, while two were consultants or affiliated experts for firms. In their academic publications none (and in their public commentaries very few) acknowledged their private affiliations between 2005 and 2009, even when they were assessing policies that might have a direct impact on these interests. Reuters found the problem was not restricted to economists – roughly one-third of the 82 academics who offered testimonies to the United States Senate Banking Committee and the House Financial Services Committee between late 2008 and early 2010 failed to disclose the relevant financial interests that could be identified on their online resumés (Flitter et al., 2010). Carrick-Hagenbarth and Epstein sought greater transparency not in the belief this might fix the economic system but in order to contribute to 'stripping away some of the veneer of objectivity from those who wield academic economics to support the special interests of finance' (p. 59). The American Economic Association (AEA) had not had an ethical code or guidelines. In January 2011, 300 economists signed a letter to the AEA calling for greater engagement in ethical matters. By April 2011, Carrick-Hagenbarth and Epstein noted a marked improvement in the levels of disclosure among one group of economists that they had investigated. In 2012, the AEA added to its conflicts of interest policy, stating authors in its journals should disclose financial support above a certain threshold from or roles with interested parties, and urging academics to adopt similar behaviour for other publications, commentaries and official testimonies.

Another example reveals financial problems in my own discipline of criminology, a less obvious field than economics. The University of Florida established a private prisons research unit headed by Charles Thomas. The unit was partly funded by large corporations with interests in private prisons. At the same time, Thomas worked as a paid consultant for Florida's Correctional Privatization Commission (CPC), a body created separate from the Department of Corrections to oversee the private prison system in that state. Under Florida law, CPC consultants were not supposed to have worked for the private sector in related fields within two years. However, Thomas provided advice for stock market analysts involved in advising firms developing private prisons and reportedly owned US$660,000 worth of shares in companies involved in private prisons. In 1997, Thomas accepted a paid position on the board of CCA Realty Trust, a real estate investment trust established by CCA specializing in buying and leasing correctional institutions. In 1999, he acted as a consultant on the merger between CCA and the Prison Realty Trust, apparently earning US$3 million in the process. In 1997, the Florida Police Benevolent Association complained to the Florida Commission on Ethics about Thomas' conflicts of interest. The chair of Wackenhut, a competitor of CCA, demanded Thomas be removed as a CPC consultant. Thomas' position at the CPC was terminated. In 1998, the Benevolent Association complained about the merger fee. The following year, Thomas admitted a conflict of interest and offered to stop his university research, pay a US$2,000 fine and resign as director of the University of Florida's Private Corrections Project. However, he maintained he had never disregarded his public duties to obtain private benefit, nor had he acted with corrupt intent or tried to hide his connections with the private corrections industry, having made disclosures to both the CPC and his own university. This fine was rejected as too low by Florida's ethics commission and Thomas later offered to pay US$20,000. Trenchant criticism of this arrangement by Gil Geis and his colleagues (Geis et al., 1999) was contested by Thomas and two collaborators from the University of Florida (Lanza-Kaduce et al., 2000).

A combination of three factors may result in a greater likelihood both that events like these will occur and that we are more likely to interpret this activity as conflict of interest. First, the public sector is expanding its notion of what constitutes conflict of interest. Second, ethics governance structures are becoming more interventionist. Finally, many of the institutions within which social scientists work are developing more of an enterprise culture, as more traditional views of academic freedom are threatened by the need for researchers and their institutions to adopt new governance structures, obtain funding and link to end-users.

Given the threat posed by conflicts of interest, various agencies have developed their own responses (American Sociological Association, 1999; National Health and Medical Research Council, Australia, 2007 a and b). In its report for the United States Institute of Medicine in 2002, the Committee on Assessing Integrity in Research Environments argued in favour of transparency, urging researchers to disclose conflicts of interest to their institution as well as in all presentations and publications that arise from the research. The National Committees for Research Ethics in Norway (2006) went further than mere transparency and asserted a need to take action 'to avoid a degree of congruence between self-interests and the principal's interests that is large enough to threaten one's ability to behave impartially' (p. 30). Other reports also recognize a need to prohibit particular conflicts in order to protect the research institution or the public interest (Institute of Medicine, 2009). However, studies in both Australia and the United States have found institutions struggling to provide practical guidance on how to manage particular financial relationships, even where conflicts oversight committees exist (Boyd and Bero, 2007). In Australia, Simon Chapman and his colleagues reported a:

> lack of clarity regarding what should be declared and the frequency of declarations; absence of clear guidance regarding the management of competing interests; few attempts to audit compliance with COI policies; no guidance on the implications of non-compliance; and reluctance to maintain and make publicly available registers of competing interests. (Chapman et al., 2012, p. 455)

In 2014, the American Association of University Professors (AAUP) published Recommended Principles and Practices to Guide Academy–Industry Relationships. AAUP urged universities to require academics and administrators to disclose financial conflicts of interest on publicly accessible websites (Principle 31).

Even if individual researchers are not directly compromised by corporate sponsorship, they may either 'be influenced by an awareness that their own institution's financial health may be affected by the results of their research' (National Human Research Protections Advisory Committee, 2001, p. 9) or, at the very least, be perceived as being influenced. Consequently, universities have come under heavy criticism for accepting money from particular sources, be they American or British counter-insurgency programmes (Attwood, 2007; Berreman, 1991; Horowitz, 1967), tobacco companies or foreign politicians facing allegations of corruption (Matthews, 2012).

In 2011, the London School of Economics was censured for its links to the Libyan government. These included allegations of academic misconduct by one of Gaddafi's sons, Saif, while he was a doctoral student at the institution, and suspicion a donation from the Gaddafi International Charity and Development Foundation may have been funded by bribes paid by multinational companies. The institution's Director resigned at the height of the scandal. An independent inquiry found internal governance structures had failed to keep pace with the growth in the institution's size and international reach. It recommended the institution adopt and embed a code and establish a committee to deal with institutional ethics and reputational risk (Woolf, 2011).

In the context of arts sponsorship, Gray and Kendzia (2009) warned of the dangers of creeping, passively followed, organizational self-censorship. This idea can easily be applied within social sciences. For example, Kjærnet (2010) critiqued the influence of the Norwegian government and the State oil company in channelling Norwegian social-science-based research on petroleum. Similarly, it is possible to be wary of the impact of corporate and state foreign funding on universities across the world via the creation of cultural institutes or endowed chairs without even identifying direct means of controlling research (Jensen, 2012; Marcus, 2013). While universities may have little choice but to look for new sources of funding and accept some of the conditions that go with that, as Cho and her colleagues noted (2000), it is difficult to avoid the conclusion that corporate sponsorship or funding from foreign governments may have an effect on the trust the wider community is prepared to place in universities and researchers.

Institutional conflict of interest operates at a different level to that of the individual researcher or research team. It involves situations where the institution's research, teaching or service are unduly influenced by external financial or business relationships held at the institutional level. Prior to their review of the institutional policies of 60 research-intensive universities in the United States, Sheila Slaughter and her collaborators identified several levels at which conflict might occur. The first and third are most relevant here:

> (1) *university as firm* in which institutional officers are economic actors who manage university technology transfer activities to maximize commercial interest;
> (2) *'sand and gravel'* in which an officer acts to maximize their own self-interest;
> (3) exchanges in which institutional officers engage in broad, unspecified *quid pro quo* arrangements with industry. (Slaughter et al., 2009, p. 4)

They called for systems that promoted transparency through the public declaration of university investments and other interests, separated functions and duties so that walls existed between those who handled investment and those who managed endowments and technology transfer, and clarity about the situations that might trigger an independent review for institutional conflicts of interest.

These systems are directly relevant to research ethics. Indeed, the relationship between researchers and their institutions can break down over ethical matters. While research ethics committees may play an important role in regulating unethical conduct, Lowman and Palys (2000) were deeply troubled by the institutional conflict of interest that underlay use of ethics approval processes to manage other risks (see Chapter 6). They have not been the only social scientists who feared that ethically acceptable research proposals might be blocked by the ethics review process because of, for example, a desire by the institution to avoid the possibility of legal action (Israel, 2004b).

Other relationships

While most work on research ethics is based on universal notions of justice, since the late 1970s, feminist writers such as Gilligan, Baier and Noddings have elaborated an ethics of care (see Chapter 2). For such writers, people develop and act as moral agents embedded in social relationships based on care, compassion and willingness to listen, include and support those people with whom one has significant relationships. An ethics of care has obvious implications for ethics in research (Mauthner et al., 2002) and how we relate to people with whom we come into contact during our lives. Among other things, it forces us to think about relationships that fall well beyond those with research participants and the academy, the traditional focus for most codes of research ethics. First, however, I want to consider the wellbeing of the individual researcher.

Safety and relationships

Researchers may find they have little choice but to take physical and emotional risks in their work. This might be a consequence of the location of their work, the nature of participants, the sensitivity of the topic, underfunding, or even professional 'pressures to venture into ever more remote, exotic, bizarre, and, importantly, unresearched settings' (Sampson and Thomas, 2003, p. 171). We have very little idea about how widespread risks to researchers are. The working assumption of Paterson and her colleagues (Paterson et al., 1999) probably remains reasonable: 'threats to the safety of researchers are few and occur infrequently in most research projects ... but those that do occur are traumatic to those involved' (p. 260).

Until recently, institutions and disciplines have largely ignored, denied, or assumed researcher safety. Scholars have been expected to look after themselves and handle whatever the research field throws at them, with little support or training (Johnson and Clarke, 2003; Lee-Treweek and Linkogle, 2000). Clark (2013) cautioned academics to treat with care some claims by researchers that their record of speaking truth to power has placed them at risk from authoritarian regimes. Clark suggested these assertions might be overstated either to lend cachet to the claimants or to warn would-be competitors off their intellectual turf. Nevertheless, following their survey of 46 researchers, Kenyon and Hawker (2000) concluded many 'individual researchers, project leaders and institutions appear to be in a state of denial' (p. 326) about researchers' safety. Sampson and Thomas (2003) condemned institutions for paying insufficient attention to the safety of researchers and charged them with 'thrusting young and inexperienced researchers unprepared, and unprotected, into the field' (p. 182). Unfortunately, although the safety of participants is often the primary consideration of ethical guidelines, few consider the safety of researchers themselves. In this sphere at least, machismo may have trumped an ethics of care. This appears odd for a couple of reasons. First, it seems anomalous that documents concerned with the well-being of a myriad of possible stakeholders stopped short of caring for the welfare of the one group of people who are always involved in the research. Second, researchers who are poorly equipped to take care of themselves are perhaps less likely to be in a position to secure the safety of others. Third, in some countries the sector should have been prompted to assume its responsibilities by occupational health and safety legislation.

While academia is still a long way behind aid and development work and journalism in assessing the safety of the research workforce, there have been some important moves to understand and respond to risks (Dickson-Swift et al., 2007; Johnson and Clarke, 2003). In his 1995 book, Raymond Lee distinguished between ambient and situational danger. In the former, risks are part of the setting – research might be located in a conflict zone or entail immersion in violent cultures or dangerous activities. Situational danger, on the other hand, stems from the very presence of the researcher triggering additional risks. Applying the distinction to work on-board ocean-going cargo vessels as part of their study of transnational seafarer communities, Sampson and Thomas (2003) identified the ambient risks of injuries linked to industrial accidents in unsafe work environments as well as the potential for piracy on some routes, and situational risks based on possible hostility from a strong male occupational culture aboard merchant cargo vessels that defined itself in opposition to outsiders, and particularly female outsiders.

A small number of researchers have lost their lives as a direct result of their research activities. Ken Pryce, a British sociologist of race relations, disappeared while investigating organized crime in Jamaica. Myrna Mack, a

Guatemalan anthropologist probing military abuses against the indigenous rural population, was fatally stabbed in an attack outside her home in 1990 (Oglesby, 1995). In 2002, three colonels were convicted of instigating her murder. Social scientists have also been subject to surveillance and harassment by security agencies and paramilitary organizations. For example Miguel Angel Beltrán, a Colombian sociologist, was arrested while on sabbatical in Mexico. He was returned to Bogotá where, charged with incitement to violence after two of his published papers were found on a Revolutionary Armed Forces of Colombia (FARC) laptop, he spent two years in prison before being acquitted in 2011 (Grove, 2012). Japanese-based Chinese history scholars have been detained during trips to their native China. In 2013, Zhu Jianrong of the Toyo Gakuen University was detained for six months before being released.

The Rwandan government ended Susan Thomson's interviews with prisoners accused of genocide and confiscated her Canadian passport until she had been 'reeducated' in the achievements of the state in promoting national unity and reconciliation (Thomson, 2009). While never feeling physically endangered herself, she was concerned for the safety of her research assistants and participants and so, following 'reeducation', she left Rwanda on another passport. Shervin Malekzadeh (2011), an Iranian-American doctoral student, was visited by Iranian security during fieldwork in Tehran. Jeffrey Sluka (1995) was threatened by an Ulster Loyalist paramilitary after he completed fieldwork in Belfast with a Republican paramiltary group.

Research work can also be emotionally stressful. Scholars may be operating in unfamiliar and challenging environments and encountering sensitive, emotionally confronting material.

> So-called participant observation has a way of drawing the ethnographer into spaces of human life where she or he might really prefer not to go at all and once there doesn't know how to go about getting out except through writing, which draws others there as well ... (Scheper-Hughes, 1992, p. xii)

Research can change how researchers view themselves, leave them exhausted or desensitized to the suffering of others, or feeling guilty for extracting information without offering reciprocity. Investigators may be affected through exposure to the experiences of research participants in the form of vicarious traumatization or even retraumatization if the trauma resonates with events of their own history:

> The work of interviewing can bring back a flood of memories and feelings that interviewers are not always able to articulate; these may manifest themselves, indirectly, in headaches, stomach aches, or difficulty getting tasks accomplished in a timely manner. (Kitson et al., 1996, p. 185)

Those working with secondary data have also reported emotional distress. Sharon Jackson and her colleagues described adverse reactions after analysing quantitative and qualitative data on sexual and physical abuse garnered from the call records of ChildLine Scotland (Jackson et al., 2013). After reading thousands of transcripts of children describing how they were being abused, analysts found themselves hearing the children's voices or picturing the events. One researcher struggled to 'regulate, control, reduce, and/or displace feelings of immense sadness and bewilderment, and to quite often fight back tears' (p. 5). Those transcribing or analysing sensitive material may also be affected emotionally. One higher degree student working on domestic violence (McCosker et al., 2001) recognized the need to provide debriefing for her transcriber who had reported feeling nauseated and had limited her daily exposure to the tapes.

Stresses may be exacerbated if participants lean on researchers for emotional, financial or logistical support. Qudsiya Contractor (2008) described the frustration felt by her colleagues working as action researchers in a slum resettlement programme near Mumbai. The team were investigating the impact of involuntary resettlement on the life and well-being of former slum dwellers, and attempting to support the community in responding to its own needs. They found that women often became distressed at the end of interviews that administered a World Health Organization self-rating survey on well-being. Participants were upset when reflecting on how their already difficult lives had been emotionally and mentally traumatized by the move. During the project, the municipal water supply to the community was cut off, forcing the poorest to drink from a stream, and the team 'felt increasingly distressed by the fact that they could not do anything to resolve the situation' (p. 22).

Many researchers struggle to manage role conflicts and avoid becoming the professional or supporter that research participants need (be it as a therapist, aid-worker, teacher, nurse or friend) or other professionals seek. Other academics have found it difficult to avoid coming into conflict with participants who hold repellent political views (Gallaher, 2009), or behave as total 'bastards' (Hubbard et al., 2001).

Like everyone else, social scientists may well cope with their emotions. However, their roles as researchers may leave them particularly vulnerable. Hochschild (1983) argued that, in order to conform to dominant ideologies, there are limits to the kinds of emotions deemed appropriate for professionals to feel or display. As a result, they are required to manage their emotions in various social contexts. It may take effort to mask surface displays and tackle deeper feelings. Extensive emotion work may result in burnout or stress, particularly where there is continued dissonance between internal feelings and external display.

The nature and levels of risk are gendered. There is an emerging literature of how women have responded to the additional dangers of fieldwork, which includes accounts of sexism, sexual intimidation and assault (Moreno, 1995; Stanko, 1992; Winkler with Hanke, 1995). Women may carry additional burdens of 'emotional labour' partly as a result of traditional gender expectations and partly because of the commitments of feminist research methodologies (Bloor et al., 2007). However, men are also vulnerable in their own way, either because of the assumption that they can handle themselves in physical confrontations (Peterson, 2000) or because they find themselves isolated in situations where the majority of violence is between men. For example, Bruce Jacobs (1998) was ripped off when a 17-year-old street-level crack dealer who had been feeding him information threatened him with a gun, and who then over the next six weeks repeatedly harassed, threatened, baited and taunted him.

When researching violence and conflict, it can be challenging to insulate researchers from ambient risk:

> Is it possible to be safe in an unsafe world? How can one seek safety, when trying specifically to study the absence of security? It is, I believe, necessary to look after one's own safety, but also incredibly presumptuous. Why should the researcher be safe while everyone else suffers fear and the consequences of violence? At its worst, security-seeking behaviour on the part of a researcher can put others at risk. (Ross, 2009, p. 179)

Nevertheless, there are ways of preparing for some dangerous situations. Paterson et al. (1999) and Adams and Moore (2007) recommended researchers create a fieldwork safety protocol that ran from the beginning to the end of a project, allowing for: assessment of the situation such as the safety of research locations; preventative strategies including identifying exit routes and reviewing research materials for anything potentially inflammatory that might raise the level of risk; identifying and responding to a threat, perhaps by designating a safety contact who would be aware of a researcher's movements; and followup such as integrating debriefings into the research design, perhaps to handle the shock of re-entry to the field or return to 'normal' life.

Konstantin Belousov and his collaborators (Belousov et al., 2007) warned against risk assessments that were divorced from knowledge of the context. The team was forced to reassess the risk posed to their fieldworkers in St Petersburg following the murder of the Captain of the Port. Having found professional international risk assessors were always likely to identify fieldworkers conducting criminological research in post-Communist Russia as being 'at risk', the team created a more contextually informed framework. Their framework recognized the characteristics of engaging in research on sensitive subjects in 'risk-saturated spaces' where social order was breaking down in the face of weakened state control and various social and institutional crises.

Social scientists can also learn from other professions when it comes to responding to emotional stressors. Saakvitne and Pearlman's recommendations on self-care in the face of vicarious traumatization (1996) might be applied more generally. They called for those at risk to heighten their sense of self-awareness, creating balance and connection to protect themselves against isolation. So, when Wager started exploring child sexual assault, she reflected on how she might look after herself:

> I am banning myself from sleeping with my work on the bed, ensuring that Friday night to Sunday morning is a 'work free zone', avoiding films at the cinema or theatre productions that have the theme of interpersonal violence and resuming old passions for dance and engaging with nature. (2011, p. 167)

Rebecca Campbell (2002) led a team that spent two years interviewing over 100 survivors of rape. During this investigation, Campbell studied her own emotions and those of her staff. Her book was remarkably honest: she found it 'costly – emotionally expensive – to engage in this work' (p. 144). Campbell drew on feminist epistemology to argue an ethics of care needed to be extended to the research team. In practice, this meant leaders needed to address the emotional needs of their research teams. First, team members should be selected for emotional maturity and self-awareness as well as for the kinds of demographic diversity that might allow the team to draw on different support strategies. Second, the team should be able to share any distress they experienced, possibly through formal debriefing. Third, the team should be organized so staff could rotate through more stressful tasks. Finally, the departure of team members should be marked by an opportunity for 'final release, reflection, integration of what has been learned and witnessed' (p. 148), perhaps involving individual exit interviews or group writing projects.

Responsibility for ensuring the safety of the scholar does not simply fall upon the individual researcher. Funders, employing institutions and research managers all should play some role in managing risk. The Social Research Association (n.d.) in the United Kingdom has adopted a code of practice on safety, mostly in relation to interviewing or observation in private settings. Dickson-Swift and her co-authors (2007) urged funding councils and research institutions to adopt guidelines for researchers' safety and suggested ethics committees should require researchers to reflect on their self-care, where appropriate. However, there is evidence some ethics committees might not have the skills to handle researcher safety and may allow over-protective, paternalist and ill-informed risk assessment to enter the ethics review process (Israel, 2004b). It may be sensible to create a broader capacity to tackle safety systematically by also introducing the issue into postgraduate curricula, institutional health and safety audits, and the peer review of grants (Bloor et al., 2007).

Research teams

Some of the examples given relate to working in teams. Some ethical issues relating to teams are simply variations on those familiar to individual researchers. However, some are more complex and responsibilities may be more diffuse. Team leaders have responsibility for the ethical behaviour of members of their staff and for ensuring that team members are appropriately briefed. Members, like research participants, need to be 'informed fully about the purpose, methods and intended possible uses of the research, what their participation in the research entails and what risks, if any, are involved' (Economic and Social Research Council, 2005). Team leaders must also ensure the physical safety and emotional well-being of their staff, who may face threats ranging from extreme physical dangers to sexual harassment from colleagues during fieldwork.

Research leaders should help team members negotiate their safety. Williams et al. (1992) wrote how they provided training for their fieldworkers who, while investigating crack distribution networks, 'spent an average of 15–20 hours per week in several of New York City's most dangerous locales' (p. 346). Despite their best efforts, other researchers can do little to protect their fieldworkers in the face of uncooperative state institutions. In a study of intravenous drug users, Buchanan et al. (2002) asked their fieldworkers to collect discarded syringes so that they could be analysed for HIV antibodies. Many fieldworkers were recovering addicts with criminal records. Moreover, possession of syringes is illegal in Massachusetts and, if the syringes contained residues of illicit drugs, fieldworkers could be charged with both possession of syringes and narcotics. Attempts to reach agreements with the local police and the State Department of Public Health failed. Not every supervisor tries, though, and some appear to be shockingly complacent. One community research worker in the United States told reviewers that her supervisor had shown very little interest in her safety:

> I did this study and I was in a bad neighborhood and there was a gunfight and what happened was the traffic was like locked ... All I could do was duck and hope the bullets don't hit me. I told my manager; she said, 'Okay, did you get any studies?' (quoted in True et al., 2011, p. 8)

Within health research, greater use is being made of community members as research workers, often in order to improve participant recruitment and follow-up. In focus groups with indigenous community research workers, two United States researchers (Alexander and Richman, 2008) discovered community members were more likely to reject strict ethical rules than more experienced researchers. Further work with other groups by the same researchers (True et al., 2011) discovered community research workers were more likely to report engaging in or witnessing ethical misconduct in research than traditional research assistants. The study found examples of fieldworkers fabricating responses by finishing off incomplete questionnaires, pressurizing people to participate and enrolling ineligible participants in order to meet recruitment quotas or enable people they regarded as deserving to access services.

Dorcas Kamuya and her colleagues (2013b) identified the important role fieldworkers in Kenya have played in obtaining access for teams to research participants and adding to the research team's understanding and ability to work within the appropriate languages and cultures. However, fieldworkers are also vulnerable to exploitation by their employers and by their own communities. In the face of such pressures, fieldworkers

> can be facilitative of research ethics through creating environments of better discussion and understanding of the research, or undermine research ethics if those relations hinder or infringe on individual freedoms to make choices. (p. 2)

Of course, principal researchers need to ensure they do not exploit their fieldworkers, their fieldworkers do not exploit research participants, and even that their fieldworkers do not exploit researchers. The Indian *Ethical Guidelines for Social Science Research in Health* explained that the first situation would occur if in their relationships with juniors, assistants, trainees and students, researchers attempted to 'seek personal, sexual or economic gain' (National Committee for Ethics in Social Science Research in Health, 2000, s.III.3.3) or sought to coerce those people into acting as 'cheap labour' (2000, s.III.3.4).

The third situation is also worth considering. A team investigating robbery in St Louis in the United States (Jacobs with Wright, 2000) used street-based field recruiters who were involved in crime to locate active drug robbers who would talk to the researchers about their activities. Both recruiters and participants received US$50 for each interview. However, the team found recruiters were trying to scam the researchers by disguising and re-presenting people who had already been interviewed and were also skimming off part of the interviewees' participation fee. Although the researchers attempted to stop these practices, they were not surprised they were happening:

> We hired these individuals because they were known criminals with a history of exploiting friends and strangers; it would have been suspicious had they not tried to deceive us. (p. 12)

Robert Morrell and his colleagues studied gender and sexuality and their relationship to high levels of HIV in South African schools. Their team included teachers as both co-researchers and as research participants, as teachers were helping to gain access to the school community and were also collecting data. Researchers heard stories suggesting one of these teachers might be having sex with a school student. The team had promised anonymity to participants and believed they owed a duty of care to the teacher, recognizing that if they reported the accusation to the school principal, the teacher might lose his job whether or not the story turned out to be accurate. This was a high cost in a region with high unemployment and where the teacher was responsible for a large extended family. The team acknowledged not all sex between male teachers and female students might be coercive, many female students in the school were adults, and the relationship might be viewed as acceptable in the local community. However, the team also had a political commitment to combatting gender inequality. The researchers approached the teacher indirectly, ascertained his and his colleagues' views generally on teacher–student sexual relationships, and found they believed that such matters should be dealt with informally together with a warning to desist. The team chose not to report their suspicions 'after much angst-ridden discussion' (Morrell et al., 2012, p. 624) but to publish on their decision-making and adapt their future plans to focus on the impact of teacher–student relationships on gender equity:

> While not wishing to fall into complete relativism, or abrogate our own duty to make moral judgements, we found this particular call very difficult. Was it more ethical to adhere to the collectivism of *ubuntu* as expressed by the teachers we interviewed and not report? Or would it have been more ethical to ignore these local views and report our suspicions? We are not convinced that we made the right choices, but neither would we accept that we made the wrong ones. (p. 625)

Family

Many researchers do not enter the field alone; yet we hear little about the risks posed to partners and children (Cassell, 1987; Howell, 1990). Andrew Goldsmith is an Australian criminologist who has undertaken research on policing in Colombia. Following fieldwork, Goldsmith (2003) wrote about the difficulties of juggling research with family and other commitments which meant that he could only spend short periods in Latin America. His decision to base his family in Toronto rather than Bogotá was made on security grounds and necessitated compromises in the methodology he adopted. Nadia Wager (2011) postponed her investigation of child sexual abuse until she believed her own children were sufficiently mature for her work to have a lesser impact. Philippe Bourgois discussed dangers associated with his work on drug dealers. Yet even he made only the briefest of references to his friends' rather than his own concerns for his family:

> most people still consider me crazy and irresponsible for having 'forced' my wife and infant son to live for three and a half years in an East Harlem

tenement. When we left the neighbourhood in mid-1990, several of my friends congratulated us, and all of them breathed a sigh of relief. (1995, p. 32)

Other researchers have been concerned that stigma associated with interacting with marginalized groups might either affect a researcher's relationship with his or her family or the way the family was treated by others. Avril Taylor (1993) worked with intravenous drug users in Scotland. Her family and friends were horrified when they discovered she planned to hang out with drug users. She was told of cases where children of health professionals who worked with clients with AIDS were shunned by classmates:

Anxious that this should not happen, particularly to my youngest son, still at primary school, I had not only to be vigilant myself but also to ensure that my children, too, were circumspect in their conversations. (p. 21)

Finally, Ben Fincham and his co-researchers (Fincham et al., 2008) became aware of the impact on their own lives of their work on suicide files held in a British coroner's office. They replaced an informal habit of offloading at home with a means for researchers to leave the archive and talk about their work, a decision that they described as beneficial to researchers, their families and friends.

Conclusion

Researchers can face pressures from both their employers and their sponsors. As the burdens increase on academics to obtain external funding for their research, and as the centre of academic enterprise has moved towards 'an entrepreneurial periphery' (Slaughter and Leslie, 1997, p. 208), many university-based social scientists find themselves working for clients. This may be portrayed as unproblematic. A broader shift to a client-centred research agenda may have significant implications for researchers. As two American anthropologists commented succinctly, 'without tenure, one's daily bread depends on pleasing the employer ... in the immediate present' (Frankel and Trend, 1991, p. 185). This entails compromises as

one is likely to learn very early that despite the way the official codes of ethics say it is supposed to be, one would be well advised to place the interests of the employer or sponsor before the interests of the people studied, their communities, one's own colleagues, students, host governments, own government, or the general public ... (p. 188)

However, these are not the only relationships that should concern researchers and their institutions. Institutions, research leaders and researchers need to pay attention to the physical and emotional safety of themselves, their colleagues and employees on research projects, as well as the impact their research activities might have on those around them, matters rarely encountered in the research literature or governance documents. Frankel and Trend argued we need to pay attention lest the protections of official codes be subverted by institutional interests. We may need to take at least as much care where no such codes exist.

TEN

Beyond Regulatory Compliance

Throughout this book, I have drawn attention to difficulties social scientists face in conducting ethical research. Sometimes complications arise as a result of the methodologies chosen. Sometimes they are caused by the actions of participants, colleagues or gatekeepers. Often, however, problems are triggered by the regulatory environment: the practices and procedures adopted by a local committee or the bureaucratic context within which committees operate. Consequently, social scientists face two distinct challenges. Not only do we have to develop ways of working that can be defended as ethical but we have to meet the demands of regulators without compromising ethical conduct.

These requirements operate simultaneously and throughout the entire research process. Social scientists might be tempted to see research ethics approval as a gate to be passed through but most committees intend their decisions to have an impact on what follows and would imagine their work shapes what occurs before the formal review process.

More-junior researchers may approach projects by identifying both the key intellectual debates they wish to consider and the means by which they expect to investigate them. This might involve some broad and tentative explorations of the ethical implications of choosing particular methodologies but little in the way of rigorous contemplation. This should not come as much of a surprise, given the training social scientists have provided and received. Most guides to, and I suspect courses on, research – if they discuss ethics at all – do so as a separate chapter or week. Ethics are rarely integrated into the material as a whole. Typically then, it is not until junior researchers are compelled to respond to research ethics committee requirements that they give detailed consideration to ethical issues. It is at this point that investigators with little experience may confront serious difficulties. For instance, the biomedically derived, hard architecture of some ethics forms can lead social scientists to adopt particular kinds of responses to committee demands because they cannot conceive or justify any alternative.

In short, for a junior researcher, the formal process of an ethics review offers both disadvantages and advantages: it can unreasonably restrict ethical responses, but it can also offer a significant mechanism for stimulating ethical reflection. Sadly, having received the formal stamp of regulatory approval, some researchers can believe the time for ethical reflection is over. However, no matter how well organized they are, no matter how thoroughly they have prepared their research project, and no matter how properly they behave, social scientists are likely to have to deal with a variety of unanticipated ethical dilemmas and problems once their research commences. Indeed, in some instances, researchers may need to depart from the agreement they reached with their ethics committee. Ethical consideration is never a 'done deal'.

More-experienced researchers can draw on their knowledge of how they and their colleagues have developed research plans, interpreted ethical guidelines, engaged with research ethics committees, and managed the practicalities of negotiating ethics in the field. From the outset of their research, they can anticipate problems they are likely to encounter in their research as well as the issues they may face in having their proposed work accepted by a research ethics committee. By comparison with more-junior colleagues, they may have broader scholarly networks to draw on for advice and greater negotiating power with regulators, though some very well-respected senior social scientists have expressed on record their frustration with review processes. More-experienced researchers know that ethics needs to be designed into a project from the outset; that it is 'what happens in every interaction' (Komesaroff, in Guillemin and Gillam, 2004, p. 266) and continues well after the research is concluded.

Since Iain Hay and I published *Research Ethics for Social Scientists* in 2006, much has changed. The work of academics and, of course, the world within which we operate have evolved. There may be more chance we will find ourselves in interdisciplinary or international teams (Hirsch Hadorn et al., 2010), a greater expectation we keep one eye on the relationship between our research, strategies of dissemination and the needs of end users (Bastow et al., 2014; Rickinson et al., 2011), and more likelihood we have to engage with intercultural and indigenous issues (Denzin et al., 2008). Far more researchers see working through or on internet research as an integral part of contemporary practice (Social Sciences and Humanities Research Ethics Special Working Committee, 2008), and our attention is more likely to be drawn to issues of integrity, if not through the policies of our institutions or journals (Resnik et al., 2010) then as the result of another scandal hitting the popular media (Woolf, 2011). Of course, my understanding of the challenges faced by social scientists has also evolved and it is possible that a more perceptive commentator might well have identified trends I missed a decade ago. As a critical social scientist, I am surprised how little I engaged with critical theory in the first book. However, even now the difficulty in finding researchers who have applied post-modernist or postcolonial theory to research ethics remains. The paucity of published reflection in some countries is troubling, and I remain deeply impressed by the collection Donna Mertens and Pauline Ginsberg gathered in 2009. If my own book evolves further in the next ten years, I would hope to continue to track greater public engagement with research ethics from a broader range of disciplines, countries and theoretical and cultural traditions. However, there is a danger such reflection will be preceded by and also shaped by regulatory creep. Restricting guidance in ethics to bureaucratic compliance has serious limitations, as prescriptive approaches to ethics and ethics education may stand in opposition to sound moral thinking and ethical outcomes.

Conduct or compliance?

Marilys Guillemin and Lynn Gillam (2004) distinguish between what they call 'ethics in practice' and procedural ethics. Procedural ethics are typically associated with compliance processes. In contrast, the term ethics in practice refers to everyday issues that occur while we conduct research. Ethical research can be compromised by bureaucratic procedural demands. Though reflection on, and commitment to, ethical research go together, '[t]his process is jeopardised when researchers see ethics as a combination of research hurdle, standard exercise, bureaucratic game and meaningless artefact' (Holbrook, 1997, p. 59). Bosk and De Vries (2004) suggested medical researchers in North America responded to ethics oversight by adopting 'a policy of weary, self-resigned compliance coupled with minor or major evasion' (p. 254). Will van den Hoonaard (2011) argued social scientists were following a similar pattern. For two British criminologists,

> The surface image of rigorous oversight ... masks the hollowing-out of faith in and commitment to the process of doing ethical research, and its replacement by a world-weary, cynical engagement deprived of the very substance that would make the process real and valuable. (Winlow and Hall, 2012, pp. 411–412)

If current regulatory trajectories continue, more social scientists may either ignore research ethics committees or retreat into safer research territories. Other forms of evasion may develop. There is some evidence of forum shopping, where applicants choose to submit to committees known to be sympathetic to their kind of research. Other researchers may disguise their real intentions or fail to alert research ethics committees to methodological changes made after receiving approval. In some environments, the last thing that will happen will be for a researcher to approach a committee for advice on how to conduct ethical research. Researchers may also find it difficult to tell committees that their requirements are impossible to meet, for fear of encountering an even less sympathetic reaction.

Advocates of committee-based review recognize ethics review will not promote reflection unless the process of review itself is reflexive – 'committees need to be willing to enter into a dialogue with applicants and be willing to listen to what applicants say' (Jennings, 2012, p. 92). Where possible, I would hope this book would help both reviewers and researchers to enter that dialogue with a better idea of how their colleagues have approached ethics in the social sciences. However, critics of committee-based review conclude this cannot happen given current regulatory approaches. Writing about the experience in the United States, Scott Burris (2008) argued the regime failed to promote virtuous conduct as 'the logic of virtue promotion is inconsistent with the enforcement of rules that fetishize formalities or treat the subject as bad or amoral, if not idiotic' (p. 75). We need therefore to generate a regulatory space where researchers are given equal weight as autonomous ethical deliberators rather than being reduced to acting out a set of sanctioned behaviours.

Social scientists can only benefit from contributing to the creation of an environment where they operate ethically, and where review mechanisms are conducted by respected, knowledgeable and experienced people who can help researchers develop better practice. As a result, individual social scientists would do well to expand their knowledge of, and engagement with, the review process, undertake empirical investigations of the ethics review boards, and educate board members. Iain Hay and I argued for this in 2006 and many of us have been doing just that:

> Over the last decade, as researchers, regulators and bureaucrats we have been able to influence the redrafting of the National Statement, help some institutions that already had HRECs to improve their practices, and ensure that others about to introduce ethical review did not repeat the mistakes of the past. (Israel et al., under review).

However, there are limits to what an individual researcher might achieve and a more collective response is certainly warranted. First, professional groups could monitor problems members have with research ethics committees and put pressure on institutions to adopt helpful, consistent, transparent and appropriate practices. They might also make available resources such as completed application forms and correspondence with committees (Tumilty et al., under review). Second, professional bodies and research organizations could lobby funding, host and regulatory agencies to support more-appropriate governance.

We may have allies in these agencies. Many government bodies employ the research services of social scientists and are dismayed to see research founder on inappropriate ethical regulations. Third, professional associations and learned societies could engage with the processes of law reform so that legislators consider the impact of their activities on social research. Fourth, professional bodies might broker the development of ethics training materials, some of which could be used to help educate ethics committee members about discipline-specific matters. Fifth, it could be useful to exchange information and resources with other professional associations either bilaterally or multilaterally.

When confronted with tensions between our own ethical consciences and the demands of regulators, there may be moments when it seems we have a stark choice: follow what we think is right, or comply passively with regulatory edict. Throughout this book, I have pointed to examples of social scientists who have faced such a decision and, in part, the new subtitle for this book represents a recognition of the level of impatience and frustration among scholars, even among people who have spent much of their lives engaging with regulators. The strategies I have suggested might reduce these tensions but will not in themselves move the debate around ethics beyond regulatory compliance.

Conclusion

The starting point for this book is that ethical conduct is not the same as regulatory compliance. There are strong practical and philosophical reasons for social scientists to take ethics seriously, even more seriously than regulators and administrators. As social scientists, we are committed to improving the lives of those people involved in our research, and we believe in the virtues of maintaining trust and integrity. We also know that research by social scientists has not always led to a better society; researchers have intentionally or unintentionally harmed participants, and our research has been co-opted to unpleasant ends.

Despite broad agreement among social scientists that behaving ethically is a good thing, research ethics regulators have achieved the seemingly impossible. They have given ethics a bad name. As scandals were revealed, largely in the field of biomedical research, ethical codes and guidelines were introduced. Regulatory mechanisms were established and multiplied.

In the beginning, it seemed that these new practices had little to do with social science. They were not our scandals, they were not our codes. We were rarely involved in their development and the language of 'experimentation' and 'procedures' and 'non-therapeutic research' was alien to many in the social sciences. On those occasions where social scientists first encountered emerging regulatory frameworks, it was possible to ignore them, change topics or even disguise what they were doing.

And then things started changing. Ethics creep led to both net-widening and intensification of the regulatory mesh. The language used in research ethics frameworks suggested that their provisions applied to all research involving humans. Funding bodies began requiring every institution that received their money to abide by such regulations – for all research. In turn, institutions concerned by the threat to their resource streams established review structures whose decisions cut to the heart of social science research. Most troubling of all, much of this happened with minimal consultation with social scientists and little recognition that social science is not the same as biomedical research. As a result, regulation of research ethics in many countries is now underpinned by an unsettling combination of biomedical research and institutional risk minimization models. In particular, social scientists have faced problems with regulatory practices associated with informed consent, confidentiality, beneficence and various research relationships and, not surprisingly, an adversarial culture has emerged between researchers and regulators.

Of course, different things have happened in different countries. Social scientists in the United States were the first to encounter 'ethics creep' and be overwhelmed by waves of bioethically influenced regulation. In many other countries similar regimes emerged, with varying impact on social sciences. Where uniform regulation clearly extended beyond the health sciences, it has taken a while in countries like Canada and Australia to slowly and painfully recognise and engage with the distinctive challenges for social science methodologies. Other nations like Brazil, Qatar, South Africa, Sweden and Thailand are yet to do so, though their regulations already appear to capture much of the research in our disciplines. In Norway and Finland, national guidelines have been created specifically for social scientists. In the United Kingdom, the Framework for Research Ethics (Economic and Social Research Council, 2010) results from a pre-emptive bid to avoid bioethically based regulatory capture. However, for many social scientists even these guidelines still bear the hallmarks of bioethics and principlism. In most other countries, including Hong Kong and New Zealand, regulation has been left to the individual research institution. Finally, in Denmark, social scientists appear to have been left out of the regulatory process completely.

Why have social scientists found it so hard to avoid the imposition of bioethically derived models of research ethics governance? Part of the answer lies in the history just outlined. Bioethics had a head start, was often well resourced and developed both high-quality analytical material and a flood of regulatory detail. For social scientists, research ethics governance often became yet another institutional or governmental move to manage the nature of research – one more bureaucratic task distracting them from their passion. First, ethics forms, regulations and protocols look very much like every other time-consuming administrative task. Second, like other work on methodology and pedagogy that is central to the quality and reproduction of our disciplines, work on research ethics and regulatory reform may not be seen by many colleagues in individual disciplines as 'real' research.

The difficulty is that an approach based on rules and their enforcement appears unable to invest similar resources in promoting the virtues that underpin ethical conduct. We took issues of ethics seriously before regulatory regimes were established. We have spent several decades grappling with the requirements and frustrations of regulations. We have traced the rise of the ensuing adversarial culture and it is time now to plot its demise. We now must move beyond regulatory compliance.

We must reflect on our ethical conduct, act on the basis of these reflections, and then explain and justify our actions through public debate (Carter, 1996). This may well entail challenging regulations and regulators that cannot accommodate our decisions. As social scientists, we need to work with regulators to develop resources and review processes that encourage and enhance ethical practice. Sadly, while there is much of value in contemporary regulations, so much has been transplanted from bioethics and so little has emerged from our own disciplines. It is frightening so many countries have imported regimes from the global North that appear incapable of respecting different ethical traditions, learning from local knowledge of context, or engaging with local researchers, institutions, participants and other stakeholders in the world of research. The challenge is to resist the temptation to allow the frustrating and often sterile debates over regulation to diminish our ethical imagination, and to divert us from the valuable goals we always set out to achieve in our research.

References

Abdur Rab M, Afzal M, Abou-Zeid A and Silverman H (2008) Ethical practices for health research in the Eastern Mediterranean region of the World Health Organization: a retrospective data analysis. *PLoS ONE*, 3(5): e2094.

Aboriginal Research Ethics Initiative (AREI) of the Interagency Advisory Panel on Research Ethics (PRE), Canada (2008) Issues and Options for Revisions to the Tri-Council Policy Statement on Ethical Conduct of Research Involving Humans (TCPS): Section 6: Research Involving Aboriginal Peoples. Available at: http://www.pre.ethics.gc.ca/policy-politique/initiatives/docs/AREI_-_February_2008_-_EN.pdf (accessed 23 December 2013).

Abou-Zeid A, Afzal M and Silverman H (2009) Capacity mapping of the National Bioethics Committees in the Eastern Mediterranean region. *BMC Medical Ethics* 10(8). Available at: http://www.biomedcentral.com/1472–6939/10/8 (accessed 23 December 2013).

Academy of Medical Sciences (2011) A new pathway for the regulation and governance of health research. Report, Academy of Medical Sciences, London. Available at: http://www.acmedsci.ac.uk/download.php?i = 13646&f = file (accessed 23 December 2013).

Academy of Social Sciences (2013) Academy of Social Sciences Response to the HEFCE Consultation on the Research Integrity Concordat. Available at: http://acss.wpengine.com/wp-content/uploads/2014/01/Concordat-Final1-March-2013.pdf (accessed 11 June 2014).

Academy of Social Sciences Working Group (2014) Towards common principles for social science research ethics? A discussion document. In: *Finding Common Ground?*, Academy of Social Sciences conference, London, UK, 10 January 2014. Available at: https://dl.dropboxusercontent.com/u/36654333/Towards%20Common%20Principles%20for%20Social%20Science%20Research%20Ethics.pdf (accessed 23 December 2013).

Adair JG (2001) Ethics of psychological research: new policies; continuing issues; new concerns. *Canadian Psychology* 42(1): 25–37.

Adams M and Moore G (2007) Participatory action research and researcher safety. In: Kindon S, Pain R and Kesby M (eds) *Participatory Action Research: Approaches and Methods*. Hoboken: Taylor and Francis, pp. 41–48.

Adams RA, Dollahite DC, Gilbert KR and Keim, RE (2001) The development and teaching of the ethical principles and guidelines for family scientists. *Family Relations* 50(1): 41–49.

Adler PA (1985) *Wheeling and Dealing: An Ethnography of an Upper-level Drug Dealing and Smuggling Community.* New York: Columbia University Press.

Adler PA and Adler P (2002) The reluctant respondent. In: Gubrium JF and Holstein JA (eds) *Handbook of Interview Research: Context and Method.* Thousand Hills, CA: Sage Publications, pp. 515–537.

Aftab N (2011) Peshawar University VC found involved in plagiarism. *The News*, 17 August. Available at: http://www.thenews.com.pk/TodaysPrintDetail.aspx?ID=63174&Cat=6 (accessed 23 December 2013).

Alahmad G, Al-Jumah M and Dierickx K (2012) Review of national research ethics regulations and guidelines in Middle Eastern Arab countries. *BMC Medical Ethics* 13(34). Available at: http://www.biomedcentral.com/1472-6939/13/34 (accessed 23 December 2013).

Albert T and Wager E (2003) How to handle authorship disputes: a guide for new researchers. Report, Committee on Publication Ethics, UK.

Albright JJ (2011) Privacy protection in social science research: possibilities and impossibilities. *PS: Political Science & Politics* 44(4): 777–782.

Aldridge J (2012) The participation of vulnerable children in photographic research. *Visual Studies* 27(1): 48–58.

Alexander L and Richman K (2008) Ethical dilemmas in evaluations using indigenous research workers. *American Journal of Evaluation* 29(1): 73–85.

Alix J-P (2011) France: how to improve a decentralized, ambiguous national system. In: Mayer T and Steneck N (eds) *Promoting Research Integrity in a Global Environment*. Singapore: Imperial College Press/ World Scientific Publishing, pp. 33–36.

Allen A, Anderson K, Bristol L, Downs Y, Watts O'Neill D and Wu Q (2009) Resisting the unethical in formalised ethics: perspectives and experiences. In: Satterthwaite J, Piper J and Sikes, P (eds) *Power in the Academy*. Stoke-on-Trent: Trentham Books, pp. 135–152.

Allen AL (1997) Genetic privacy: emerging concepts and values. In: Rothstein MA (ed) *Genetic Secrets: Protecting Privacy and Confidentiality in the Genetic Era*. New Haven: Yale University Press, pp. 31–60.

Allen B (2009) Are researchers ethically obligated to report suspected child maltreatment? A critical analysis of opposing perspectives. *Ethics & Behavior* 19(1): 15–24.

Allen C (1996) What's wrong with the 'Golden Rule'? Conundrums of conducting ethical research in cyberspace. *The Information Society: An International Journal* 12(2): 175–188.

Allmark P (1995) Can there be an ethics of care? *Journal of Medical Ethics* 21(1): 19–24.

American Anthropological Association (1971) Statement on Ethics. Available at: http://www.aaanet.org/profdev/ethics/ (accessed 23 December 2013).

American Anthropological Association (1998) Code of Ethics. Available at: http://www.aaanet.org/profdev/ethics/ (accessed 23 December 2013).

American Anthropological Association (2007) Executive Board Statement on the Human Terrain System Project. Arlington VA: American Anthropological Association.

American Anthropological Association (2009) Code of Ethics of the American Anthropological Association. Available at: http://www.aaanet.org/issues/policy-advocacy/upload/AAA-Ethics-Code-2009.pdf (accessed 23 December 2013).

American Anthropological Association (2012) AAA Statement on Ethics: Principles of Professional Responsibility. Available at: http://ethics.aaanet.org/category/statement/ (accessed 9 June 2014).

American Anthropological Association Commission on the Engagement of Anthropology with the US Security and Intelligence Communities (CEAUSSIC) (2007) Final Report. American Anthropological Association, Arlington VA. Available at: http://www.aaanet.org/pdf/FINAL_Report_Complete.pdf (accessed 23 December 2013).

American Anthropological Association Commission on the Engagement of Anthropology with the US Security and Intelligence Communities (CEAUSSIC) (2009) Final Report on the Army's Human Terrain System Proof of Concept Program. American Anthropological

Association, Arlington VA. http://www.aaanet.org/cmtes/commissions/ceaussic/upload/ceaussic_hts_final_report.pdf (accessed 23 December 2013).

American Association of University Professors (2001) Institutional Review Boards and Social Science Research. Available at: http://www.aaup.org/report/institutional-review-boards-and-social-science-research (accessed 27 January 2014).

American Association of University Professors (2014) Summary of Recommendations. In: Recommended Principles and Practices to Guide Academy–Industry Relationships. Washington DC: American Association of University Professors. Available at: http://www.aaup.org/report/recommended-principles-guide-academy-industry-relationships (accessed 16 January 2013).

American Economic Association (2012) American Economic Association adopts extensions to principles for author disclosure of conflict of interest. Available at: http://www.aeaweb.org/PDF_files/PR/AEA_Adopts_Extensions_to_Principles_for_Author_Disclosure_01-05-12.pdf (accessed 23 December 2013).

American Historical Association (2011) Statement on Standards of Professional Conduct. Washington DC: American Historical Association. Available at: http://www.historians.org/pubs/Free/Statement-on-Standards-2011_FINAL.pdf (accessed 23 December 2013).

American Psychological Association (1963) Ethical standards of psychologists. *American Psychologist* 18: 56–60.

American Sociological Association (1970) Code of Ethics. Washington DC: American Sociological Association.

American Sociological Association (1999) Code of Ethics. Available at: http://www.asanet.org/images/asa/docs/pdf/CodeofEthics.pdf (accessed 10 June 2014).

Ana J, Koehlmoos T, Smith R and Yan LL (2013) Research misconduct in low- and middle-income countries. *PLoS Med* 10(3): e1001315.

Andoh C (2011) Bioethics and the challenges to its growth in Africa. *Open Journal of Philosophy* 1(2): 67–75.

Annas J (2005) Virtue ethics. In: Copp D (ed) *The Oxford Handbook of Ethical Theory*. Oxford: Oxford University Press, pp. 515–536.

Anscombe GEM (1958) Modern moral philosophy. *Philosophy* 33: 1–19.

Appiah KA (2008) *Experiments in Ethics*. Cambridge MA: Harvard University Press.

Ardalan F, Arfaei H, Mansouri R, Balalimood M, Farhud D, Malekzadeh R, Firouzabadi H, Izadpanah-Jahromi K, Safavi A, Kaveh A, Saidi F, Shafiee A and Sobouti Y (2009) Correspondence: Iran's scientists condemn instances of plagiarism. *Nature* 462: 847.

Aristotle (350 BCE/2003) *Nicomachean Ethics*. New York: Penguin Books.

Assembly of First Nations (n.d.) First Nations Ethics Guide on Research and Aboriginal Traditional Knowledge. Available at: http://www.afn.ca/uploads/files/env/atk_protocol_book.pdf (accessed 23 December 2013).

Associação Nacional de Pós-Graduação e Pesquisa em Ciências Sociais (2013) Por uma regulamentação específica da ética em pesquisa nas ciências humanas e sociais. Available at: http://portal.anpocs.org/portal/index.php?option = com_content&view = article&id = 1149:por-uma-regulamentacao-especifica-da-etica-em-pesquisa-nas-ciencias-humanas-e-sociais-&catid = 1136:destaques&Itemid = 433 (accessed 23 December 2013).

Association of Universities in the Netherlands (Vereniging van Universiteiten, VSNU) (2004, revised 2012) The Netherlands Code of Conduct for Scientific Practice. Available at: http://www.tue.nl/fileadmin/content/universiteit/Over_de_universiteit/

integriteit/The_Netherlands_Code_of_Conduct_for_Scientific_Practice_2012.pdf (accessed 23 December 2013).

Atran S (2007) Research police – how a university IRB thwarts understanding of terrorism. In: *Institutional Review Blog*, 28 May. Available at: http://www.institutionalreviewblog.com/2007/05/scott-atran-research-police-how.html (accessed 23 December 2013).

Attwood R (2007) ESRC 'ignores' danger fears. *Times Higher Education*, 20 July. Available at: http://www.timeshighereducation.co.uk/news/esrc-ignores-danger-fears/209666.article (accessed 10 June 2014).

Aultman JM (2013) Abuses and apologies: irresponsible conduct of human subjects research in Latin America. *The Journal of Law, Medicine & Ethics* 41(1): 353–368.

Australian Health Ethics Committee (2002) Ethical and Practical Issues Concerning Ashed Bones from the Commonwealth of Australia's Strontium 90 Program 1957–1978, Advice of the Australian Health Ethics Committee to the Commonwealth Minister for Health and Ageing, Senator the Honourable Kay Patterson, March.

Australian Institute of Aboriginal and Torres Strait Islander Studies (AIATSIS) (2012) Guidelines for Ethical Research in Australian Indigenous Studies (GERAIS). Available at: http://www.aiatsis.gov.au/_files/research/ethics/GERAIS.pdf (accessed 10 June 2014).

Autor DH (2011) Correspondence: David H. Autor and Bruno S. Frey. *Journal of Economic Perspectives* 25(3): 239–240.

Baez B (2002) Confidentiality in qualitative research: reflections on secrets, power and agency. *Qualitative Research* 2(1): 35–58.

Baier A (1994) *Moral Prejudices: Essays on Ethics*. Cambridge, MA: Harvard University Press.

Bailey CD, Hasselback JR and Karcher JN (2001) Research misconduct in accounting literature: a survey of the most prolific researchers' actions and beliefs. *Abacus* 37(1): 26–54.

Baker TD (2012) Confidentiality and electronic surveys: how IRBs address ethical and technical issues. *IRB: Ethics & Human Research* 34(5): 8–15.

Bakker M and Wicherts JM (2011) The (mis)reporting of statistical results in psychology. *Behavior Research Methods* 43: 666–678.

Bamber GJ and Sappey J (2007) Unintended consequences of human research ethics committees: au revoir workplace studies? *Monash Bioethics Review* 26(3): 26–36.

Barboza M, Minaya G and Fuentes D (2010) Hacia una comisión nacional de ética de la investigación en salud en perú: apuntes acerca de rutas y procesos en perspectiva comparada (Towards a national ethics committee of health research in Peru: Notes about routes and processes in comparative perspective). *Revista Peruana de Medicina Experimental y Salud Publica* 27(4): 621–628.

Barchifontaine CP (2010) Bioethics in Latin America. *International Journal of Bioethics* 21(1): 57–68.

Barnes C (2009) An ethical agenda in disability research: rhetoric or reality. In: Mertens DM and Ginsberg PE (eds) *Handbook of Social Research Ethics*. Thousand Oaks, CA: Sage, pp. 458–473.

Barnes M and Bero LA (1998) Why review articles on the health effects of passive smoking reach different conclusions. *Journal of the American Medical Association* 279: 1566–1570.

Barter C and Renold E (2003) Dilemmas of control: methodological implications and reflections of foregrounding children's perspectives on violence. In: Lee RM and

Stanko EA (eds) *Researching Violence: Essays on Methodology and Measurement*. London: Routledge, pp. 88–106.

Bartlett, T (2008) Investigation finds that Columbia U. professor plagiarized repeatedly. *The Chronicle of Higher Education*, 20 February.

Bartoszko A (2011) Writing an anthropological detective story – interview with Nancy Scheper-Hughes Part 3/3. *Antropologi.info*, 11 November. Available at: http://www.antropologi.info/blog/anthropology/2011/nancy-scheper-hughes-new-book (accessed 23 December 2013).

Bastow S, Dunleavy P and Tinkler, J (2014) *The Impact of the Social Sciences: How Academics and Their Research Make a Difference*. London: Sage.

Battles HT (2010) Exploring ethical and methodological issues in internet-based research with adolescents. *International Journal of Qualitative Methods* 9(1): 27–39. Available at: http://ejournals.library.ualberta.ca/index.php/IJQM/article/view File/5017/6480 (accessed 23 December 2013).

Baud M, Legêne S and Pels P (2013) *Draaien om de werkelijkheid*. Rapport over het antropologisch werk van prof. em. M M G Bax. Amsterdam: Vrije Universiteit Amsterdam. Available at: http://www.vu.nl/nl/Images/20130910_RapportBax_tcm9-356928.pdf?utm_source=sub_persbericht&utm_medium=e-mail&utm_term=&utm_content=&utm_campaign=pb13107 (accessed 23 December 2013).

Bauman Z (1993) *Postmodern Ethics*. Oxford: Blackwell.

Beach D and Eriksson A (2010) The relationship between ethical positions and methodological approaches: a Scandinavian perspective. *Ethnography and Education* 5(2): 129–142.

Beauchamp T (2005) The origins and future of the Belmont Report. In: Childress JF, Meslin EM and Shapiro HT (eds) *Belmont Revisited: Ethical Principles for Research with Human Subjects*. Washington DC: Georgetown University Press, pp. 12–25.

Beauchamp TL (2008) Codes, declarations, and other ethical guidance for human subjects research: the Belmont Report. In: Emanuel EJ, Grady CC, Crouch RA, Lie RK, Miller FG and Wendler DD (eds) *The Oxford Textbook of Clinical Research Ethics*. New York: Oxford University Press, pp. 149–155.

Beauchamp TL and Childress JF (1994) *Principles of Biomedical Ethics* (4th edition). New York: Oxford University Press.

Beauchamp TL and Childress JF (2001) *Principles of Biomedical Ethics* (5th edition). New York: Oxford University Press.

Beauchamp TL and Childress JF (2009) *Principles of Biomedical Ethics* (6th edition). New York: Oxford University Press.

Beauchamp TL, Walters L, Kahn JP and Mastroianni AC (2008) *Contemporary Issues in Bioethics* (7th edition). Belmont, CA: Thompson Wadsworth.

Bebeau MJ and Monson V (2011) Authorship and publication practices in the social sciences: historical reflections on current practices. *Science and Engineering Ethics* 17: 365–388.

Becker HC (1964) To the editor: against the code of ethics. *American Sociological Review* 29: 409–410.

Becker-Blease KA and Freyd KA (2006) Research participants telling the truth about their lives: the ethics of asking and not asking about abuse. *American Psychologist* 61: 218–226.

Bedeian AG, Taylor SG and Miller AN (2010) Management science on the credibility bubble: cardinal sins and various misdemeanors. *Academy of Management Learning & Education* 9(4): 715–725.

Beecher HK (1966) Ethics and clinical research. *New England Journal of Medicine* 274(24): 1354–1360.

Bell K (under review, 2014) The more things change, the more they stay the same: TCPS2 and the institutional oversight of social science research in Canada. In: van den Hoonaard W and Hamilton A (eds) *Ethics Rupture: Exploring Alternatives to Formal Research-Ethics Review*.

Belousov K, Horlick-Jones T, Bloor M, Gilinsky Y, Golbert V, Kostikovsky Y, Levi M and Pentsov D (2007) Any port in a storm: fieldwork difficulties in dangerous and crisis-ridden settings. *Qualitative Research* 7(2): 155–175.

Benham B (2007) The ubiquity of deception and the ethics of deceptive research. *Bioethics* 22(3): 147–56.

Benham B (2008) Moral accountability and debriefing. *Kennedy Institute of Ethics Journal* 18(3): 253–273.

Bentham J (1781/2000) *An Introduction to the Principles of Morals of Legislation*. Kitchener: Batoche Books.

Bento SF, Hardy E, Hebling EM, de Pádua KS and Osis MJD (2011) The Brazilian ethics research review system: an evaluation from the perspectives of institutional review boards. *AJOB Primary Research* 2(3): 28–37.

Bernhard JK and Young JEE (2009) Gaining institutional permission: researching precarious legal status in Canada. *Journal of Academic Ethics* 7: 175–191.

Berreman G (1991) Ethics versus 'realism'. In: Fluehr-Lobban C (ed) *Ethics and the Profession of Anthropology: Dialogue for a New Era*. Philadelphia: University of Philadelphia Press, pp. 38–71.

Bishop L (2009) Ethical sharing and reuse of qualitative data. *Australian Journal of Social Issues* 44(3): 255–272.

Bishop R (2008) Te Kotahitanga: Kaupapa Māori in mainstream classrooms. In: Denzin NK, Lincoln YS and Smith LT (eds) *Handbook of Critical and Indigenous Methodologies*. Los Angeles: Sage, pp. 439–458.

Blass T (2004) *The Man Who Shocked the World: The Life and Legacy of Stanley Milgram*. New York: Basic Books.

Blee KM (1998) White-knuckle research: emotional dynamics in fieldwork with racist activists. *Qualitative Sociology* 212: 381–99.

Bloor M, Fincham B and Sampson H (2007) Qualiti (NCRM) commissioned inquiry into the risk to well-being of researchers in qualitative research. Cardiff: School of Social Sciences. Available at: http://www.cf.ac.uk/socsi/qualiti/CIReport.pdf (accessed 23 December 2013).

Boden R, Epstein D and Latimer J (2009) Accounting for ethos or programmes for conduct? The brave new world of research ethics committees. *The Sociological Review* 57(4): 727–749.

Boga M, Davies A, Kamuya D, Kinyanjui SM, Kivaya E, Kombe F, Lang T, Marsh V, Mbete B, Mlamba A, Molyneux S, Mulupi S and Mwalukore S (2011) Strengthening the informed consent process in international health research through community engagement: The KEMRI–Wellcome Trust research programme experience. *PLoS Med* 8(9): e1001089. Available at: http://www.plosmedicine.org/article/info%3Adoi%2F10.1371%2Fjournal.pmed.1001089 (accessed 23 December 2013).

Bok S (1983) *Secrets: The Ethics of Concealment and Revelation*. New York: Random House.

Borgatti SP and Molina JL (2003) Ethical and strategic issues in organizational social network analysis. *Journal of Applied Behavioral Science* 39(3): 337–349.

Boschma, G, Yonge O and Mychajlunow L (2003) Consent in oral history interviews: unique challenges. *Qualitative Health Research* 13(1): 129–135.

Bosk CL and De Vries RG (2004) Bureaucracies of mass deception: Institutional Review Boards and the ethics of ethnographic research. *Annals of the American Academy of Political and Social Science* 595: 249–263.

Bošnjak S (2001) The Declaration of Helsinki: the cornerstone of research ethics. *Archive of Oncology* 9(3): 179–184.

Bosworth M, Campbell D, Demby B, Ferranti S and Santos M (2005) Doing prison research: views from inside. *Qualitative Inquiry* 11: 249–264.

Bourgois P (1995) *In Search of Respect: Selling Crack in El Barrio.* Cambridge: Cambridge University Press.

Bower RT and de Gasparis P (1978) *Ethics in Social Research: Protecting the Interests of Human Subjects.* New York: Praeger.

Boyd EA and Bero LA (2007) Defining financial conflicts and managing research relationships: an analysis of university conflict of interest committee decisions. *Science and Engineering Ethics* 13(4): 415–435.

Brabeck MM and Brabeck KM (2009) Feminist perspectives on research ethics. In: Mertens DM and Ginsberg PE (eds) *Handbook of Social Research Ethics.* Thousand Oaks, CA: Sage, pp. 39–53.

Brady HE, Grand SA, Powell MA and Schink W (2001) Access and confidentiality issues with administrative data. In: Ver Ploeg M, Moffitt RA and Citro CF (eds) *Studies of Welfare Populations: Data Collection and Research Issues.* Washington, DC: National Academy of Sciences, pp. 220–274.

Brajuha M and Hallowell L (1986) Legal intrusion and the politics of fieldwork: the impact of the Brajuha case. *Journal of Contemporary Ethnography* 14(4): 454–478.

Bretag T and Carapiet S (2007) A preliminary study to identify the extent of self-plagiarism in Australian academic research. *Plagiary: Cross-Disciplinary Studies in Plagiarism, Fabrication, and Falsification* 2: 92–103.

Brewster Smith M (1979) Some perspectives on ethical/political issues in social science research. In: Wax ML and Cassell J (eds) *Federal Regulations: Ethical Issues and Social Research.* Boulder: Westview Press, pp. 11–22.

British Academy (2007) *Peer Review: The Challenges for the Humanities and Social Sciences.* London: British Academy.

British Educational Research Association (2011) Ethical Guidelines for Educational Research. Available at: http://www.bera.ac.uk/wp-content/uploads/2014/02/BERA-Ethical-Guidelines-2011.pdf (accessed 10 June 2014).

British Psychological Society (1992) Council Statement: the late Sir Cyril Burt. *The Psychologist* 5: 147.

British Sociological Association (1968) Statement of Ethical Principles and Their Application to Sociological Practice. London: British Sociological Association.

British Sociological Association (2002) Statement of Ethical Practice for the British Sociological Association. Available at: http://www.britsoc.co.uk (accessed 23 December 2013).

Brotsky SR and Giles D (2007) Inside the 'pro-ana' community: a covert online participant observation. *Eating Disorders: The Journal of Treatment & Prevention* 19: 93–109.

Brown T (2006) Did the U.S. Army distribute smallpox blankets to Indians? Fabrication and falsification in Ward Churchill's genocide rhetoric. *Plagiary: Cross-Disciplinary Studies in Plagiarism, Fabrication, and Falsification* 1: 100–129.

Bryan J (2010) Force multipliers: geography, militarism, and the Bowman expeditions. *Political Geography* 29(8): 414–416.

Brydon-Miller M, Greenwood D and Maguire P (2003) Why action research? *Action Research* 1(1): 9–28.

Buchanan D, Khosnood K, Stopka T, Shaw S, Santelices C and Singer M (2002) Ethical dilemmas created by the criminalization of status behaviors: case examples from ethnographic field research with injection drug users. *Health Education & Behavior* 29(1): 30–42.

Buchanan E (2011) Internet research ethics: past, present, future. In: Ess C and Consalvo M (eds) *The Handbook of Internet Studies*. Hoboken, NJ: Wiley-Blackwell, pp. 83–108.

Buchanan E, Aycock J, Dexter S, Dittrich D and Hvizdak E (2011) Computer science security research and human subjects: emerging considerations for Research Ethics Boards. *Journal of Empirical Research on Human Research Ethics: An International Journal* 6(2): 71–83.

Buchanan EA and Hvizdak EE (2009) Online survey tools: ethical and methodological concerns of human research ethics committees. *Journal of Empirical Research on Human Research Ethics* 4(2): 37–48.

Bull T (2002) Kunnskapspolitikk, forskningsetikk og det samiske samfunnet. In: *Samisk forskning og forskningsetikk*. Oslo: De nasjonale forskningsetiske komiteer, pp. 6–21.

Burger JM (2009) Replicating Milgram: would people still obey today? *American Psychologist* 64(1): 1–11.

Burgess RG (1989) Ethical dilemmas in educational ethnography. In: Burgess RG (ed) *The Ethics of Educational Research*. London: Falmer Press, pp. 60–76.

Burr J and Reynolds P (2010) The wrong paradigm? Social research and the predicates of ethical scrutiny. *Research Ethics Review* 6(4):128–133.

Burris S (2008) Regulatory innovation in the governance of human subjects research: a cautionary tale and some modest proposals. *Regulation and Governance* 2: 65–84.

Cage MC (1996) University of Chicago Panel finds professor guilty of plagiarism. *Chronicle of Higher Education* 9: A18.

Callahan D (2003) Principlism and communitariansm. *Journal of Medical Ethics* 29: 287–291.

Callaway E (2011) Report finds massive fraud at Dutch universities. *Nature* 479: 15.

Campbell R (2002) *Emotionally Involved: The Impact of Researching Rape*. London: Routledge.

Campbell R, Adams AE, Wasco SM, Ahrens CE and Sefl T (2010) 'What has it been like for you to talk with me today?': the impact of participating in interview research on rape survivors. *Violence Against Women* 16(1): 60–83.

Canadian Sociological Association (2012) Statement of Professional Ethics. Available at: http://www.csa-scs.ca/files/www/csa/documents/codeofethics/2012Ethics.pdf (accessed 27 January 2014).

Cannella G and Lincoln Y (2011) Ethics, research regulations and critical social science. In: Denzin N and Lincoln Y (eds) *The Sage Handbook of Qualitative Research* (4th edition). Thousand Oaks, CA: Sage, pp. 81–89.

Caplan P (2003) *Ethics of Anthropology: Debates and Dilemmas*, London: Routledge.

Caplan P (2010) Something for posterity or hostage to fortune? Archiving anthropological field material. *Anthropology Today* 26(4): 13–17.

Carlson RV, Boyd KM and Webb DJ (2004) The revision of the Declaration of Helsinki: past, present and future. *British Journal of Clinical Pharmacology* 57(6): 695–713.

Carrick-Hagenbarth J and Epstein GA (2012) Dangerous interconnectedness: economists' conflicts of interest, ideology and financial crisis. *Cambridge Journal of Economics* 36(1): 43–63.

Carter SL (1996) *Integrity*. New York: Harper Perennial.

Cassell J (1982) Does risk–benefit analysis apply to moral evaluation of social research. In: Beauchamp TL, Faden RR, Wallace RJ and Walters L (eds) *Ethical Issues in Social Science Research*. London: John Hopkins University Press, pp. 144–162.

Cassell J (ed) (1987) *Children in the Field: Anthropological Experiences.* Philadelphia: Temple University Press.

Castleden H, Morgan VS and Neimanis A (2010) Researchers' perspectives on collective/community co-authorship in community-based participatory indigenous research. *Journal of Empirical Research on Human Research Ethics* 5: 23–32.

Castro R and Bronfman MN (1997) *Algunos problemas no resueltos en la integracion de métodos cualitativos y cuantitativos en la investigacion social en salud.* Cocoyoc, México: IV Congreso Latinoamericano de Ciencias Sociales y Medicina.

Cauce AM and Nobles RH (2006) With all due respect: ethical issues in the study of vulnerable adolescents. In: Tromble JE and Fisher CB (eds) *The Handbook of Ethical Research with Ethnocultural Populations and Communities.* Thousand Oaks, CA: Sage, pp. 197–215.

Cerulli C (2011) Research ethics in victimization studies: widening the lens. *Violence Against Women* 17(12): 1525–1535.

Chalmers D (2004) Ethical and policy issues in research involving human participants. Available at: http://www.onlineethics.org/cms/8069.aspx (accessed 27 January 2014).

Chalmers R and Israel M (2005) Caring for data: law, professional codes and the negotiation of confidentiality in Australian criminological research. Report for the Criminology Research Council (Australia). Available at: http://www.criminologyre searchcouncil.gov.au/reports/200304-09.html (accessed 27 January 2014).

Chapman S, Morrell B, Forsyth R, Kerridge I and Stewart C (2012) Policies and practices on competing interests of academic staff in Australian universities. *Medical Journal of Australia* 196: 452–456.

Charatan FB (1997) Psychologist wins damages over theft of research. *British Medical Journal* 315: 501.

Chattopadhyay S (2011) Facing up to the hard problems: Western bioethics in the Eastern land of India. In: Myser C (ed) *Bioethics Around the Globe.* Oxford: Oxford University Press, pp. 19–38.

Chen XP (2011) Author ethical dilemmas in the research publication process. *Management and Organization Review* 7(3): 423–432.

Cherry MJ (2009) UNESCO, 'universal bioethics', and state regulation of health risks: a philosophical critique. *The Journal of Medicine and Philosophy* 34: 274–295.

Chicago Tribune Editorial (2011) NU vs. Protess. *Chicago Tribune*, 8 April. Available at: http://articles.chicagotribune.com/2011-04-08/news/ct-edit-protess-20110408_1_ medill-innocence-project-david-protess-subpoena (accessed 23 December 2013).

Childress JF (1982) *Who Should Decide? Paternalism in Health Care.* New York: Oxford University Press.

Chilisa B (2009) Indigenous African-centered ethics: contesting and complementing dominant models. In: Mertens DM and Ginsberg PE (eds) *Handbook of Social Research Ethics.* Thousand Oaks, CA: Sage, pp. 407–425.

Chilisa B and Preece J (2005) *Research Methods for Adult Educators in Africa.* Cape Town: Pearson/UNESCO.

Cho MK, Shohara R, Schissel A and Rennie D (2000) Policies on faculty conflicts of interest at US universities. *Journal of the American Medical Association* 284(17): 2203–2208.

Christie M with Guyula Y, Gotha K and Gurruwiwi D (2010) The ethics of teaching from country. *Australian Aboriginal Studies* 2010(2): 69–80.

Citro CF, Ilgen DR and Marrett CB (eds) (2003) *Protecting Participants and Facilitating Social and Behavioral Sciences Research.* Washington, DC: The National Academies Press.

Clark P (2013) Must academics researching authoritarian regimes self-censor? *Times Higher Education*, 28 November. Available at http://www.timeshighereducation.co.uk/features/must-academics-researching-authoritarian-regimes-self-censor/2009275.fullarticle (accessed 23 December 2013).

Clegg JW and Slife BD (2009) Research ethics in the postmodern context. In: Mertens DM and Ginsberg PE (eds) *Handbook of Social Research Ethics*. Thousand Oaks, CA: Sage, pp. 23–38.

Coimbra C, Baldini C, Silveira C, Cerveny CMO, Bonilha EA and Concone MHVB (2007) *Relatório da reunião sobre ética em pesquisa qualitativa em saúde* (Report on the meeting on ethics and qualitative research in health). São Paulo: Comitê de Ética em Pesquisa da Secretaria Municipal de Saúde (Research Ethics Committee of the Municipal Secretary of Health). Available at: http://www.fsp.usp.br/rsp/noticias/070417p.pdf (accessed 27 January 2014).

Colorado Conference of the American Association of University Professors (2011) Report on the termination of Ward Churchill. Available at: http://www.aaup.org/sites/default/files/files/JAF/2012%20JAF/ConferenceReport.pdf (accessed 23 December 2013).

Committee on Assessing Integrity in Research Environments (2002) Integrity in Scientific Research: Creating an Environment that Promotes Responsible Conduct. Washington, DC: National Academic Press.

Committee on Publication Ethics (2003) *Guidelines on Good Publication Practice*. London: Committee on Publication Ethics.

Coney S and Bunkle P (1987) An 'unfortunate experiment' at National Women's. *Metro*, June, 47–65.

Conselho Nacional de Saúde (1996) Resolution 196/6 (Resolução n.196, de 10 de outubro de 1996). Diretrizes e Normas Regulamentado-ras de Pesquisas Envolvendo Seres Humanos, CNS, Brasília. Available at: http://conselho.saude.gov.br/resolucoes/1996/Res196_en.pdf (accessed 27 January 2014).

Conselho Nacional de Saúde (2000) Resolution 304/2000 (Resolution n.304, 9 August, 2000). Diretrizes e Normas Regulamentado-ras de Pesquisas Envolvendo Seres Humanos, CNS, Brasília. Available at: http://conselho.saude.gov.br/resolucoes/2000/Res304_en.pdf (accessed 9 June 2014).

Conselho Nacional de Saúde (2012) Resolution 466/12 (Resolução n.466, de 12 de dezembro de 2012). Diretrizes e Normas Regulamentado-ras de Pesquisas Envolvendo Seres Humanos, CNS, Brasília. Available at: http://conselho.saude.gov.br/resolucoes/2012/Reso466.pdf (accessed 9 June 2014).

Contractor Q (2008) Fieldwork and social science research ethics. *Indian Journal of Medical Ethics* 5(1): 22–23.

Cook KS and Yamagishi T (2008) A defense of deception on scientific grounds. *Social Psychology Quarterly* 71(3): 215–220.

Cordner C and Thomson C (2007) No need to go! Workplace studies and the resources of the Revised National Statement. *Monash Bioethics Review* 26(3): 37–48.

Cossette P (2004) Research integrity: an exploratory survey of administrative science faculties. *Journal of Business Ethics* 49: 213–234.

Council for International Organizations of Medical Sciences (CIOMS) (2002) International Ethical Guidelines for Biomedical Research Involving Human Subjects. Available at http://www.cioms.ch/publications/layout_guide2002.pdf (accessed 27 January 2014).

Coutinho L, Raje G and Bisht S (2000) Numerical narratives and documentary practices: vaccines, targets and reports of the immunization programme. *Economic & Political Weekly* 35(8–9): 656–666.

Cramer CE (2006) Why footnotes matter: checking *Arming America*'s claims. *Plagiary: Cross-Disciplinary Studies in Plagiarism, Fabrication, and Falsification* 1: 149–177. Available at: http://quod.lib.umich.edu/p/plag/5240451.0001.016?rgn=main;view=fulltext (accessed 23 December 2013).

Creed-Kanashiro H, Ore B, Scurrah M, Gil A and Penny M (2005) Conducting research in developing countries: experiences of the informed consent process from community studies in Peru. *The Journal of Nutrition* 135: 925–928.

Cromwell PF, Olson JN and Wester Avary D (1991) *Breaking and Entering: An Ethnographic Analysis of Burglary*. London: Sage.

Czymoniewicz-Klippel MT, Brijnath B and Crockett B (2010) Ethics and the promotion of flexibility within international qualitative research: case examples from Asia and the Pacific. *Qualitative Inquiry* 16(5): 332–341.

D'Andrade R (1995) Moral models in anthropology. *Current Anthropology* 36(3): 399–408.

Dahl, D (2012) The future of human subjects research regulation. *Harvard Law Today*, June 14. Available at: http://today.law.harvard.edu/the-future-of-human-subjects-research-regulation/ (accessed 10 June 2014).

Dalen K (2007) Ethics review in Norway: psychologists and psychology projects. *Research Ethics* 3(19): 19–21.

Daley K (2012) Gathering sensitive stories: using care theory to guide ethical decision-making in research interviews with young people. *Youth Studies Australia* 31(3): 27–34.

Dallari SG (2008) A proteção do direito à intimidade, a confidencialidade e o sigilo nas pesquisas em saúde. In: Guerriero ICZ, Schmidt MLS and Zicker F (eds) *Ética nas pesquisas em ciências humanas e sociais na saúde*. São Paulo: Aderaldo and Rothschild, pp. 53–82.

Dancy J (1993) An ethic of prima facie duties. In: Singer P (ed) *A Companion to Ethics*. Oxford: Blackwell, pp. 219–229.

Danish Committees on Scientific Dishonesty (2009) *Guidelines on Good Scientific Practice* (unauthorised translation). Available at: http://ufm.dk/en/publications/2009/files-2009/guidelines-for-good-scientific-practice.pdf (accessed 10 June 2014).

Darou WG, Hum A and Kurtness J (1993) An investigation of the impact of psychosocial research on a Native population. *Professional Psychology: Research and Practice* 24(3): 325–329.

David M, Edwards R and Alldred P (2001) Children and school-based research: 'informed consent' or 'educated consent'. *British Educational Research Journal* 27(3): 347–365.

Davis P (2012) The emergence of a citation cartel. *The Scholarly Kitchen*, 10 April. Available at: http://scholarlykitchen.sspnet.org/2012/04/10/emergence-of-a-citation-cartel/ (accessed 23 December 2013).

De Vries R and Rott LM (2011) Bioethics as missionary work: the export of western ethics to developing countries. In: Myser C (ed) *Bioethics Around the Globe*. Oxford: Oxford University Press, pp. 3–18.

Dearden A (2013) See no evil? Ethics in an interventionist ICTD. *Information Technologies & International Development* 9(2): 1–17.

Decker SH and van Winkle B (1996) *Life in the Gang: Family, Friends and Violence*. Cambridge, Cambridge University Press.

Decoo W (2002) *Crisis on Campus: Confronting Academic Misconduct*. London: MIT Press.

Denscombe M, Dingwall G and Hillier T (2009) Ethics first: reflections on the role of research ethics at the initial stages of an investigation into taxi drivers' experiences of crime. *International Review of Victimology* 16(3): 301–308.

Denzin N, Lincoln YS and Smith LT (2008) Introduction: critical methodologies and indigenous inquiry. In: Denzin NK, Lincoln YS and Smith LT (eds) *Handbook of Critical and Indigenous Methodologies*. Los Angeles: Sage, pp. 1–20.

DePalma R (2010) Socially just research for social justice: negotiating consent and safety in a participatory action research project. *International Journal of Research & Method in Education* 33(3): 215–227.

Dickert N and Grady C (1999) What's the price of a research subject? Approaches to payment for research participation. *New England Journal of Medicine* 341(3): 198–203.

Dickson-Swift V, James EL, Kippen S and Liamputtong P (2007) Doing sensitive research: what challenges do qualitative researchers face? *Qualitative Research* 7(3): 327–353.

Dingwall R (2012) How did we ever get into this mess? The rise of ethical regulation in the social sciences. In: Love K (ed) *Ethics in Social Research*. Bingley: Emerald, pp. 3–26.

Dodds S (2000) Human research ethics in Australia: ethical regulation and public policy. *Monash Bioethics Review* 19(2): 4–21.

Doherty M (1998) Redundant publication. Report, COPE. Available at: http://bmj.bmj-journals.com/miosc/cope/tex5.shtml (accessed 23 December 2013).

Doumbo KO (2005) It takes a village: medical research and ethics in Mali. *Science* 307: 679–681.

Dranseika V, Gefenas E, Cekanauskaite A, Hug K, Mezinska S, Peicius E, Silis V, Soosaar A and Strosberg M (2011) Twenty years of human research ethics committees in the Baltic States. *Developing World Bioethics* 11(1): 48–54.

Dreger A (2011) Darkness's descent on the American Anthropological Association. *Human Nature* 22(3): 225–246.

Duncan GT, Elliot M and Salazar-González J-J (2011) *Statistical Confidentiality Principles and Practice*. New York, NY: Springer.

Duncan RE, Drew SE, Hodgson J and Sawyer SM (2009) 'Is my mum going to hear this?' Methodological and ethical challenges in qualitative health research with young people. *Social Science & Medicine* 69(11): 1691–1699.

Dworkin R (1978) *Taking Rights Seriously*. Cambridge, MA: Harvard University Press.

Dwyer E (2012) Neurological patients as experimental subjects: epilepsy studies in the United States. In: Jacyna LS and Casper ST (eds) *The Neurological Patient in History: Vol. 20*. New York: Boydell & Brewer, University of Rochester Press, pp. 44–60.

Eckstein S (2004) Efforts to build capacity in research ethics: an overview. *Science and Development Network*, 1 June. http://www.scidev.net/global/policy-brief/efforts-to-build-capacity-in-research-ethics-an-ov.html (accessed 27 January 2014).

Economic and Social Research Council (ESRC) (United Kingdom) (2010, revised 2012) Framework for Research Ethics. Swindon: Economic and Social Research Council. Available at: http://www.esrc.ac.uk/about-esrc/information/research-ethics.aspx (accessed 23 December 2013).

Economic and Social Research Council (United Kingdom) (2005) Research Ethics Framework. Swindon: Economic and Social Research Council.

Eden L (2010) Letter from the Editor-in-Chief: scientists behaving badly. *Journal of International Business Studies* 41(4): 561–566.

El Dorado Task Force (2002) Final Report. Report, American Anthropological Association, Arlington VA. Available at: http://www.aaanet.org/edtf/final/preface.htm (accessed 13 January 2014).

Ellen RF (1984) *Ethnographic Research: A Guide to General Conduct*. London: Academic Press.

Ellis C (1986) *Fisher Folk. Two Communities on Chesapeake Bay*. Lexington: University Press of Kentucky.

Ellis C (2007) Telling secrets, revealing lives: relational ethics in research with intimate others. *Qualitative Inquiry* 13(1): 3–29.

Ellsberg M and Heise L (2002) Bearing witness: ethics in domestic violence research. *The Lancet* 359: 1599–1604.

Emanuel EJ (1995) The beginning of the end of principlism. *The Hastings Center Report* 25(4): 37.

Emanuel EJ (2008) Benefits to host countries. In: Ezekiel EJ (ed) *The Oxford Textbook of Research Ethics*. New York: Oxford University Press, pp. 719–728.

Emanuel EJ and Weijer C (2005) Protecting communities in research: from a new principle to rational protections. In: Childress JF, Meslin EM and Shapiro HT (eds) *Belmont Revisited: Ethical Principles for Research with Human Subjects*. Washington DC: Georgetown University Press, pp. 165–183.

Emmerich N (2013) An overview and summary of the ethical codes of the learned society members of the UK's Academy of Social Sciences. Paper written for Generic Ethics Principles in Social Science Research Symposia. http://acss.org.uk/wp-content/uploads/2014/01/Summaries-of-LS-Members-Statements-of-Research-Ethics.pdf (accessed 27 January 2014).

Enders W and Hoover GA (2004) Whose line is it? Plagiarism in economics. *Journal of Economic Literature* 42(3): 487–493.

Enders W and Hoover GA (2006) Plagiarism in the economics profession: a survey. *Challenge* 49(5): 92–107.

Engerman DC (2009) *Know Your Enemy: The Rise and Fall of America's Soviet Experts*. New York: Oxford University Press.

Enserink M (2012a) Rotterdam marketing psychologist resigns after university investigates his data. *ScienceInsider*, 25 June. Available at: http://news.sciencemag.org/scienceinsider/2012/06/rotterdam-marketing-psychologist.html?ref=hp (accessed 23 December 2013).

Enserink M (2012b) Final report: Stapel affair points to bigger problems in social psychology. *ScienceInsider*, 28 November. Available at: http://news.sciencemag.org/scienceinsider/2012/11/final-report-stapel-affair-point.html (accessed 23 December 2013).

Erasmus University Rotterdam (2012) Universiteit trekt artikelen terug. *Erasmus University Rotterdam News*, 25 June. Available at: http://www.eur.nl/nieuws/detail/article/38616-universiteit-trekt-artikelen-terug/ (accessed 23 December 2013).

Ethical Practices of Journal Editors (2012) Voluntary Code of Conduct. Available at: http://editorethics.uncc.edu/ (accessed 23 December 2013).

European Commission (2005) Facing the Future Together: Conference on Research Ethics Committees in Europe, Brussels, Belgium, 27–28 January 2005. Brussels: Directorate-General for Research.

European Research Council (2010) Guidance Note for Researchers and Evaluators of Social Sciences and Humanities Research. Available at: http://ec.europa.eu/research/participants/data/ref/fp7/89867/social-sciences-humanities_en.pdf (accessed 27 January 2014).

European Science Foundation (2011) A European Code of Conduct for Research Integrity. ALLEA. Available at: http://www.allea.org/Content/ALLEA/Scientific%20Integrity/A%20European%20Code%20of%20Conduct%20for%20Research%20Integrity_final.10.10.pdf (accessed 27 January 2014).

Evans JH (2000) A sociological account of the growth of principlism. *The Hastings Center Report* 30(5): 31–38.

Evans M (2004) Ethics, anonymity, and authorship in community centred research or anonymity and the island cache. *Pimatisiwin* 2(1): 59–75. Available at: www.pima tisiwin.com/uploads/810119208.pdf (accessed 23 December 2013).

Experts Committee for Human Research Participant Protection in Canada (2008) Moving Ahead: Final Report. Available at: http://noveltechethics.ca/files/files/Policy/ Research_Ethics/Moving_Ahead.pdf (accessed 23 December 2013).

Eysenbach G and Till JE (2001) Ethical issues in qualitative research on internet communities. *British Medical Journal* 323: 1103–1105.

Fadare JO and Porteri C (2010) Informed consent in human subject research: a comparison of current international and Nigerian guidelines. *Journal of Empirical Research on Human Research Ethics* 5(1): 67–73.

Faden RR and Beauchamp TL (1986) *A History and Theory of Informed Consent.* New York: Oxford University Press.

Fanelli D (2011) The black, the white and the grey areas: towards an international and interdisciplinary definition of scientific misconduct. In: Mayer T and Steneck N (eds) *Promoting Research Integrity in a Global Environment.* Singapore: Imperial College Press/World Scientific Publishing, pp. 79–84.

Feagin J (1999) Soul-searching in sociology: is the discipline in crisis? *Chronicle of Higher Education* 15 October: B4.

Federman DD, Hanna KE and Rodriguez LL (eds) (2002) *Responsible Research: A Systems Approach to Protecting Research Participants.* Washington DC: The National Academies Press.

Feenan D (2002) Legal issues in acquiring information about illegal behaviour through criminological research. *British Journal of Criminology* 42: 762–781.

Feinberg J (1984) *Harm to Others.* Oxford: Oxford University Press.

Feinberg J (1986) *Harm to Self.* New York: Oxford University Press.

Feldman D (2005) Writing and reviewing as sadomasochistic rituals. *Journal of Management* 31 (3): 325–329.

Fielding N (1982) Observational research on the National Front. In: Bulmer M (ed) *Social Research Ethics: An Examination of the Merits of Covert Participant Observation.* London: Macmillan, pp. 80–104.

Figueiredo V (2004) Ética e ciência: comissões de ética em pesquisa científica. In: Victora C, Oliven RG, Maciel ME and Oro AP (eds) *Antropologia Ética. O debate atual no Brasil.* Niterói: Editora da Universidade Federal Fluminense, pp. 113–118.

Fincham B, Scourfield J and Langer S (2008) The impact of working with disturbing secondary data: reading suicide files in a coroner's office. *Qualitative Health Research* 18(6): 853–862.

Fine M (2005) Contesting research: rearticulation and 'thick democracy' as political projects of method. In: Dimitriadis G, McCarthy C and Weis L (eds) *Ideology, Curriculum, and the New Sociology of Education: Revisiting the Work of Michael Apple.* New York: Routledge, pp. 146–166.

Fine S (2014) Researcher's taped interview with alleged killer Magnotta off-limits to police. *The Globe and Mail,* 22 January.

Finn P and Jakobsson K (2007) Designing ethical phishing experiments. *IEEE Technology and Society Magazine* 26(1): 45–58.

Fisher CB and Ragsdale K (2006) Goodness-of-fit ethics for multicultural research. In: Tromble JE and Fisher CB (eds) *The Handbook of Ethical Research with Ethnocultural Populations and Communities.* Thousand Oaks, CA: Sage, pp. 3–25.

Fitzgerald J and Hamilton M (1996) The consequences of knowing: ethical and legal liabilities in illicit drug research. *Social Science & Medicine* 43(11): 1591–1600.

Fitzgerald J and Hamilton M (1997) Confidentiality, disseminated regulation and ethico-legal liabilities in research with hidden populations of illicit drug users. *Addiction* 92(9): 1099–1107.

Fitzpatrick S (2010) Red-handed plagiarism brings down Flinders-trained professor in Indonesia. *The Australian*, 17 February, 21–22.

Flitter E, Cooke K and da Costa P (2010) Special report: for some professors, disclosure is academic. Reuters. Available at: http://www.reuters.com/article/2010/12/20/us-academics-conflicts-idUSTRE6BJ3LF20101220 (accessed 23 December 2013).

Fluehr-Lobban C (2000) How anthropology should respond to an ethical crisis. *Chronicle of Higher Education* 47(6): B 24.

Fontes LA (1998) Ethics in family violence research: cross-cultural issues. *Family Relations* 47(1): 53–61.

Fontes LA (2004) Ethics in violence against women research: the sensitive, the dangerous, and the overlooked. *Ethics & Behavior* 14: 141–174.

Foot P (1978) *Virtues and Vices and Other Essays in Moral Philosophy*. Berkeley, CA: University of California Press.

Forbat L and Henderson J (2003) 'Stuck in the middle with you': the ethics and process of qualitative research with two people in an intimate relationship. *Qualitative Health Research* 13(10): 1453–1462.

Frankel B and Trend MG (1991) Principles, pressures and paychecks: the anthropologist as employee. In: Fluehr-Lobban C (ed) *Ethics and the Profession of Anthropology: Dialogue for a New Era*. Philadelphia: University of Philadelphia Press, pp. 177–197.

Frankena WK (1973) *Ethics*. Englewood Cliffs, NJ: Prentice-Hall.

Freedman B (1987) Scientific value and validity as ethical requirements for research: a proposed explication. *IRB: A Review of Human Subjects Research* 9(6): 7–10.

Freidson E (1964) To the editor: against the code of ethics. *American Sociological Review* 29: 410.

Freyd JJ (2011) Journal vitality, intellectual integrity, and the problems of McEthics. *Journal of Trauma & Dissociation* 12(5): 475–481.

Gallagher M, Haywood SL, Jones M and Milne S (2010) Negotiating informed consent with children in school-based research: a critical review. *Children & Society* 24(6):471–482.

Gallaher C (2009) Researching repellent groups: Some methodological considerations on how to represent militants, radicals, and other belligerents. In: Sriram CL, King JC, Mertus J, Martin-Ortega O and Hermann J (eds) *Surviving Field Research: Working in Violent and Difficult Situations*. London: Routledge, pp. 127–146.

Galliher JF (1973) The protection of human subjects: a re-examination of the professional code of ethics. *American Sociologist* 8: 93–100.

Garrett B (2014) Place-hacker Bradley Garrett: research at the edge of the law. *Times Higher Education*, 5 June. Available at: http://www.timeshighereducation.co.uk/story.aspx?storyCode=2013717 (accessed 9 June 2014).

Geelhoed RJ, Phillips JC, Fischer AR, Shpungin E, Gong Y (2007) Authorship decision making: an empirical investigation. *Ethics & Behavior* 17(2): 95–115.

Geis G, Mobley A and Schichor D (1999) Private prisons, criminological research, and conflict of interest: a case study. *Crime & Delinquency* 45: 372–388.

Gellman R (2009) Privacy in the clouds: risks to privacy and confidentiality from cloud computing. Report prepared for the World Privacy Forum. Available at: http://www.worldprivacyforum.org/2011/11/resource-page-cloud-privacy/ (accessed 27 January 2014).

Genders E and Player E (1995) *Grendon: A Study of a Therapeutic Prison*. Oxford: Clarendon Press.

Gill J (2013) Leader: rotten to the core? Far from it. *Times Higher Education*, 28 February. Available at: http://www.timeshighereducation.co.uk/comment/leader/rotten-to-the-core-far-from-it/2002085.article (accessed 27 January 2014).

Gilligan C (1977) In a different voice: women's conceptions of self and of morality. *Harvard Educational Review* 47(4): 481–503.

Gilligan C (1982) *In a Different Voice: Psychological Theory and Women's Development*. Cambridge: Harvard University Press.

Gillon R (1994) Medical ethics: four principles plus attention to scope. *British Medical Journal* 309: 184–188.

Gledhill J (1999) Moral ambiguities and competing claims to justice: exploring the dilemmas of activist scholarship and intervention in complex situations. Available at: http://jg.socialsciences.manchester.ac.uk/Moral%20Ambiguities.pdf (accessed 27 January 2014).

Godlee F and Wager E (2012) Research misconduct in the UK: time to act. *British Medical Journal* 344:d8357.

Goldsmith A (2003) Fear, fumbling and frustration: reflections on doing criminological fieldwork in Colombia. *Criminal Justice* 3(1): 103–125.

Gong Y (2005) China Science Foundation takes action against 60 grantees. *Science* 309(5742): 1798–1799.

Gontcharov I (2013) Methodological crisis in the social sciences: the New Brunswick Declaration as a new paradigm in research ethics governance? *Transnational Legal Theory* 4(1): 146–156.

Gontcharov I (under review, 2014) The eclipse of 'human subjects' and the rise of 'human participants' in research involving humans. In: van den Hoonaard W and Hamilton A (eds) *Ethics Rupture: Exploring Alternatives to Formal Research-Ethics Review*.

Goodstein D (2002) Scientific misconduct. *Academe* 1: 28–31.

Government of Mozambique (2007) Science and technology ethics code (Decree n° 71/2007, 24 December).

Government of Senegal (2009) Code of ethics for health research (Law 2009-17, 9 March).

Gracia D (1995) Hard times, hard choices: founding bioethics today. *Bioethics* 9(3–4): 183–206.

Grassley CE (2010) Ghostwriting in medical literature. Minority Staff Report, 111th Congress, United States Senate Committee on Finance, Washington, DC. Available at: http://www.grassley.senate.gov/about/upload/Senator-Grassley-Report.pdf (accessed 23 December 2013).

Graves W III and Shields MA (1991) Rethinking moral responsibility in fieldwork: the situated negotiation of research ethics in anthropology and sociology. In: Fluehr-Lobban C (ed) *Ethics and the Profession of Anthropology: Dialogue for a New Era*. Philadelphia: University of Pennsylvania Press, pp. 132–151.

Gray GC and Kendzia VB (2009) Organizational self-censorship: corporate sponsorship, nonprofit funding, and the educational experience. *Canadian Review of Sociology* 46(2): 161–177.

Griffin M, Resick P, Waldrop A and Mechanic M (2003) Participation in trauma research: is there evidence of harm? *Journal of Traumatic Stress* 16: 221–227.

Grove J (2012) Arrested, beaten, caged – but the state could not break him. *Times Higher Education*, 5 July. Available at: http://www.timeshighereducation.co.uk/420433.article (accessed 14 March 2014).

Guerriero ICZ (under review, 2014) Ethics in social science and humanities research: Brazilian strategies to improve guidelines. In: van den Hoonaard W and Hamilton A (eds) *Ethics Rupture: Exploring Alternatives to Formal Research-Ethics Review*.

Guerriero ICZ and Dallari SG (2008) The need for adequate ethical guidelines for qualitative health research. *Ciência & Saúde Coletiva*, Marzo–Abril: 303–311.

Guillemin M and Gillam L (2004) Ethics, reflexivity and 'ethically important moments' in research. *Qualitative Inquiry* 10(2): 261–280.

Gunsalus CK, Bruner EM, Burbules NC, Dash L, Finkin M, Goldberg JP, Greenough WT, Miller GA, Pratt MG, Iriye M and Aronson D (2007) The Illinois White Paper: improving the system for protecting human subjects: counteracting IRB 'mission creep'. *Qualitative Inquiry* 13: 617–649.

Gustafsson B, Rydén L, Tibell G and Wallensteen P (1984) The Uppsala Code of Ethics for Scientists. *Journal of Peace Research* 21(4): 311–316.

Guta A, Nixon SA and Wilson MG (2013) Resisting the seduction of 'ethics creep': using Foucault to surface complexity and contradiction in research ethics review. *Social Science & Medicine* 98: 301–310.

Haggerty, K. (2004) Ethics creep: governing social science research in the name of ethics, *Qualitative Sociology* 27(4): 391–414.

Hall SM (2009) 'Private life' and 'work life': difficulties and dilemmas when making and maintaining friendships with ethnographic participants. *Area* 41(3): 263–272.

Halse C and Honey A (2005) Unraveling ethics: illuminating the moral dilemmas of research ethics. *Signs: Journal of Women in Culture and Society* 30(4): 2141–2162.

Hammersley M (2009) Against the ethicists: on the evils of ethical regulation. *International Journal of Social Research Methodology* 12(3): 211–225.

Hammersley M (2013) A response to 'Generic ethics principles in social science research' by David Carpenter. Generic Ethics Principles in Social Science Research Symposium 1: Principles. Available at: http://acss.org.uk/wp-content/uploads/2014/01/Hammersley-AcSS-Response-to-Carpenter-5-March-2013-Principles-for-Generic-Ethics-Principles-in-Social-Science-Research.pdf (accessed 27 January 2014).

Hammersley M and Traianou A (2012) *Ethics in Qualitative Research: Controversies and Contexts*. London: Sage.

Hammett D and Sporton D (2012) Paying for interviews? Negotiating ethics, power and expectation. *Area* 44(4): 496–502.

Hancock L (2001) *Community, Crime and Disorder: Safety and Regeneration in Urban Neighbourhoods*. London: Palgrave.

Harding S (1991) *Whose Science? Whose Knowledge?* New York: Cornell University Press.

Hardy E, Bento SF, Hebling EM, Faúndes A, Osis MJD and Sousa MH (2010) Twelve years of the Brazilian initiative to create a network of IRBs for the ethical evaluation of research studies involving human subjects. *AJOB Primary Research* 1(4): 19–27.

Harkness J, Lederer SE and Wikler D (2001) Laying ethical foundations for clinical research. *Bulletin of the World Health Organization* 79(4): 365–372.

Hart RA (1992) Children's participation: from tokenism to citizenship. *Innocenti Essay* 4, Florence: UNICEF ICDC. Available at: http://www.unicef-irc.org/publications/100 (accessed 27 January 2014).

Hazelgrove J (2002) The old faith and the new science: the Nuremberg Code and human experimentation ethics in Britain, 1946–73. *Social History of Medicine* 15(1): 109–135.

Health and Development Policy Project (1995) Measuring violence against women cross-culturally: notes from a meeting, June 29, Maryland, USA. Unpublished.

Hearnshaw LS (1979) *Cyril Burt: Psychologist*. London: Hodder and Stoughton.

Heath C, Hindmarsh J and Luff P (2010) *Video in Qualitative Research*. London: Sage.

Heath E (2001) Ethical and policy issues in research involving human participants: the history, function and future of independent institutional review boards (Volume 2). Report, National Bioethics Advisory Committee (USA). Available at: http://bioethics.georgetown.edu/nbac/human/overvol2.html (accessed 27 January 2014).

Hedayat KM (2007) The possibility of a Universal Declaration of Biomedical Ethics. *Journal of Medical Ethics* 33: 17–20.

Hedgecoe A (2008) Research ethics review and the sociological research relationship. *Sociology* 42: 873–886.

Hegtvedt KA (2007) Ethics and experiment. In: Webster M Jr and Sell J (eds) *Laboratory Experiments in the Social Sciences*. Burlington: Academic Press, pp. 141–172.

Heitman E and Litewka S (2011) International perspectives on plagiarism and considerations for teaching international trainees. *Urologic Oncology* 29(1): 104–108.

Held V (ed) (1995) *Justice and Care*. Boulder: Westview Press.

Henderson M, Johnson NF and Auld G (2013) Silences of ethical practice: dilemmas for researchers using social media. *Educational Research and Evaluation: An International Journal on Theory and Practice* 19(6): 546–560.

Herrera CD (1999) Two arguments for 'covert methods' in social research. *British Journal of Sociology* 50(2): 331–343.

Hertwig R and Ortmann A (2001) Experimental practices in economics: a methodological challenge for psychologists? *Behavioral and Brain Sciences* 24: 383–451.

Hertwig R and Ortmann A (2008) Deception in social psychological experiments: two misconceptions and a research agenda. *Social Psychology Quarterly* 71(3): 222–227.

Hett G and Hett J (2013) Ethics in intercultural research: reflections on the challenges of conducting field research in a Syrian context. *Compare: A Journal of Comparative and International Education* 43(4): 496–515.

Hickling Arthurs Low (2009) The state of research integrity and misconduct policies in Canada. Report prepared for the Canadian Research Integrity Committee. Available at: http://www.nserc-crsng.gc.ca/_doc/NSERC-CRSNG/HAL_Report_e.pdf (accessed 23 December 2013).

Hirsch Hadorn GH, Bammer G and Pohl C (2010) Solving problems through transdisciplinary research. In: Frodeman R, Klein JT and Mitcham C (eds) *The Oxford Handbook of Interdisciplinarity*. Oxford: Oxford University Press, pp. 431–452.

Hlavka H, Kruttschnitt C and Carbone-Lopez K (2007) Revictimizing the victims? Interviewing women victims of interpersonal violence. *Journal of Interpersonal Violence* 22: 894–920.

Hochschild A (1983) *The Managed Heart: Commercialisation of Human Feeling*. Berkeley: University of California Press.

Holbrook A (1997) Ethics by numbers? An historian's reflection of ethics in the field. In: Bibby M (ed) *Review of Australian Research in Education*. Australian Association for Research in Education: Ethics and Education Research (4), pp. 49–66.

Holm S (2001) The Danish research ethics committee system – overview and critical assessment. In: National Bioethics Advisory Committee (USA) (ed) *Ethical and Policy Issues in Research Involving Human Participants, Volume 2*. Available at: http://bioethics.georgetown.edu/nbac/human/overvol2.html (accessed 27 January 2014).

Hornblum AM (1998) *Acres of Skin: Human Experimentation at Holmesburg Prison*. New York: Routledge.

Horowitz IL (ed) (1967) *The Rise and Fall of Project Camelot: Studies in the Relationship Between Social Science and Practical Politics*. Cambridge, MA: MIT Press.

House of Commons Science and Technology Committee, United Kingdom (2011) *Peer review in scientific publications, Eighth Report of Session 2010–12, Volume I: Report, together with formal minutes, oral and written evidence*. London: The Stationery Office.

Howell N (1990) Surviving fieldwork: a report of the Advisory Panel on Health and Safety in Fieldwork. Report, American Anthropological Association, Washington, DC.

Hsiung P (2012) The globalization of qualitative research: challenging Anglo American domination and local hegemonic discourse. *Forum Qualitative Sozialforschung/Forum: Qualitative Social Research*. 13(1). Available at: http://www.qualitative-research.net/index.php/fqs/article/view/1710 (accessed 27 January 2014).

Hubbard G, Backett-Milburn K and Kemmer D (2001) Working with emotion: issues for the researcher in fieldwork and teamwork. *International Journal of Social Research Methodology* 4(2): 119–137.

Hudson M, Milne M, Reynolds P, Russell K and Smith B (2010) *Te Ara Tika*, Guidelines for Māori Research Ethics: a framework for researchers and ethics committee members. Final Draft. Available at: www.hrc.govt.nz/sites/default/files/Te%20Ara%20Tika%20Guidelines%20for%20Maori%20Research%20Ethics.pdf (accessed 23 December 2013).

Hudson ML and Russell K (2009) The Treaty of Waitangi and research ethics in Aotearoa. *Bioethical Inquiry* 6: 61–68.

Huggins MK and Glebbeek M-L (2003) Women studying violent male institutions: Cross-gendered dynamics in police research on secrecy and danger. *Theoretical Criminology* 7(3): 363–387.

Hugman R, Pittaway E and Bartolomei L (2011) When 'do no harm' is not enough: the ethics of research with refugees and other vulnerable groups. *British Journal of Social Work* 41: 1271–1287.

Hume D (1740/1967) *A Treatise of Human Nature*. Oxford: Oxford University Press.

Humphreys L (1970) *Tearoom Trade: A Study of Homosexual Encounters in Public Places*. London: Duckworth.

Humphreys M (2011) Ethical challenges of embedded experimentation. *Comparative Democratization* 9(3): 10, 23–29.

Hungarian Academy of Sciences (2010) Science Ethics Code of the Hungarian Academy of Sciences. Budapest: Hungarian Academy of Sciences. Available at: http://www.allea.org/Content/ALLEA/Scientific%20Integrity/ScienceEthicsCode-HAS.pdf (accessed 23 December 2013).

Hurdley R (2010) In the picture or off the wall? Ethical regulation, research habitus, and unpeopled ethnography. *Qualitative Inquiry* 16(6): 517–528.

Hussein G (2008) The Sudan experience. *Journal of Academic Ethics* 6: 289–293.

Hvinden B (2002) Ansvar for oppfølgingen av resultater Sammenliknende perspektiver og utfordringer i forskning om minoriteter (Responsibility for monitoring the results: comparative perspectives and challenges in research on minorities) In: *Samisk forskning og forskningsetikk* (*Sami research and research ethics*). Oslo: De nasjonale forskningsetiske komiteer, pp. 134–150. Available at: http://www.etikkom.no/Documents/Publikasjoner-som-PDF/Samisk%20forskning%20og%20forskningse-tikk%20(2002).pdf (accessed 27 January 2014).

Hyder AA, Zafar W, Ali J, Ssekubugu R, Ndebele P and Kass N (2013) Evaluating institutional capacity for research ethics in Africa: a case study from Botswana. *BMC Medical Ethics* 14(31).

IJsselmuiden C, Marais D, Wassenaar D and Mokgatla-Moipolai B (2012) Mapping African ethical review committee activity onto capacity needs: the MARC initiative and HRWeb's interactive database of RECs in Africa. *Developing World Bioethics* 12(2): 74–86.

Imbens GW and Lemieux T (2008) Regression discontinuity designs: a guide to practice. *Journal of Econometrics*, 142(2): 615–635.

Indian Council of Medical Research (ICMR) (1980) Policy Statement on Ethical Considerations Involved in Research on Human Subjects. New Delhi: ICMR.

Indian Council of Medical Research (ICMR) (2000) Ethical Guidelines for Biomedical Research on Human Subjects. New Delhi: ICMR.

Indian Council of Medical Research (ICMR) (2006) Ethical Guidelines for Biomedical Research on Human Participants. New Delhi: ICMR. Available at: http://icmr.nic.in/ethical_guidelines.pdf (accessed 9 June 2014).

Institute for Employment Studies (2004) The RESPECT Code of Practice. Available at: http://www.respectproject.org/code/ (accessed 13 January 2014).

Institute of Medicine (2009) Conflict of Interest in Medical Research, Education, and Practice. Washington DC: National Academies Press.

Institute of Science and Ethics (2004) Draft Final Report: Provision of Support for Producing a European Directory of Local Ethics Committees (LECs). Report, The Institute for Science and Ethics, Bonn.

International Bioethics Committee of UNESCO (2008) Report on Consent. UNESCO Social and Human Sciences Sector, Division of Ethics of Science and Technology, Bioethics Section, Paris.

International Committee of Medical Journal Editors (2013) Recommendations for the Conduct, Reporting, Editing, and Publication of Scholarly Work in Medical Journals. Available at: http://www.icmje.org/icmje-recommendations.pdf (accessed 23 December 2013).

Iphofen R (under review, 2014) Professional research ethics: helping to balance individual and institutional integrity. In: van den Hoonaard W and Hamilton A (eds) *Ethics Rupture: Exploring Alternatives to Formal Research-Ethics Review*.

Israel M (1998) Crimes of the state: victimisation of South African political exiles in the United Kingdom. *Crime, Law and Social Change* 29(1): 1–29.

Israel M (1999) *South African Political Exiles in the United Kingdom*. London: Macmillan.

Israel M (2000) The commercialisation of university-based criminological research in Australia. *Australian & New Zealand Journal of Criminology* 33(1): 1–20.

Israel M (2004a) Strictly confidential? Integrity and the disclosure of criminological and socio-legal research. *British Journal of Criminology* 44(5): 715–740.

Israel M (2004b) Ethics and the governance of criminological research in Australia. Report, New South Wales Bureau of Crime Statistics and Research, Sydney, October.

Israel M (2011) The key to the door? Teaching awards in Australian higher education. Sydney: Australian Learning and Teaching Council. Available at: http://www.olt.gov.au/system/files/resources/Israel%2C%20M%20UWA%20Fellowship%20report%202011_0.pdf (accessed 23 December 2013).

Israel M and Hay I (2006) *Research Ethics for Social Scientists: Between Ethical Conduct and Regulatory Compliance*. London: Sage.

Israel M (2014) Gerry Adams arrest: when is it right for academics to hand over information to the courts? *The Conversation*, 6 May. Available at: https://theconversation.com/gerry-adams-arrest-when-is-it-right-for-academics-to-hand-over-information-to-the-courts-26209 (accessed 9 June 2014).

Israel M, Allen G and Thomson C (under review, 2014) Australian research ethics governance: plotting the demise of the adversarial culture. In: van den Hoonaard W and

Hamilton A (eds) *The Ethics Rupture: Exploring Alternatives to Formal Research-Ethics Review*.

Jabeen T (2009) 'But I've never been asked!' Research with children in Pakistan. *Children's Geographies* 7(4): 405–419.

Jackson S, Backett-Milburn K and Newall E (2013) Researching distressing topics: emotional reflexivity and emotional labor in the secondary analysis of children and young people's narratives of abuse. *SAGE Open*, April–June, 1–12. Available at: http://sgo.sagepub.com/content/3/2/2158244013490705.

Jacobs BA (1998) Researching crack dealers: dilemmas and contradictions. In: Ferrell J and Hamm MS (eds) *Ethnography at the Edge: Crime, Deviance and Field Research*. Boston: Northeastern University Press, pp. 160–177.

Jacobs BA with Wright R (2000) Researching drug robbery. In: Jacobs BA (ed) *Robbing Drug Dealers: Violence Beyond the Law*. New York: Aldine de Gruyter, pp. 1–21.

Jeffery, R (2013) Authorship in multi-disciplinary, multi-national North–South research projects: issues of equity, capacity and accountability. *Compare: A Journal of Comparative and International Education*, doi: 10.1080/03057925.2013.829300.

Jennings S (2012) Response to Schrag: What are ethics committees for anyway? A defence of social science research ethics review. *Research Ethics* 8(2): 87–96.

Jensen LM (2012) Culture industry, power, and the spectacle of China's 'Confucius Institutes'. In: Weston TB and Jensen LM (eds) *China in and beyond the Headlines*. Lanham, MD: Rowman and Littlefield, pp. 271–299.

Jesani A (2004) Preface to the first reprint. In: National Committee for Ethics in Social Science Research in Health (NCESSRH), Ethical Guidelines for Social Science Research in Health. Mumbai: CEHAT.

Jesani A and Barai-Jaitly T (2005) Ethics of social science research in health. In: Jesani A and Barai-Jaitly T (eds) *Ethics in Health Research: A Social Science Perspective*. Mumbai: Centre for Studies in Ethics and Rights, pp. 9–19.

Joanou J P (2009) The bad and the ugly: ethical concerns in participatory photographic methods with children living and working on the streets of Lima, Peru. *Visual Studies* 24(3): 214–223.

Johnson B and Clarke JM (2003) Collecting sensitive data: the impact on researchers. *Qualitative Health Research* 13(3): 421–434.

Johnson H (2004) Investigating the dilemmas of ethical social research. *Journal of International Women's Studies* 6(1): 41–53.

Jones RA (1994) The ethics of research in cyberspace. *Internet Research* 4(3): 30–35.

Jonsen A (2005) The origins and evolution of the Belmont Report. In: Childress JF, Meslin EM and Shapiro HT (eds) *Belmont Revisited: Ethical Principles for Research with Human Subjects*. Washington, DC: Georgetown University Press, pp. 3–11.

Jonsen A (2007) Interview with Zachary M. Schrag. San Francisco, 24 October.

Jonsen AR (1998) *The Birth of Bioethics*. New York: Oxford University Press.

Jordan SR and Gray PW (2013) Research integrity in Greater China: surveying regulations, perceptions and knowledge of research integrity from a Hong Kong perspective. *Developing World Bioethics* 13(3): 125–137.

Jorgensen JG (1971) On ethics and anthropology. *Current Anthropology* 12(3): 321–333.

Joungtrakul J, Sheehan B and Allen BM (2011) Research ethics in practice: a comparative study of qualitative doctoral dissertations submitted to universities in the USA and Thailand 2001–2010. *Asian Forum on Business Education Journal* 4(3): 437–454.

Joynson RB (2003) Selective interest and psychological practice: a new interpretation of the Burt Affair. *British Journal of Psychology* 94: 409–426.

Kaiser K (2009) Protecting respondent confidentiality in qualitative research. *Qualitative Health Research* 19(11): 1632–1641.

Kamuya D, Marsh V and Molyneux S (2011) What we learned about voluntariness and consent: incorporating 'background situations' and understanding into analyses. *The American Journal of Bioethics* 11(8): 31–33.

Kamuya D, Marsh V, Kombe FK, Geissler PW and Molyneux SC (2013a) Engaging communities to strengthen research ethics in low-income settings: selection and perceptions of members of a network of representatives in coastal Kenya. *Developing World Bioethics* 13(1): 10–20.

Kamuya D, Theobald SJ, Munywoki PK, Koech D, Geissler WP and Molyneux SC (2013b) Evolving friendships and shifting ethical dilemmas: fieldworkers' experiences in a short term community based study in Kenya. *Developing World Bioethics* 13(1): 1–9.

Kant I (1785/2005) *Groundwork for the Metaphysics of Morals* with Denis L (ed). Orchard Park, NY: Broadview Press.

Kapur R (2005) *Erotic Justice: Law and the New Politics of Postcolonialism*. London: Glass House Press.

Kass NE, Hyder AA, Ajuwon A, Appiah-Poku J and Barsdorf N (2007) The structure and function of research ethics committees in Africa: a case study. *PLoS Medicine* 4(1): e3.

Katyal KR (2011) Gate-keeping and the ambiguities in the nature of 'informed consent' in Confucian societies. *International Journal of Research & Method in Education* 34(2): 147–159.

Katz SN, Gray HH and Ulrich LT (2002) Report of the investigative committee in the matter of Professor Michael Bellesiles. Report, Emory University. Available at: http://www.emory.edu/news/Releases/Final_Report.pdf (accessed 27 January 2014).

Kaufman J (2008) Blog comment from October 2, 'Michael – we did not consult'. In: Michael Zimmer (Blog author) *On the 'Anonymity' of the Facebook Dataset (Updated)*. Available at: http://michaelzimmer.org/2008/09/30/on-the-anonymity-of-the-facebook-dataset/ (accessed 13 January 2014).

Kaufman SR (1997) The World War II plutonium experiments: contested stories and their lessons for medical research and informed consent. *Culture, Medicine and Psychiatry* 21: 161–197.

Kellehear A (1989) Ethics and social research. In: Perry J (ed) *Doing Fieldwork: Eight Personal Accounts of Social Research*. Waurn Ponds, Vic: Deakin University Press, pp. 61–72.

Kelly P (1989) Utilitarianism and distributive justice: the civil law and the foundation of Bentham's economic thought. *Utilitas* 1(1): 62–81.

Kenyon E and Hawker S (2000) 'Once would be enough': some reflections on the issue of safety for lone researchers. *International Journal of Social Research Methodology* 2(4): 313–327.

Kerr NL (1998) HARKing: hypothesizing after the results are known. *Personality and Social Psychology Review* 2(3): 196–217.

Kershaw D and Fair J (1976) *The New Jersey Negative Income-Maintenance Experiment. Volume 1: Operations, Surveys and Administration*. New York: Academic Press.

Kim J and Park K (2013) Ethical modernization: research misconduct and research ethics reforms in Korea following the Hwang Affair. *Science and Engineering Ethics* 19(2): 355–380.

Kimmel AJ (1988) *Ethics and Values in Applied Social Research*. London: Sage.

Kimmelman J (2006) Review of *Belmont Revisited: Ethical Principles for Research with Human Subjects*. *Journal of the American Medical Association* 296(5): 589–594.

King PA (2005) Justice beyond Belmont. In: Childress JF, Meslin EM and Shapiro HT (eds) *Belmont Revisited: Ethical Principles for Research with Human Subjects*. Washington, DC: Georgetown University Press, pp. 136–147.

Kirigia JM, Wambebe C and Baba-Moussa A (2005) Status of national research bioethics committees in the WHO African region. *BMC Medical Ethics* 6(10) doi:10.1186/1472-6939-6-10. Available at: www.biomedcentral.com/1472-6939/6/10.

Kirkman BL and Chen G (2011) Maximizing your data or data slicing? Recommendations for managing multiple submissions from the same dataset *Management and Organization Review* 7(3): 433–446.

Kishore RR (2003) End of life issues and moral certainty. A discovery through Hinduism. *Eubios Journal of Asian and International Bioethics* 13: 210–213.

Kitchener KS and Kitchener RF (2009) Social science research ethics: historical and philosophical issues. In: Mertens DM and Ginsberg PE (eds) *Handbook of Social Research Ethics*. Thousand Oaks, CA: Sage, pp. 5–22.

Kitchin H (under review, 2014) The internet as a stage: dramaturgy, research ethics boards, and privacy as 'performance'. In: van den Hoonaard W and Hamilton A (eds) *Ethics Rupture: Exploring Alternatives to Formal Research-Ethics Review*.

Kitson GC, Clark RD, Rushforth NB, Brinich PM, Sudak HS and Zyzanski SJ (1996) Research on difficult family topics: helping new and experienced researchers cope with research on loss. *Family Relations* 45(2): 183–188.

Kjærnet H (2010) At arm's length? Applied social science and its sponsors. *Journal of Academic Ethics* 8(3): 161–169.

Kopelman LM (2009) Bioethics as public discourse and second-order discipline. *The Journal of Medicine and Philosophy* 34: 261–273.

Korn JH (1997) *Illusions of Reality: A History of Deception in Social Psychology*. Albany NY: State University of New York Press.

Kotch JB (2000) Ethical issues in longitudinal child maltreatment research. *Journal of Interpersonal Violence* 15(7): 696–709.

Kovats-Bernat JC (2002) Negotiating dangerous fields: pragmatic strategies for fieldwork amid violence and terror. *American Anthropologist* 104(1): 208–222.

Krimsky S, Rothenberg LS, Stott P and Kyle G (1996) Financial interests of authors in scientific journals: a pilot study of 14 publications. *Science and Engineering Ethics* 2: 395–410.

Kubar OI and Asatryan AG (2007) Establishment of the ethical review system and ethics committees in the region. In: Kubar O, Mikirtichan G and Nikitina A (eds) *Ethical Review of Biomedical Research in the CIS Countries (Social and Cultural Aspects)*. Saint-Petersburg: Phoenix, pp. 71–88.

Kuper A (1995) Comment. *Current Anthropology* 36(3): 424–426.

Kuula A (2010/11) Methodological and ethical dilemmas of archiving qualitative data. *IASSIST Quarterly* 34–35: 12–17.

Kuyper L, de Wit J, Adam P and Woertman L (2012) Doing more good than harm? The effects of participation in sex research on young people in the Netherlands. *Archives of Sexual Behavior* 41: 497–506.

LaFrance J and Crazy Bull C (2009) researching ourselves back to life: taking control of the research agenda in Indian country. In: Mertens DM and Ginsberg PE (eds) *Handbook of Social Research Ethics*. Thousand Oaks, CA: Sage, pp. 135–149.

Landman W and Schuklenk U (2005) From the editor. *Developing World Bioethics* 5(3): iii–vi.

Langdon EJ, Maluf S and Tornquist CS (2008) Ética e política na pesquisa: os métodos qualitativos e seus resultados. In: Guerriero ICZ, Schmidt MLS and Zicker S (eds) *Ética nas pesquisas em ciências humanas e sociais na saúde*. São Paulo, Aderaldo and Rothschild, pp. 128–147.

Langlois A (2008) The UNESCO Universal Declaration on Bioethics and Human Rights: perspectives from Kenya and South Africa. *Health Care Analysis* 16: 39–51.

Langlois AJ (2011) Political research and human research ethics committees. *Australian Journal of Political Science* 46(1): 141–156.

Lanza-Kaduce L, Parker KF and Thomas CW (2000) The Devil in the details: the case against the case study of private prisons, criminological research, and conflict of interest. *Crime and Delinquency* 46(1): 92–136.

Largcnt E, Grady C, Miller FG and Wertheimer A (2012) Money, coercion, and undue inducement: attitudes about payments to research participants. *IRB: Ethics & Human Research* 34(1): 1–8.

Lavery JV, Bandewar SV, Kimani J, Upshur RE, Plummer FA and Singer PA (2010) 'Relief of oppression': an organizing principle for researchers' obligations to participants in observational studies in the developing world. *BMC Public Health* 10: 384 doi:10.1186/1471-2458-10-384. Available at: http://www.biomedcentral.com/1471-2458/10/384 (accessed 14 January 2014).

Lawson D (2004) Blurring the boundaries: ethical considerations for online research. In: Buchanan E (ed) *Readings in Virtual Research Ethics: Issues and Controversies*. Hershey PA: Idea Group, pp. 80–100.

Leaning J (1996) War crimes and medical science. *British Medical Journal* 313: 1413–1415.

Lederman R (2006) The perils of working at home: IRB 'mission creep' as context and content for an ethnography of disciplinary knowledges. *American Ethnologist* 33(4): 482–491.

Lederman R (2007) Comparative 'research': a modest proposal concerning the object of ethics regulation. *PoLAR: Political and Legal Anthropology Review* 30(2): 305–327.

Lee I (2008) *A Survey on Research Ethics Activities in Korea*. Ministry of Education, Science, and Technology, Seoul. (in Korean)

Lee RM (1995) *Dangerous Fieldwork*. London: Sage.

Lee-Treweek G and Linkogle S (2000) Putting danger in the frame. In: Lee-Treweek G and Linkogle S (eds) *Danger in the Field: Risk and Ethics in Social Research*. London: Routledge, pp. 8–25.

Leung K (2011) Presenting post hoc hypotheses as a priori: ethical and theoretical issues. *Management and Organization Review* 7(3): 471–479.

Levin JR (2011) Ethical issues in professional research, writing and publishing. In: Panter AT and Sterba SK (eds) *Handbook of Ethics in Quantitative Evaluation*. New York: Routledge, pp. 463–492.

Levine, RJ (1988) Ethics and Regulation of Clinical Research (2nd edition). New Haven CT: Yale University Press.

Levine RJ (1993) New international ethical guidelines for research involving human subjects. *Annals of Internal Medicine* 119(4): 339–341.

Levine C (1996) Changing views of justice after Belmont: AIDS and the inclusion of 'vulnerable' subjects. In: Vanderpool HY (ed) *The Ethics of Research Involving Human Subjects: Facing the 21st Century*. Frederick, MD: University Publishing, pp. 105–126.

Leviton LC (2011) Ethics in program evaluation. In: Panter AT and Sterba SK (eds) *Handbook of Ethics in Quantitative Evaluation*. New York: Routledge, pp. 241–264.

Lewis G, Brown N, Holland S and Webster A (2003) A review of ethics and social science research for the Strategic Forum for the Social Sciences. Summary of the Review, Science and Technology Studies Unit, York, September.

Lexchin J, Bero LA and Djulbegovic B (2003) Pharmaceutical industry sponsorship and research outcome and quality: systematic review. *British Medical Journal* 326: 1167–1170.

Light D and Warburton R (2008) In focus: ethical standards for health care journal editors: a case report and recommendations. *Harvard Health Policy Review* 9(1): 58–67.

List JA, Bailey CD, Euzent PJ and Martin TL (2001) Academic economists behaving badly? A survey on three areas of unethical behaviour. *Economic Inquiry* 391: 162–170.

Liu X (2008) Research on the Na and academic integrity. *Critique of Anthropology* 28(3): 297–320.

Lloyd M, Preston-Shoot M, Temple B and Wuu R (1996) Whose project is it anyway? Sharing and shaping the research and development agenda. *Disability & Society* 11(3): 301–315.

London AJ (2005) Justice and the human development approach to international research. *The Hastings Center Report* 35(1): 24–37.

London AJ and Zollman KZ (2010) Research at the auction block: problems for the fair benefits approach to international research. *The Hastings Center Report* 40(4): 34–45.

Louisy P (1997) Dilemmas of insider research in a small-country setting. In: Crossley M and Vulliamy G (eds) *Qualitative Educational Research in Developing Countries: Current Perspectives*. New York: Garland, pp. 199–220.

Louw B and Delport R (2006) Contextual challenges in South Africa: the role of a research ethics committee. *Journal of Academic Ethics* 4: 39–60.

Lowman J and Palys T (1999) Going the distance: lessons for researchers from jurisprudence on privilege (a third submission to the SFU Research Ethics Policy Revision Task Force). Available at: http://www.sfu.ca/~palys/Distance.pdf (accessed 16 January 2014).

Lowman J and Palys T (2000) Ethics and institutional conflict of interest: the research confidentiality controversy at Simon Fraser University. *Sociological Practice: A Journal of Clinical and Applied Sociology* 2(4): 245–264.

Lowman J and Palys T (2001) Limited confidentiality, academic freedom, and matters of conscience: where does CPA stand? *Canadian Journal of Criminology* 43(4): 497–508.

Loyle CE (2011) Overcoming research obstacles in Rwanda. *Comparative Democratization* 9(2): 17–19.

Luna F (2006) *Bioethics and Vulnerability: A Latin American View*. Amsterdam: Rodolpi.

Lundy P and McGovern M (2006) The ethics of silence: action research, community 'truth-telling' and post-conflict transition in the North of Ireland. *Action Research*, 4(1): 49–64.

Lyotard J-F (1979) *The Postmodern Condition: A Report on Knowledge*. Paris: Minuit.

Macfarlane B (2008) *Researching with Integrity: The Ethics of Academic Inquiry*. New York: Routledge.

Macfarlane B (2010) Researching with integrity. *Chronicle of Higher Education* 56(3): A30.

Macfarlane B and Saitoh Y (2008) Research ethics in Japanese higher education: faculty attitudes and cultural mediation. *Journal of Academic Ethics* 6: 181–195.

MacFarlane D (2011) Copycat academic 'quits' Oz post. *Mail & Guardian Online*, 29 April. Available at: http://mg.co.za/article/2011-04-29-copycat-academic-quits-oz-post (accessed 23 December 2013).

MacIntyre A (1982) Risk, harm, and benefit assessments as instruments of moral evaluation. In: Beauchamp TL, Faden RR, Wallace RJ and Walters L (eds) *Ethical Issues in Social Science Research*. London: John Hopkins University Press, pp. 175–188.

MacIntyre A (1984) *After Virtue*. South Bend, IN: University of Notre Dame Press.

Mackenzie C, McDowell C and Pittaway E (2007) Beyond 'do no harm': the challenge of constructing ethical relationships in refugee research. *Journal of Refugee Studies* 20(2): 299–319.

Mackie C and Bradburn N (eds) (2000) Improving access to and confidentiality of research data: report of a workshop. Report, Committee on National Statistics, National Research Council, Washington DC.

Macklin R (1982) The problem of adequate disclosure in social science research. In: Beauchamp TL, Faden RR, Wallace RJ and Walters L (eds) *Ethical Issues in Social Science Research*. London: Johns Hopkins University Press, pp. 193–214.

Macklin R (2004) *Double Standards in Medical Research in Developing Countries*. Cambridge: Cambridge University Press.

Madden J (2002) Closing the book on a career. *The Australian*, 13 July, pp. 1, 4.

Madhiwalla N, Pilgaonkar A and Bandewar S (2005) Institutional ethics committees: experience of CEHAT, 2001–02. In: Jesani A and Barai-Jaitly T (eds) *Ethics in Health Research: A Social Science Perspective*. Mumbai: Centre for Studies in Ethics and Rights, pp. 241–257.

Maffly B (2011) 'Pattern of plagiarism' costs University of Utah scholar his job. *Salt Lake Tribune*, 18 August. Available at: http://www.sltrib.com/sltrib/cougars/52378377-78/bakhtiari-university-panel-plagiarism.html.csp (accessed 23 December 2013).

Maiter S, Simich L, Jacobson N and Wise J (2008) Reciprocity: an ethic for community-based participatory action research. *Action Research* 6(3): 305–325.

Malekzadeh S (2011) Paranoia and perspective ... research in the Islamic Republic of Iran. *Comparative Democratization* 9(2): 3, 20–22.

Mamotte N and Wasenaar D (2009) Ethics review in a developing country: a survey of South African social scientists' experience. *Journal of Empirical Research on Human Research Ethics* 4(4): 69–78.

Marcus J (2013) West's universities reconsider China-funded Confucius Institutes. *The Times Higher Education*, 4 April.

Marcuse P (1985) Professional ethics and beyond: values in planning. In: Wachs M (ed) *Ethics in Planning*. New Brunswick, NJ: Center for Urban Policy Research, Rutgers University, pp. 3–24.

Mark A (2011) Written evidence submitted by Professor Annabelle Mark (PR12). In: House of Commons Science and Technology Committee, United Kingdom (2011) *Peer review in scientific publications, Eighth Report of Session 2010–12, Volume II: Additional written evidence*. London: The Stationery Office, Ev w25-27.

Mark MM and Lenz-Watson AL (2011) Experiments and quasi-experiments in field settings. In: Panter AT and Sterba SK (eds) *Handbook of Ethics in Quantitative Evaluation*. New York: Routledge, pp. 185–209.

Markham A (2012) Fabrication as ethical practice. *Information, Communication & Society* 15(3): 334–353.

Markham A and Buchanan E (2012) Ethical decision-making and internet research recommendations from the AoIR Ethics Working Committee (Version 2.0). Available at: http://www.aoir.org/reports/ethics2.pdf (accessed 23 December 2013).

Martinson B, Anderson MA, and De Vries R (2005) Scientists behaving badly. *Nature* 435(9): 737–738.

Maruši A, Bošnjak L, Jeroni A (2011) A systematic review of research on the meaning, ethics and practices of authorship across scholarly disciplines. *PLoS ONE* 6(9): e23477.

Marzano M (2007) Informed consent, deception, and research freedom in qualitative research: a cross-cultural comparison. *Qualitative Inquiry* 13: 417–436.

Maslen G (2011) Australia-SA: plagiarising academic loses job twice. *University World News*, 24 April, 76.

Masui T (2011) The integrity of researchers in Japan. In: Mayer T and Steneck N (eds) *Promoting Research Integrity in a Global Environment*. Singapore: Imperial College Press/World Scientific Publishing, pp. 49–54.

Matthews D (2012) Tobacco gift to Durham caused turmoil at the top. *Times Higher Education*, 8 November, 22.

Mauthner M, Birch M, Jessop J and Miller T (2002) *Ethics in Qualitative Research*. London: Sage.

Maxwell SE and Kelley K (2011) Ethics and sample size planning. In: Panter AT and Sterba SK (eds) *Handbook of Ethics in Quantitative Evaluation*. New York: Routledge, pp. 159–184.

Mayer-Schönberger V and Cukier K (2013) *Big Data: A Revolution that Will Transform How We Live, Work and Think*. London, UK: John Murray.

Mazonde IN and Msimanga-Ramatabele SH (2006) Research coordination and ethical considerations in Botswana. In: Rwomire A and Nyamnjoh FB (eds) *The Organization for Social Science Research in Eastern and Southern Africa*. Addis Ababa, pp. 191–197.

McCollum K (1999) Appeals court cites researchers' rights in denying Microsoft's request for notes. *Chronicle of Higher Education*, 8 January, A31.

McCosker H, Barnard A and Gerber R (2001) Undertaking sensitive research: issues and strategies for meeting the safety needs of all participants. *Forum Qualitative Sozialforschung/ Forum: Qualitative Social Research* 2(1), article 22. Available at: http://www.qualitative-research.net/index.php/fqs/article/view/983 (accessed 27 January 2014).

McIndoe WA, McLean MR, Jones RW and Mullen PR (1984) The invasive potential of carcinoma in situ of the cervix. *Obstetrics & Gynecology* 64: 451–458.

McKee HA (2008) Ethical and legal issues for writing researchers in an age of media convergence. *Computers and Composition* 25: 104–122.

McKenzie J, Herbison GP, Roth P and Paul C (2010) Obstacles to researching the researchers: a case study of the ethical challenges of undertaking methodological research investigating the reporting of randomised controlled trials. *Trials* 11: 28. Available at: http://www.trialsjournal.com/content/11/1/28 (accessed 23 December 2013).

McLaughlin RH (1999) From the field to the courthouse: should social science research be privileged? *Law & Social Inquiry* 24(4): 927–965.

McNeill PM, Berglund CA and Webster IW (1990) Reviewing the reviewers: a survey of Institutional Ethics Committees in Australia. *Medical Journal of Australia* 152(6): 289–296.

Medical Research Council of South Africa (2001) Guidelines on Ethics for Medical Research. Available at: http://www.mrc.ac.za/ethics/ethicsbook1.pdf (accessed 28 January 2014).

Medical Review and Ethics Committee (2006) Guidelines for Ethical Review of Clinical Research or Research Involving Human Subjects. Kuala Lumpur, Malaysia: Ministry of Health. Available at: http://www.nccr.gov.my/index.cfm?menuid=26&parentid=17 (accessed 23 December 2013).

Mertens DM and Ginsberg PE (eds) (2009) *Handbook of Social Research Ethics*. Thousand Oaks, CA: Sage.

Meth P with Malaza K (2003) Violent research: the ethics and emotions of doing research with women in South Africa. *Ethics, Place and Environment* 6(2): 143–159.

Metz T (2013) The western ethic of care or an Afro-communitarian ethic? Specifying the right relational morality. *Journal of Global Ethics* 9(1): 77–92. Available at: http://dx.doi.org/10.1080/17449626.2012.756421 (accessed 23 December 2013).

Milgram S (1974) *Obedience to Authority*. New York: Harper and Row.

Milgram S (1977) Ethical issues in the study of obedience. In: Milgram S (ed) *The Individual in a Social World*. Reading, MA: Addison–Wesley, pp. 188–199.

Mill JS (1863) *Utilitarianism*. Adelaide: University of Adelaide (e-book). Available at: http://etext.library.adelaide.edu.au/m/mill/john_stuart /m645u/index.html (accessed 16 January 2014).

Miller FG and Wertheimer A (2007) Facing up to paternalism in research ethics. *The Hastings Center Report* 37(3): 24–34.

Miller FG, Gluck JP and Wendler D (2008) Debriefing and accountability in deceptive research. *Kennedy Institute of Ethics Journal* 18(3): 235–251.

Miller RB (2003) How the Belmont Report fails. *Essays in Philosophy* 4(2) Article 6. Available at: http://commons.pacificu.edu/cgi/viewcontent.cgi?article = 1089& context = eip (accessed 28 January 2014).

Miller S and Selgelid M (2007) Ethical and philosophical consideration of the dual use dilemma in the biological sciences. *Science and Engineering Ethics* 13: 523–580.

Millum J, Wendler D and Emanuel EJ (2013) The 50th anniversary of the Declaration of Helsinki: progress but many remaining challenges. *Journal of the American Medical Association* 310(20): 2143–2144.

Ministry of Health, Jamaica (2012) Guidelines for the Conduct of Research on Human Subjects: Under Review – 1st Draft (Revised: 1 October 2012 by Ms. Tameka Clough, Director, Investigation and Enforcement Branch).

Mitchell A (2013) Escaping the 'field trap': exploitation and the global politics of educational fieldwork in 'conflict zones'. *Third World Quarterly* 34(7): 1247–1264.

Moczydłowski, P (1992) *The Hidden Life of Polish Prisons*. Bloomington and Indianapolis: Indiana University Press. [Originally published in Polish in 1982.]

Moe H and Larsson AO (2012) Methodological and ethical challenges associated with large-scale analyses of online political communication. *NORDICOM Review: Nordic Research on Media and Communication* 33(1): 117–124.

Moewaka Barnes HE, McCreanor TN, Edwards S and Borell BA (2009) Epistemological domination, social science research ethics in Aotearoa. In: Mertens DM and Ginsberg PE (eds) *Handbook of Social Research Ethics*. Thousand Oaks, CA: Sage, pp. 442–457.

Mohatt GV and Thomas LR (2006) 'I wonder, why would you do it that way?' Ethical dilemmas in doing participatory research with Alaska native communities. In: Tromble JE and Fisher CB (eds) *The Handbook of Ethical Research with Ethnocultural Populations and Communities*. Thousand Oaks, CA: Sage, pp. 93–115.

Molyneux CS, Wassenaar D, Peshu N and Marsh K (2005) 'Even if they ask you to stand by a tree all day, you will have to do it!': community voices on the notion and practice of informed consent. *Social Science & Medicine* 61(2): 443–454.

Molyneux C, Goudge J, Russell S, Chuma J, Gumede T and Gilson L (2009) Conducting health-related social science research in low income settings: ethical dilemmas faced in Kenya and South Africa. *Journal of International Development* 21(2): 309–326.

Montreal Statement on Research Integrity in Cross-Boundary Research Collaborations (2013) Available at: http://www.cehd.umn.edu/olpd/MontrealStatement.pdf (accessed 23 December 2013).

Moodley K and Myer L (2007) Health research ethics committees in South Africa 12 years into democracy. *BMC Medical Ethics* 8(1).

Moodley K and Rennie, S (2011) Advancing research ethics training in Southern Africa (ARESA). *South African Journal of Bioethics and Law* 4: 104–105.

Moore A (2011) New Zealand research ethics committee matters. *Research Ethics* 7(4): 132–135.

Moosa D (2013) Challenges to anonymity and representation in educational qualitative research in a small community: a reflection on my research journey. *Compare: A Journal of Comparative and International Education* 43(4): 483–495.

Moreno E (1995) Rape in the field: reflections from a survivor. In: Kulick D and Willson M (eds) *Taboo: Sex, Identity and Erotic Subjectivity in Anthropological Fieldwork*. London: Routledge, pp. 219–250.

Morrell R, Epstein D and Moletsane R (2012) Doubts, dilemmas and decisions: towards ethical research on gender and schooling in South Africa. *Qualitative Research* 12(6): 613–629.

Morrison K (2006) Sensitive educational research in small states and territories: the case of Macau. *Compare: A Journal of Comparative and International Education* 36(2): 249–264.

Morrow V and Richards M (1996) The ethics of social research with children: an overview. *Children and Society* 10: 90–105.

Mowatt G, Shirran L, Grimshaw JM, Rennie D, Flanagin A, Yank V, MacLennan G, Gotzsche PC and Bero LA (2002) Prevalence of honorary and ghost authorship in Cochrane reviews. *Journal of the American Medical Association* 287(21): 2769–2771.

Mulder SS, Rance S, Suárez MS and Condori MC (2000) Unethical ethics? Reflections on intercultural research practices. *Reproductive Health Matters* 8(15): 104–112.

Muzvidziwa VN (2006) Ethical issues in a study of how urban women deal with impoverishment. In: Rwomire A and Nyamnjoh FB (eds) *Challenges and Responsibilities of Social Research in Africa: Ethical Issues*. Addis Ababa: The Organization for Social Science Research in Eastern and Southern Africa (OSSREA), pp. 143–154.

Nama N and Swartz L (2002) Ethical and social dilemmas in community-based controlled trials in situations of poverty: a view from a South African project. *Journal of Community & Applied Social Psychology* 12: 286–297.

National Advisory Board on Research Ethics, Finland (2009) Ethical Principles of Research in the Humanities and Social and Behavioural Sciences and Proposals for Ethical Review. Helsinki: National Advisory Board on Research Ethics. Available at: http://www.tenk.fi/sites/tenk.fi/files/ethicalprinciples.pdf (accessed 28 January 2014).

National Commission for the Protection of Human Subjects of Biomedical and Behavioral Research (NCPHSBBR) (1979) Belmont Report: Ethical Principles and Guidelines for the Protection of Human Subjects of Research. Report, Department of Health, Education and Welfare, Office of the Secretary, Protection of Human Subjects, Michigan. Available at: http://www.hhs.gov/ohrp/humansubjects/guidance/belmont.html (accessed 28 January 2014).

National Committee for Ethics in Social Science Research in Health (NCESSRH) (2000) Ethical Guidelines for Social Science Research in Health. Mumbai: Centre for Enquiry into Health and Allied Themes (CEHAT).

National Committees for Research Ethics in Norway (2005) The Norwegian Model. Available at: http://www.etikkom.no/Engelsk (accessed 13 January 2014).

National Committees for Research Ethics in Norway (2006) Guidelines for Research Ethics in the Social Sciences, Law and the Humanities. Available at: http://www.etikkom.no/Documents/English-publications/Guidelines%20for%20research%20ethics%20in%20the%20social%20sciences,%20law%20and%20the%20humanities%20(2006).pdf (accessed 23 December 2013).

National Ethics Advisory Committee (2012) Ethical Guidelines for Observational Studies: Observational Research, Audits and Related Activities. Wellington: Ministry of Health.

National Health and Medical Research Council, Australia (1966) Statement on Human Experimentation and Supplementary Notes. Commonwealth of Australia, Canberra.

National Health and Medical Research Council, Australia (1999) National Statement on Ethical Conduct in Research Involving Humans, Commonwealth of Australia. Available at: http://www.nhmrc.gov.au/_files_nhmrc/publications/attachments/e35.pdf (accessed 28 January 2014).

National Health and Medical Research Council, Australia (2007a) Australian Code for the Responsible Conduct of Research, Canberra. Available at: http://www.nhmrc.gov.au/_files_nhmrc/publications/attachments/r39.pdf (accessed 23 December 2013).

National Health and Medical Research Council, Australia (2007b, updated 2013) National Statement on Ethical Conduct in Human Research. Available at: http://www.nhmrc.gov.au/guidelines/publications/e72 (accessed 23 December 2013).

National Human Research Protections Advisory Committee, United States (2001) Re: HHS' Draft Interim Guidance: Financial Relationships in Clinical Research: Issues for Institutions, Clinical Investigators and IRBs to Consider when Dealing with Issues of Financial Interests and Human Subjects Protection. Letter of 8 August to Secretary of US Department of Health and Human Services.

National Research Council, United States (2014) Proposed Revisions to the Common Rule for the Protection of Human Subjects in the Behavioral and Social Sciences. Committee on Revisions to the Common Rule for the Protection of Human Subjects in Research in the Behavioral and Social Sciences. Board on Behavioral, Cognitive, and Sensory Sciences, Committee on National Statistics, Division of Behavioral and Social Sciences and Education, Board on Health Sciences Policy, Institute of Medicine. Washington, DC: The National Academies Press.

National Science Foundation, United States (1995) Notice of Technical Changes to Investigator Financial Disclosure Policy: Investigator Financial Disclosure Policy, Effective 1 January 1995. Available at: http://www.ucop.edu/raohome/certs/coi-nsf.html (accessed 16 January 2014).

National Science Foundation, United States (2008) Frequently Asked Questions and Vignettes: Interpreting the Common Rule for the Protection of Human Subjects for Behavioral and Social Science Research. Available at: http://www.nsf.gov/bfa/dias/policy/hsfaqs.jsp (accessed 23 December 2013).

Neale B and Bishop L (2012) The Timescapes archive: a stakeholder approach to archiving qualitative longitudinal data. *Qualitative Research* 12(1): 53–65.

Nelson C (2012) If those who pay the pipers call the tune, make the fact public. *Times Higher Education*, 28 June, 28.

Nencel L (2001) *Ethnography and Prostitution in Peru*. London: Pluto Press.

Newman E and Kaloupek D (2009) Overview of research addressing ethical dimensions of participation in traumatic stress studies: autonomy and beneficence. *Journal of Traumatic Stress* 22: 595–602.

Newman E, Walker EA and Gefland A (1999) Assessing the ethical costs and benefits of trauma-focused research. *General Hospital Psychiatry* 21: 187–196.

Newman M (2009) Plagiarist escaped Birmingham penalty. *The Times Higher Education Supplement*, 26 November, 12.

Newman SD, Andrews JO, Magwood GS, Jenkins C, Cox MJ and Williamson DC (2011) Community advisory boards in community-based participatory research: a synthesis of best processes. *Preventing Chronic Disease* 8(3): A70.

Nickels S, Shirley J and Laidler G (eds) (2007) *Negotiating Research Relationships with Inuit Communities: A Guide for Researchers*. Inuit Tapiriit Kanatami and Nunavut Research Institute: Ottawa and Iqaluit. Available at: https://www.itk.ca/publication/negotiating-research-relationships-inuit-communities-guide-researchers (accessed 23 December 2013).

Nissenbaum H (2010) *Privacy in Context: Technology, Policy, and the Integrity of Social Life*. Stanford: Stanford University Press.

Noddings N (2003) *Caring: A Feminine Approach to Ethics & Moral Education* (2nd edition). Berkeley, CA: University of California Press.

Ntseane PG (2009) The ethics of the researcher–subject relationship: experiences from the field. In: Mertens DM and Ginsberg PE (eds) *Handbook of Social Research Ethics*. Thousand Oaks, CA: Sage, pp. 295–307.

Nyambedha EO (2008) Ethical dilemmas of social science research on AIDS and orphanhood in Western Kenya. *Social Science & Medicine* 67: 771–779.

Nyamnjoh F (2006) Towards a predicament-oriented approach to social research ethics. In: Rwomire A and Nyamnjoh FB (eds) *Challenges and Responsibilities of Social Research in Africa: Ethical Issues*. Addis Ababa: The Organization for Social Science Research in Eastern and Southern Africa (OSSREA), pp. 1–10.

Nyika A, Kilama W, Chilengi R, Tangwa G, Tindana P, Ndebele P and Ikingura J (2009) Composition, training needs and independence of ethics review committees across Africa: are the gate-keepers rising to the emerging challenges? *Journal of Medical Ethics* 35: 189–193.

O'Brien M (2001) Doing ethical research legally: research ethics and the law. In: Tolich M (ed) *Research Ethics in Aotearoa/New Zealand*. Auckland: Pearson Education, pp. 25–34.

O'Neil RM (1996) A researcher's privilege: does any hope remain? *Law and Contemporary Problems* 59(3): 35–50.

Oakes JM (2002) Risks and wrongs in social science research: an evaluator's guide to IRB. *Evaluation Review* 26(5): 443–479.

Oczak M and Nied wie ska A (2007) Debriefing in deceptive research: a proposed new procedure. *Journal of Empirical Research on Human Research Ethics* 2(3): 49–59.

Oeye C, Bjelland AK and Skorpen A (2007) Doing participant observation in a psychiatric hospital – research ethics resumed. *Social Science & Medicine* 65: 2296–2306.

Office of Research Integrity, United States (1994) ORI provides working definition of plagiarism. *ORI Newsletter* 3(1).

Office of Research Integrity, United States (2011) Annual Report 2011. Available at: http://ori.hhs.gov/images/ddblock/ori_annual_report_2011.pdf (accessed 23 December 2013).

Office of Science and Technology Policy, United States (2000) Federal Research Misconduct Policy, *Federal Register*, 65(235): 76260-76264.

Oglesby E (1995) Myrna Mack. In: Nordstrom C and Robben ACGM (eds) *Fieldwork under Fire: Contemporary Studies of Violence and Culture*. Berkeley: University of California Press, pp. 254–259.

Ohm P (2010) Broken promises of privacy: responding to the surprising failure of anonymization. *UCLA Law Review* 57: 1701–1777.

Oliveira LRC (2004) Pesquisas em versus pesquisas com seres humanos. In: Víctora C, Oliven RG, Maciel ME and Oro AP (eds) *Antropologia Ética. O debate atual no Brasil*. Niterói: Editora da Universidade Federal Fluminense, pp. 33–44.

Oliver M (1992) Changing the social relations of research production. *Disability, Handicap and Society* 7: 101–114.

Onyemelukwe, C. and Downie, J. (2011) The tunnel at the end of the light? A critical analysis of the development of the Tri-Council Policy Statement. *Canadian Journal of Law and Society* 26(1): 159–176.

Oransky M, Fisher C, Mahadevan M and Singer M (2009) Barriers and opportunities for recruitment for non-intervention studies on HIV risk: perspectives of street drug users. *Substance Use & Misuse* 44: 1642–1659.

Ortmann A and Hertwig R (2002) The empirical costs of deception: evidence from psychology. *Experimental Economics* 5: 111–131.

Paluck EL (2009) Methods and ethics with research teams and NGOs: comparing experiences across the border of Rwanda and Democratic Republic of Congo. In: Sriram CL, King JC, Mertus J, Martin-Ortega O and Hermann J (eds) *Surviving Field Research: Working in Violent and Difficult Situations*. London: Routledge, pp. 37–56.

Palys T and Atchison C (2012) Qualitative research in the digital era: obstacles and opportunities. *International Journal of Qualitative Methods* 11(4): 352–367.

Palys T and Lowman J (2000) Ethical and legal strategies for protecting confidential research information. *Canadian Journal of Law and Society* 15(1): 39–80.

Palys T and Lowman J (2001) Social research with eyes wide shut: the limited confidentiality dilemma. *Canadian Journal of Criminology* 43(2): 255–267.

Palys T and Lowman J (2010) Going boldly where no one has gone before? How confidentiality risk aversion is killing research on sensitive topics. *Journal of Academic Ethics* 8: 265–284.

Palys T and Lowman J (2011) What's been did and what's been hid: reflections on TCPS2. Canada: School of Criminology, Simon Fraser University. Available at: http://www.sfu.ca/~palys/PalysLowmanCommentsOnTCPS2-2011.pdf (accessed 23 December 2013).

Palys T and Lowman J (2012) Defending research confidentiality 'to the extent the law allows': lessons from the Boston College subpoenas. *Journal of Academic Ethics* 10: 271–297.

Pappworth MH (1962/3) Human guinea pigs: a warning. *Twentieth Century* 171: 67–75.

Pappworth MH (1967) *Human Guinea Pigs: Experimentation on Man*. London: Routledge.

Paterson BL, Gregory D and Thorne S (1999) A protocol for researcher safety. *Qualitative Health Research* 9(2): 259–269.

Peach L (1995) An introduction to ethical theory. In: Penslar RL (ed) *Research Ethics: Cases and Materials*. Bloomington: Indiana University Press, pp. 13–26.

Pearson G (2009) The researcher as hooligan: where 'participant' observation means breaking the law. *International Journal of Social Research Methodology* 12(3): 243–255.

Perry G (2012) *Behind the Shock Machine: The Untold Story of the Notorious Milgram Psychology Experiments*. Melbourne: Scribe.

Peterson J (2000) Sheer foolishness: shifting definitions of danger in conducting and teaching ethnographic field research. In: Lee-Treweek G and Linkogle S (eds) *Danger in the Field: Risk and Ethics in Social Research*. London: Routledge, pp. 182–196.

Petticrew M, Semple S, Hilton S, Creely KS, Eadie D, Ritchie D, Ferrell C, Christopher Y and Hurley F (2007) Covert observation in practice: lessons from the evaluation of the prohibition of smoking in public places in Scotland. *BMC Public Health* 7: 204.

Pettit P (1993) Consequentialism. In: Singer P (ed) *A Companion to Ethics*. Oxford: Blackwell, pp. 230–240.

Picou JS (1996) Compelled disclosure of scholarly research: some comments on high stakes litigation. *Law and Contemporary Problems* 59(3): 149–158.

Piper H and Sikes P (2010) All teachers are vulnerable but especially gay teachers: using composite fictions to protect research participants in pupil–teacher sex-related research. *Qualitative Inquiry* 16(7): 566–574.

Plankey-Videla N (2012) Informed consent as process: problematizing informed consent in organizational ethnographies. *Qualitative Sociology* 35: 1–21.

Poon JML and Ainuddin RA (2011) Selected ethical issues in the analysis and reporting of research: survey of business school faculty in Malaysia. *Journal of Academic Ethics* 9: 307–322.

Postiglione GA (2007) Editor's introduction. *Chinese Education & Society* 40(6): 3–5.

Presidential Commission for the Study of Bioethical Issues (2011a) 'Ethically Impossible' STD Research in Guatemala from 1946 to 1948. Washington DC. Available at: http://bioethics.gov/node/654 (accessed 23 December 2013).

Presidential Commission for the Study of Bioethical Issues (2011b) Moral Science: Protecting Participants in Human Subjects Research. Washington, DC: United States Department of Health and Human Services. Available at: http://bioethics.gov/node/558 (accessed 23 December 2013).

Price D (2008) *Anthropological Intelligence: The Deployment and Neglect of American Anthropology in the Second World War*. Durham, NC: Duke University Press.

Prinstein MJ (2011) Me, Myron Prinstein, and I: a troubling case of confused academic identity. *Ethics & Behavior* 21(3): 173–181.

Punch M (1986) *The Politics and Ethics of Fieldwork*. Beverley Hills, CA: Sage.

Qatar Supreme Council of Health (2009) Policies, Regulations and Guidelines for Research Involving Human Subjects. Available at: http://www.sch.gov.qa/sch/UserFiles/File/Research%20Department/PoliciesandRegulations.pdf (accessed 23 December 2013).

Quinnell S-L (2010) *Building Capacity for Biosafety in Africa: Networks of Science, Aid & Development in the Implementation of Multi-Lateral Environmental Agreements*. PhD Thesis, King's College London, UK.

Qureshi R (2010) Ethical standards and ethical environment: tension and a way forward. In: Shamim F and Qureshi R (eds) *Perils, Pitfalls and Reflexivity in Qualitative Research in Education*. Karachi, Pakistan: Oxford University Press, pp. 78–100.

Rainwater L and Pittman DJ (1967) Ethical problems in studying a politically sensitive and deviant community. *Social Problems* 14: 357–366.

Ramos AR (2004) A difícil questão do consentimento informado. In: Victora C, Oliven RG, Maciel ME and Oro AP (eds) *Antropologia Ética. O debate atual no Brasil*. Niterói: Editora da Universidade Federal Fluminense, pp. 91–96.

Ravindran D and Nikarge S (2010) Clinical trials watch job. *Indian Journal of Medical Ethics* 7(4): 259–62.

Reiss A (1978) Conditions and consequences of consent in human subject research. In: Wulff KM (ed) *Regulation of Scientific Inquiry*. Boulder, CO: Westview Press, pp. 161–184.

Reiss AJ Jr (1976) Selected Issues in Informed Consent and Confidentiality, with Special Reference to Behavioral/Social Science Research/Inquiry, 1 Feb., box 5, meeting#16(A), tab 23, National Commission for the Protection of Human Subjects of Biomedical and Behavioral Research Collection, Center for Bioethics Literature, Kennedy Institute of Ethics, Georgetown University, Washington DC.

Research Councils United Kingdom (2011) RCUK Policy and Code of Conduct on the Governance of Good Research Conduct: Integrity, Clarity and Good Management. Swindon: RCUK. Available at: http://www.rcuk.ac.uk/RCUK-prod/assets/documents/reviews/grc/goodresearchconductcode.pdf (accessed 10 June 2014).

Resnik DB (2012) Ethical virtues in scientific research. *Accountability in Research: Policies and Quality Assurance* 19(6): 329–343.

Resnik DB, Patrone D and Peddada S (2010) Research misconduct policies of social science journals and impact factor. *Accountability in Research* 17: 79–84.

Reynolds PD (1979) *Ethical Dilemmas and Social Science Research: An Analysis of Moral Issues Confronting Investigators in Research Using Human Participants*. San Francisco, CA: Jossey-Bass.

Rickinson M, Sebba J and Edwards A (2011) *Improving Research through User Engagement*. London: Routledge.

Rid A and Schmidt H (2010) The 2008 Declaration of Helsinki – first among equals in research ethics? *Journal of Law, Medicine & Ethics* 38(1): 143–148.

Ringheim K (1995) Ethical issues in social science research with special reference to sexual behaviour research. *Social Science & Medicine* 40(12): 1691–1697.

Rivera R and Ezcurra E (2001) Composition and operation of selected research ethics review committees in Latin America. *IRB: Ethics & Human Research* 23(5): 9–12.

Roberts C and Lewis J (2009) ESRC Consultation Document – Review of the ESRC Research Ethics Framework, Submission to the ESRC on behalf of the Academy of Social Sciences.

Robinson LC (2010) Informed consent among analog people in a digital world. *Language & Communication* 30: 186–191.

Robson S (2011) Producing and using video data in the early years: ethical questions and practical consequences in research with young children. *Children & Society* 25: 179–189.

Roche M and Mansvelt J (1996) Ethical research in a public good funding environment. *New Zealand Geographer* 52(1): 41–47.

Rodgers G (2004) 'Hanging out' with forced migrants: methodological and ethical challenges. *Forced Migration Review* 21: 48–49.

Rooney VM (2013) Consent in longitudinal intimacy research: adjusting formal procedure as a means of enhancing reflexivity in ethically important decisions. *Qualitative Research* epub ahead of print 9 September 2013. doi 10.1177/1468794113501686.

Rosenthal JP (2006) Politics, culture, and governance in the development of prior informed consent in Indigenous communities. *Current Anthropology* 47(1): 119–142.

Ross A (2009) Impact on research of security-seeking behaviour. In: Sriram CL, King JC, Mertus JA, Martin-Ortega O and Herman J (eds) *Surviving Field Research: Working in Violent and Difficult Situations*. London: Routledge, pp. 177–188.

Ross WD (1930) *The Right and the Good*. Oxford: Oxford University Press.

Rosser JB (2010) *Tales from the Editor's Crypt: Dealing with True, Uncertain, and False Accusations of Plagiarism*. Harrisonburg: James Madison University. Available at: http://cob.jmu.edu/rosserjb (accessed 23 December 2013).

Rowe M (2007) Tripping over molehills: ethics and the ethnography of police work. *International Journal of Social Research Methodology* 10(1): 37–48.

Ruusalepp R (2008) A comparative study of international approaches to enabling the sharing of research data. DCC and JISC. Available at: http://www.jisc.ac.uk/publica tions/reports/2008/nationaldatafinalreport.aspx (accessed 28 January 2014).

Rylko-Bauer B, Singer M and van Willigen J (2006) Reclaiming applied anthropology: its past, present, and future. *American Anthropologist* 108(1): 178–190.

Saakvitne KW and Pearlman LA (1996) *Transforming the Pain: A Workbook on Vicarious Traumatisation*. New York: Norton.

Sallaz JJ (2008) Deep plays: a comparative ethnography of gambling contests in two post-colonies. *Ethnography* 9(1): 5–33.

Sampson H and Thomas M (2003) Lone researchers at sea: gender, risk and responsibility. *Qualitative Research* 3(2): 165–189.

Sanders T (2005) *Sex Work: A Risky Business*. Cullompton: Willan.

Santi MF (2013) Aportes para una Nueva Concepción de la Vulnerabilidad en Ética de la Investigación. Available at: http://www.tcba.com.ar/PREMIO-BIOETICA/pdf/pub-licaciones/2013/segunda-mencion-bioetica-2013%202.pdf (accessed 16 February 2014).

Santos RV (2006) Indigenous peoples, bioanthropological research, and ethics in Brazil: issues in participation and consent. In: Ellison GTH and Goodman AH (eds) *The Nature of Difference: Science, Society and Human Biology*. Boca Raton, FL: CRC Taylor and Francis, pp. 181–202.

Sarvmsakova B (2009) Central Asia: developing a capacity building approach to ethical review. *Asian Bioethics Review* 1(2): 168–170.

Schenk K and Williamson J (2005) *Ethical Approaches to Gathering Information from Children and Adolescents in International Settings. Guidelines and Resources.* Available at: http://www.popcouncil.org/pdfs/horizons/childrenethics.pdf (accessed 23 December 2013).

Scheper-Hughes N (1992) *Death Without Weeping: The Violence of Everyday Life in Brazil.* Berkeley: University of California Press.

Scheper-Hughes N (1995) Propositions for a militant anthropology. *Current Anthropology* 36(3): 409–420.

Scheper-Hughes N (2000) Ire in Ireland. *Ethnography* 1(1): 117–140.

Scheper-Hughes N (2004) Parts unknown: undercover ethnography of the organs-trafficking underworld. *Ethnography* 5(1): 29–73.

Scheper-Hughes N (2009) The ethics of engaged anthropology: applying a militant anthropology in organs-trafficking research. *Anthropology News*, September, 13–14.

Schmidt P (2012) Boston College case shows weakness of researchers' confidentiality pledges. *Chronicle of Higher Education* 58(19): A13.

Schminke M (2009) Editor's comments: the better angels of our nature – ethics and integrity in the publishing process. *Academy of Management Review* 34(4): 586–591.

Schrag ZM (2010a) *Ethical Imperialism: Institutional Review Boards and the Social Sciences, 1965–2009.* Baltimore: Johns Hopkins University Press.

Schrag ZM (2010b) Belmont's ethical malpractice. *Bioethics Forum Blog*, 30 November. Available at: http://www.thehastingscenter.org/Bioethicsforum/Post.aspx?id=4999 (accessed 23 December 2013).

Schuetze CF (2011) The whiff of plagiarism again hits German elite. *The New York Times*, 24 April.

Schuler EA (1969) Toward a code of ethics for sociologists: a historical note. *American Sociologist* 4(2): 144–146.

Scott G (2008) They got their program, and I got mine: a cautionary tale concerning the ethical implications of using respondent-driven sampling to study injection drug users. *International Journal of Drug Policy* 19(1): 42–51.

Sehgal M (2009) The veiled feminist ethnographer: fieldwork amongst women of India's Hindu Right. In: Huggins M and Glebbeek M-L (eds) *Women Fielding Danger: Negotiating Ethnographic Identities in Field Research.* Lanham, MD: Rowman and Littlefield Publishers, pp. 325–352.

Seidelman WE (1996) Nuremberg lamentation: for the forgotten victims of medical science. *British Medical Journal* 313: 1463–1467.

Shamim F and Qureshi R (2013) Informed consent in educational research in the South: tensions and accommodations. *Compare: A Journal of Comparative and International Education* 43(4): 464–482.

Sheikh A (2000) Publication ethics and the Research Assessment Exercise: reflections on the troubled question of authorship. *Journal of Medical Ethics* 26: 422–426.

Sheikh S (2008) The Pakistan experience. *Journal of Academic Ethics* 6: 283–287.

Shubis K, Juma O, Sharifu R, Burgess B and Abdulla S (2009) Challenges of establishing a Community Advisory Board (CAB) in a low-income, low-resource setting: experiences from Bagamoyo, Tanzania. *Health Research Policy and Systems* 7: 16.

Shuster S (2013) Putin's Ph.D.: can a plagiarism probe upend Russian politics? *Time*, 18 February.

Sieber JE and Tolich MB (2013) *Planning Ethically Responsible Research* (2nd edition). Los Angeles: Sage.

Sieber JE, Plattner S and Rubin P (2002) How (not) to regulate social and behavioral research. *Professional Ethics Report* 15(2): 1–3.

Sikes P (2013) Working together for critical research ethics. *Compare: A Journal of Comparative and International Education* 43(4): 516–536.

Sikweyiya Y and Jewkes R (2012) Perceptions and experiences of research participants on gender-based violence community based survey: implications for ethical guidelines. *PLoS ONE* 7(4): e35495.

Simonelli J (2006) Commentary on Rosenthal. *Current Anthropology* 47(1): 135–136.

Simons H and Usher R (eds) (2000) *Situated Ethics in Educational Research*. London/New York: Routledge/Falmer.

Singapore Statement on Research Integrity (2010) Available at: http://www.singaporestatement.org/statement.html (accessed 23 December 2013).

Singer M (1993) Knowledge for use: anthropology and community-centered substance abuse research. *Social Science & Medicine* 37: 15–26.

Singer M and Easton D (2006) Ethnographic research on drugs and HIV/AIDS in ethnocultural communities. In: Tromble JE and Fisher CB (eds) *The Handbook of Ethical Research with Ethnocultural Populations and Communities*. Thousand Oaks, CA: Sage, pp. 257–278.

Singer M, Huertas E and Scott G (2000) Am I my brother's keeper? A case study of the responsibilities of research. *Human Organization* 59(4): 389–400.

Singer M, Mirhej G, Hodge D, Salaheen H, Fisher C and Mahadevan M (2008) Ethical issues in research with Hispanic drug users: participant perspectives on risks and benefits. *Journal of Drug Issues* 38(1): 351–372.

Singer P (1999) Living high and letting die. *Philosophy and Phenomenological Research* 59: 183–187.

Singer PA and Benatar SR (2001) Beyond Helsinki: a vision for global health ethics. *British Medical Journal* 322: 747–748.

Sinnott-Armstrong W (2003) Consequentialism. Available at: http://plato.stanford.edu/entries/consequentialism/ (accessed 23 December 2013).

Šipka P (2010) Letter to the Serbian Ministry of Science and Technological Development, 6 July. Available at: http://ceon.rs/pdf/dopis_mntr_plagijarizam.pdf (accessed 23 December 2013).

Sismondo S (2007) Ghost management: how much of the medical literature is shaped behind the scenes by the pharmaceutical industry? *PLoS Medicine* 4(9): e286.

Slaughter S and Leslie LL (1997) *Academic Capitalism: Politics, Policies, and the Entrepreneurial University*. London: Johns Hopkins University Press.

Slaughter S and Rhoades G (2004) *Academic Capitalism and the New Economy: Markets, State, and Higher Education*. London: Johns Hopkins University Press.

Slaughter S, Feldman M and Thomas S (2009) Research universities' institutional conflict of interest policies. *Journal of Empirical Research on Human Research Ethics* 4(3): 3–20.

Sluka JA (1989) *Hearts and Minds, Water and Fish: Support for the IRA and INLA in a Northern Irish Ghetto*. Greenwich, CT: JAI Press.

Sluka JA (1995) Reflections on managing danger in fieldwork: dangerous anthropology in Belfast. In: Nordstrom C and Robben ACGM (eds) *Fieldwork under Fire: Contemporary Studies of Violence and Survival*. London: University of California Press, pp. 276–294.

Smeltzer S (2012) Asking tough questions: the ethics of studying activism in democratically restricted environments. *Social Movement Studies: Journal of Social, Cultural and Political Protest* 11(2): 255–271.

Smith DM (1998) How far should we care? On the spatial scope of beneficence. *Progress in Human Geography* 22(1): 15–38.

Smith LT (2001) *Decolonising Methodologies: Research and Indigenous Peoples.* Dunedin: University of Otago Press.

Smith MD (2010) FAS Dean Smith confirms scientific misconduct by Marc Hauser. *Harvard Magazine*, 20 August. Available at: http://harvardmagazine. com/2010/08/harvard-dean-details-hauser-scientific-misconduct (accessed 23 December 2013).

Smith NC, Kimmel AJ and Klein JG (2009) Social contract theory and the ethics of deception in consumer research. *Journal of Consumer Psychology* 19: 486–496.

Smith R (2006) The trouble with medical journals. *Journal of the Royal Society of Medicine* 99: 115–119.

Smith R (2008) A ripping yarn of editorial misconduct. *BMJ Group Blogs*, 21 October. Available at: http://blogs.bmj.com/bmj/2008/10/21/richard-smith-a-ripping-yarn-of-editorial-misconduct/ (accessed 23 December 2013).

Smith SS and Richardson D (1983) Amelioration of deception and harm in psychological research: the important role of debriefing. *Journal of Personality and Social Psychology* 44: 1075–1082.

Social and Behavioral Sciences Working Group on Human Research Protections (United States) (2004) Risk and Harm. Available at: http://www.aera.net/Portals/38/docs/About_AERA/humansubjects_risk_harm.pdf (accessed 28 January 2014).

Social Research Association (n.d.) A Code of Practice for the Safety of Social Researchers. Available at: http://the-sra.org.uk/sra_resources/safety-code/ (accessed 23 December 2013).

Social Science Research Council (SSRC) (2008) The Minerva Controversy. Available at: http://essays.ssrc.org/minerva/ (accessed 23 December 2013).

Social Sciences and Humanities Research Ethics Special Working Committee, Canada (SSHWC) (2004) *Giving Voice to the Spectrum.* Ottawa: Interagency Advisory Panel on Research Ethics.

Social Sciences and Humanities Research Ethics Special Working Committee, Canada (SSHWC) (2008) SSHWC Recommendations Regarding Privacy and Confidentiality. Report for the Federal Interagency Advisory Panel on Research Ethics. Available at: http://www.pre.ethics.gc.ca/policy-politique/initiatives/docs/SSHWC_PC_Policy_Recommendations_-_January_2008_-_EN.pdf (accessed 23 December 2013).

Society for Applied Anthropology (1948/1951) Code of Ethics of the Society for Applied Anthropology. *Human Organization* 10(2): 32.

Society for Research in Child Development (2007) Ethical Standards for Research with Children. Available at: http://www.srcd.org/about-us/ethical-standards-research (accessed 28 January 2014).

Socio-Legal Studies Association (2009) Statement of Principles of Ethical Research Practice. Available at: http://www.slsa.ac.uk/index.php/ethics-statement (accessed 10 June 2014).

Sonin K (2013) A small victory over academic plagiarism. *The Moscow Times*, Issue 5063, 7 February. Available at: http://www.themoscowtimes.com/opinion/article/ a-small-victory-over-academic-plagiarism/475159.html (accessed 23 December 2013).

Southall J (2009) 'Is this thing working?' – The challenge of digital audio for qualitative research. *Australian Journal of Social Issues* 44(3): 321–334.

Spelman EV (1988) *Inessential Woman: Problems of Exclusion in Feminist Thought.* Boston: Beacon Press.

Spicker P (2011) Ethical covert research. *Sociology* 45: 118–133.

Stanko EA (1992) Intimidating education: sexual harassment in criminology. *Journal of Criminal Justice Education* 3(2): 331–340.

Stanley L and Wise S (2010) The ESRC's 2010 Framework for Research Ethics: fit for research purpose? *Sociological Research Online* 15(4): 12. Available at: http://www.socresonline.org.uk/15/4/12.html (accessed 28 January 2014).

Stapel D (2012) Written Press Statement (in Dutch), 28 November. Available at: http://content1a.omroep.nl/2fc983f7470ca99d7a667e79b0813211/50b838d8/nos/docs/281112_verklaring_stapel.pdf (accessed 23 December 2013).

Stein A (2010) Sex, truths, and audiotape: anonymity and the ethics of exposure in public ethnography. *Journal of Contemporary Ethnography* 39: 554–568.

Sterba SK (2006) Misconduct in the analysis and reporting of data: bridging methodological and ethical agendas for change. *Ethics & Behavior* 16(4): 305–318.

Stevenson M (2010) Flexible and responsive research: developing rights-based emancipatory disability research methodology in collaboration with young adults with Down Syndrome. *Australian Social Work* 63(1) 35–50.

Stigler SM (1987) Testing hypotheses or fitting models? Another look at mass extinctions. In: Nitecki MH and Hoffman A (eds) *Neutral models in biology.* New York: Oxford University Press, pp. 147–159.

Stiles PG, Boothroyd RA, Robst J and Ray JV (2011) Ethically using administrative data in research: Medicaid administrators' current practices and best practice recommendations. *Administration & Society* 43(2): 171–192.

Stillo J (2011) Research ethics in impossibly unethical situations. *Cacaphony,* 21 December. Available at: http://cac.ophony.org/2011/12/21/research-ethics-in-impossibly-unethical-situations/ (accessed 23 December 2013).

Storbeck O (2011a) 'Journal of Economic Perspectives' rebukes Bruno Frey – plus: replies by Torgler and Frey. *Economics Intelligence,* 4 July. Available at: http://olafstorbeck.blogstrasse2.de/?p=915 (accessed 28 January 2014).

Storbeck O (2011b) Bruno Frey: more cases of self-plagiarism unveiled. *Economics Intelligence,* 12 September. Available at: http://olafstorbeck.blogstrasse2.de/?p=1277 (accessed 28 January 2014).

Street J, Rogers W, Israel M and Braunack-Mayer A (2010) Credit where credit is due? Regulation, research integrity and the attribution of authorship in the health sciences. *Social Science & Medicine* 70(9): 1458–1465.

Striefel S (2001) Ethical research issues: going beyond the Declaration of Helsinki. *Applied Psychophysiology and Biofeedback* 26(1): 39–59.

Stroebe W and Hewstone M (2013) Primed, but not suspect. *Times Higher Education* 2090: 34–39. Available at: http://www.timeshighereducation.co.uk/features/social-psychology-is-primed-but-not-suspect/2002055.article (accessed 10 June 2014).

Sudnow D (1965) Normal crimes: sociological features of the penal code in a Public Defender Office. *Social Problems* 12(3): 255–268.

Sueblinwong T, Mahaisawiriya P and Panichkul S (eds) (2007) The Ethical Guidelines for Conducting Research on Human Subject in Thailand B.E. 2550. Forum for Ethics Committees in Thailand, Bangkok. Available at: http://www.fercit.org/file/Guideline_English_version.pdf (accessed 10 June 2014).

Sveningsson Elm M (2009) How do various notions of privacy influence decisions in qualitative internet research? In: Markham A and Baym N (eds) *Internet Inquiry: Conversations about Method.* Thousand Oaks, CA: Sage, pp. 69–87.

Swedish Council for Research in the Humanities and Social Sciences (HSFR) (1990/1999) Ethical Principles for Scientific Research in the Humanities and Social Sciences. Stockholm: Swedish Council for Research in the Humanities and Social Sciences.

Swedish Research Council (2005) Project Research Grant, Humanities and Social Sciences. Stockholm: Swedish Research Council.

Swedish Research Council's Expert Group on Ethics (2011) *Good Research Practice*. Stockholm: Swedish Research Council. Available at: http://www.vr.se/download/18.3 a36c20d133af0c1295800030/1321519981391/Good + Research + Practice + 3.2011_webb.pdf (accessed 28 January 2014).

Sweeney L (2000) Uniqueness of simple demographics in the US population. Technical report, Carnegie Mellon University, Pittsburgh, PA.

Szklut J and Reed RR (1991) Community anonymity in anthropological research: a reassessment. In: Fluehr-Lobban C (ed) *Ethics and the Profession of Anthropology: Dialogue for a New Era*. Philadelphia: University of Pennsylvania Press, pp. 97–114.

Tai MC (2011) An Asian perspective of Western or Eastern principles in a globalised bioethics. *Asian Bioethics Review* 3(1): 23–30.

Tangwa GB (2004) Between universalism and relativism: a conceptual exploration of problems in formulating and applying international biomedical ethical guidelines. *Journal of Medical Ethics* 30(1): 63–67.

Tangwa GB (2009) Research with vulnerable human beings. *Acta Tropica* 112 (Supp 1): S16–S20.

Taylor A (1993) *Women Drug Users: An Ethnography of a Female Injecting Community*. Oxford: Clarendon Press.

Teixeira AAC and da Costa MF (2010) Who rules the ruler? On the misconduct of journal editors. *Journal of Academic Ethics* 8: 111–128.

Tesch F (1977) Debriefing research participants: 'Though this be method there is madness to it'. *Journal of Personality and Social Psychology* 35: 217–224.

Tester F (2006) Iglutaq: the implications of homelessness for Inuit. A case study of housing and homelessness in Kinngait, Nunavut Territory. Report for The Harvest Society, Kinngait, Nunavut Territory. Available at: http://www.tunngavik.com/documents/publications/2006-04-00-Iglutaq-The-Implications-of-Homelessness-for-Inuit.pdf (accessed 10 June 2014).

Thacher D (2004) The casuistical turn in planning ethics. *Journal of Planning Education and Research* 23: 269–285.

The Hankyoreh (2008) Education secretary appointee postpones official appointment. *The Hankyoreh*, 24 June. Available at: http://english.hani.co.kr/arti/english_edition/e_national/295067.html (accessed 23 December 2013).

Thomas J (1996) Introduction: a debate about the ethics of fair practices for collecting social science data in cyberspace. *The Information Society* 12(2): 107–117.

Thomson SM (2009) 'That is not what we authorised you to do ...': access and government interference in highly politicised research environments. In: Sriram CL, King JC, Mertus J, Martin-Ortega O and Hermann J (eds) *Surviving Field Research: Working in Violent and Difficult Situations*. London: Routledge, pp. 108–123.

Thulesius H (2010) A Swedish perspective on research ethics review. *Grounded Theory Review: An International Journal* 9(3). Available at http://groundedtheoryreview.com/2010/12/01/a-swedish-perspective-on-research-ethics-review/ (accessed 23 December 2013).

Tikly L and Bond T (2013) Towards a postcolonial research ethics in comparative and international education. *Compare: A Journal of Comparative and International Education* 43(4): 422–442.

Tindana P and Boateng O (2008) The Ghana experience. *Journal of Academic Ethics* 6: 277–281.

Tindana PO, Kass N and Akweongo P (2006) The informed consent process in a rural African setting: a case study of the Kassena-Nankana district of Northern Ghana. *IRB* 28(3): 1–6.

Tinker A and Coomber V (2004) *University Research Ethics Committees: Their Role, Remit and Conduct*. London: Kings College.

Tisdall EKM (2003) The rising tide of female violence? Researching girls' own understandings and experiences of violent behaviour. In: Lee RM and Stanko EA (eds) *Researching Violence: Essays on Methodology and Measurement*. London: Routledge, pp. 137–152.

Tolich M (2001) Beyond an unfortunate experiment: ethics for small-town New Zealand. In: Tolich M (ed) *Research Ethics in Aotearoa/New Zealand*. Auckland: Pearson Education, pp. 2–12.

Tolich M (2004) Internal confidentiality: when confidentiality assurances fail relational informants. *Qualitative Sociology* 27(1): 101–106.

Tolich M (2009) The principle of caveat emptor: confidentiality and informed consent as endemic ethical dilemmas in focus group research. *Bioethical Inquiry* 6: 99–108.

Tolich M (2014) What can Milgram and Zimbardo teach ethics committees and qualitative researchers about minimizing harm? *Research Ethics* doi: 10.1177/1747016114523771

Training and Resources in Research Ethics Evaluation (2014) Tanzanian Module. http://elearning.trree.org/mod/page/view.php?id = 172 (accessed 9 June 2014).

Traynor M (1996) Countering the excessive subpoena for scholarly research. *Law and Contemporary Problems* 59(3): 119–148.

Tri-Agency (Canadian Institutes of Health Research, National Science and Engineering Research Council of Canada, Social Sciences and Humanities Research Council of Canada) (2011) Tri-Agency Framework: Responsible Conduct of Research. Available at: http://www.rcr.ethics.gc.ca/eng/policy-politique/framework-cadre/ (accessed 11 June 2014).

Tri-Council (Canadian Institutes of Health Research, National Science and Engineering Research Council of Canada, Social Sciences and Humanities Research Council of Canada) (2010) Tri-Council Policy Statement: Ethical Conduct for Research Involving Humans. Ottawa: Public Works and Government Services. Available at: http://www.pre.ethics.gc.ca/pdf/eng/tcps2/TCPS_2_FINAL_Web.pdf (accessed 23 December 2013).

Tri-Council (Medical Research Council of Canada, National Science and Engineering Research Council of Canada, Social Sciences and Humanities Research Council of Canada) (1998) Tri-Council Policy Statement: Ethical Conduct for Research Involving Humans. Ottawa: Public Works and Government Services. Available at: http://www.pre.ethics.gc.ca/eng/archives/tcps-eptc/Default/ (accessed 28 January 2014).

Trindade ZA and Szymanski H (2008) O impacto dos comitês de ética — CEPs, na atividade de pesquisa em Psicologia. In: Guerriero ICZ, Schmidt MLS and Zicker S (eds) *Ética nas Pesquisas em Ciências Humanas e Sociais na Saúde*. São Paulo: Aderaldo and Rothschild, pp. 280–304.

Tronto J (1993) *Moral Boundaries: A Political Argument for an Ethic of Care*. New York: Routledge.

True G, Alexander L and Richman K (2011) Misbehaviors of front-line research personnel and the integrity of community-based research. *Journal of Empirical Research on Human Research Ethics* 6(2): 3–12.

Tumilty E, Tolich M and Dobson S (under review, 2014) Rupturing ethics literacy: The Ethics Applications Repository (TEAR). In: van den Hoonaard W and Hamilton A (eds) *Ethics Rupture: Exploring Alternatives to Formal Research-Ethics Review*.

Tunnell KD (1998) Honesty, secrecy, and deception in the sociology of crime: confessions and reflections from the backstage. In: Ferrell J and Hamm M (eds) *Ethnography at the Edge: Crime, Deviance, and Field Research*. Boston, MA: Northeastern University Press, pp. 206–220.

UNESCO (2005) Universal Declaration on Bioethics and Human Rights. Paris: UNESCO. Available at: http://unesdoc.unesco.org/images/0014/001461/146180E.pdf (accessed 23 December 2013).

UNESCO and International Social Science Council (2010) World Social Science Report 2010: Knowledge Divides. Paris: UNESCO and International Social Science Council. Available at: http://unesdoc.unesco.org/images/0018/001883/188395e.pdf (accessed 13 January 2014).

UNICEF Evaluation Office (2002) Children Participating in Research, Monitoring and Evaluation – Ethics and Your Responsibilities as a Manager. Available at: http://www.unicef.org/evaluation/files/TechNote1_Ethics.pdf (accessed 23 December 2013).

United Nations (1989) United Nations Convention on the Rights of the Child. Available at: http://www.ohchr.org/en/professionalinterest/pages/crc.aspx (accessed 9 June 2014).

United Nations (2007) United Nations Declaration on the Rights of Indigenous Peoples. Available at: http://www.un.org/esa/socdev/unpfii/documents/DRIPS_en.pdf (accessed 23 December 2013).

Universiteit van Tilburg (2011) Interim-Rapportage Inzake Door Prof. Dr. D.A. Stapel Gemaakte Inbreuk Op Wetenschappelijke Integriteit, 31 October. Available at: https://www.tilburguniversity.edu/upload/57315b00-9323-4ce4-80e5-265410f17299_interim-rapport.pdf (accessed 13 January 2014).

Usdin S, Christfides N, Malepe L and Aadielah M (2000) The value of advocacy in promoting social change: implementing the new Domestic Violence Act in South Africa. *Reproductive Health Matters* 8: 55–65.

van den Borne F (2007) Using mystery clients to assess condom negotiation in Malawi: some ethical concerns. *Studies in Family Planning* 2007 38(4): 322–330.

van den Eynden V (2008) Sharing research data and confidentiality: restrictions caused by deficient consent forms. *Research Ethics Review* 4(1): 37–38.

van den Hoonaard WC (2001) Is ethics review a moral panic? *The Canadian Review of Sociology and Anthropology* 38(1): 19–35.

van den Hoonaard WC (2011) *The Seduction of Ethics: Transforming the Social Sciences.* Toronto: University of Toronto Press.

van den Hoonaard WC (2013a) The 'Ethics Rupture' summit, Fredericton, New Brunswick, Canada, October 25–28, 2012. *Journal of Empirical Research on Human Research Ethics* 8(1): 3–7.

van den Hoonaard WC (2013b) The social and policy contexts of the New Brunswick declaration on research ethics, integrity, and governance: a commentary. *Journal of Empirical Research on Human Research Ethics* 8(2): 104–109.

van den Scott L-J K (2012) Science, politics, and identity in Northern research ethics licensing. *Journal of Empirical Research on Human Research Ethics* 7(1): 28–36.

Van der Geest S (2003) Confidentiality and pseudonyms – a fieldwork dilemma from Ghana. *Anthropology Today* 19(1): 14–18.

Van Maanen J (1983) The moral fix: on the ethics of fieldwork. In: Emerson RM (ed) *Contemporary Field Research: A Collection of Readings.* Boston, MA: Little, Brown, pp. 269–287.

Van Zijl S, Johnson B, Benatar S, Cleaton-Jones P, Netshidzivhani P, Ratsaka-Mothokoa M, Shilumani S, Rees H and Dhai A (eds) (2004) *Ethics in Health Research: Principles, Structures and Processes.* Pretoria: Department of Health.

van Kolfschooten, F (2014) UvA-hoogleraar manipuleerde data van onderzoek. NRC Handelsblad 29 April. Available at: http://www.nrc.nl/nieuws/2014/04/29/uva-hoogleraar-manipuleerde-data-van-onderzoek/ (accessed 9 June 2014).

VanderStaay SL (2005) One hundred dollars and a dead man: ethical decision making in ethnographic fieldwork. *Journal of Contemporary Ethnography* 34: 371–409.

VanWey LK, Rindfuss RR, Gutmann MP, Entwisle B and Balk DL (2005) Confidentiality and spatially explicit data: concerns and challenges. *Proceedings of the National Academy of Sciences of the United States of America* 102(43): 15337–15342.

Vasconcelos S, Leta J, Costa L, Pinto A and Sorenson MM (2009) Discussing plagiarism in Latin American science. *EMBo Reports* 10(7): 677–682.

Venkatesh S (1999) The promise of ethnographic research: the researcher's dilemma. *Law & Social Inquiry* 24(4): 987–991.

Venkatesh S (2008) *Gang Leader for a Day*. New York: Penguin.

Vietnam News Brief Service (2010) Society: plagiarism scandal shames Vietnam intellectuals. *Vietnam News Brief Service*, 13 May.

Vogel G (2012) German research minister faces plagiarism allegations. *ScienceInsider*, 2 May. Available at: http://news.sciencemag.org/scienceinsider/2012/05/german-research-minister-faces.html (accessed 23 December 2013).

Vollmann J and Winau R (1996) Informed consent in human experimentation before the Nuremberg code. *British Medical Journal* 313: 1445–1447.

Wager E and Kleinert S (2011) Responsible research publication: international standards for authors. A position statement developed at the 2nd World Conference on Research Integrity, Singapore, July 22–24, 2010. In: Mayer T and Steneck N (eds) *Promoting Research Integrity in a Global Environment*. Singapore: Imperial College Press/World Scientific Publishing, pp. 309–316.

Wager E, Fiack S, Graf C, Robinson A and Rowlands I (2009) Science journal editors' views on publication ethics: results of an international survey. *Journal of Medical Ethics* 35: 348–353.

Wager N (2011) Researching sexual revictimisation: associated ethical and methodological issues, and possible solutions. *Child Abuse Review* 20: 158–172.

Walker T (2009) What principlism misses. *Journal of Medical Ethics* 35(4): 229–231.

Wall C and Overton J (2006) Unethical ethics? The challenges of conducting development research in Uzbekistan. *Development in Practice* 16(1): 62–67.

Warwick DP (1982) Types of harm in social research. In: Beauchamp TL, Faden RR, Wallace RJ and Walters L (eds) *Ethical Issues in Social Science Research*. London: Johns Hopkins University Press, pp. 101–124.

Watkins J (2002) Roles, responsibilities, and relationships between anthropologists and indigenous people in the anthropological enterprise. In: *El Dorado Task Force Papers* (Volume 2). Arlington, VA: American Anthropological Association, pp. 64–79.

Weijer C (1999a) Selecting subjects for participation in clinical research: one sphere of justice. *Journal of Medical Ethics* 25: 31–36.

Weijer C (1999b) Protecting communities in research: philosophical and pragmatic challenges. *Cambridge Quarterly of Healthcare Ethics* 8: 501–513.

Weijer C, Goldsand G and Emanuel EJ (1999) Protecting communities in research: current guidelines and limits of extrapolation. *Nature Genetics* 23: 275–280.

Weinberg M (2002) Biting the hand that feeds you, and other feminist dilemmas in fieldwork. In: van den Hoonaard WC (ed) *Walking the Tightrope: Ethical Issues for Qualitative Researchers*. Toronto: University of Toronto Press, pp. 79–94.

Weisz G (1990) The origins of medical ethics in France: the International Congress of *Morale Médicale* of 1955. In: Weisz G (ed) *Social Science Perspectives in Medical Ethics*. Boston: Kluwer Academic Publishers, pp. 145–161.

West J (2013) The de-habilitation of a serial salami slicer. In: *Open Innovation Blog*, 13 September. Available at: http://blog.openinnovation.net/2013/09/the-de-habilitation-of-serial-salami.html (accessed 23 December 2013).

Whiteman N (2012) *Undoing Ethics: Rethinking Practice in Online Research*. London: Springer.

Whitty M (2003) Peering into online bedroom windows: considering the ethical implications of investigating internet relationships and sexuality. In: Buchanan E (ed) *Readings in Virtual Research Ethics: Issues and Controversies*. Hershey PA: Idea Group, pp. 203–218.

Wicherts JM (2011) Psychology must learn a lesson from fraud case. *Nature* 480(7375): 7.

Wicherts JM, Bakker M and Molenaar D (2011) Willingness to share research data is related to the strength of the evidence and the quality of reporting of statistical results. *PLoSONE* 6(11): e26828.

Wicherts JM, Borsboom D, Kats J and Molenaar D (2006) The poor availability of psychological research data for reanalysis. *American Psychologist* 61(7): 726–728.

Wikipedia (2012) VroniPlag Wiki. Available at: http://en.wikipedia.org/wiki/VroniPlag_Wiki (accessed 28 January 2014).

Wilhite AW and Fong EA (2012) Coercive citation in academic publishing. *Science* 335: 6068, 542–543.

Williams E, Guenther J and Arnott A (2011) Beyond informed consent and researcher ethics: how is it possible to ethically evaluate Indigenous programs? North Australia Research Unit paper, ANU. Available at: http://naru.anu.edu.au/__documents/seminars/2011/paper_williams_2011.pdf (accessed 28 January 2014).

Williams T, Dunlap E, Johnson BD and Hamid A (1992) Personal safety in dangerous places. *Journal of Contemporary Ethnography* 21(3): 343–374.

Winkler C with Hanke P (1995) Ethnography of the ethnographer. In: Nordstrom C and Robben ACGM (eds) *Fieldwork under Fire: Contemporary Studies of Violence and Survival*. Berkeley: University of California Press, pp. 155–185.

Winlow S and Hall S (2012) What is an 'ethics committee'? Academic governance in an epoch of belief and incredulity. *British Journal of Criminology* 52: 400–416.

Winlow S, Hobbs D, Lister S and Hadfield P (2001) Get ready to duck. Bouncers and the realities of ethnographic research on violent groups. *British Journal of Criminology* 41: 536–548.

Wolpe PR (1998) The triumph of autonomy in American bioethics: a sociological view. In: DeVries R and Subedi J (eds) *Bioethics and Society: Constructing the Ethical Enterprise*. Upper Saddle River, NJ: Prentice-Hall, pp. 38–59.

Woolf L (2011) An inquiry into the LSE's links with Libya and lessons to be learned. Available at: http://www.woolflse.com/dl/woolf-lse-report.pdf (accessed 23 December 2013).

Working Group of Indigenous Minorities in Southern Africa (n.d.) *Research Policy, Research Contract*. Windhoek, Namibia: Working Group of Indigenous Minorities in Southern Africa.

World Association of Medical Editors (2002) Reviewer Conflict of Interest. Available at: http://www.wame.org/ethics-resources/reviewer-conflict-of-interest/?search term = Reviewer%20Conflict%20of%20Interest (accessed 28 January 2014).

World Health Organization Regional Committee for Africa (2001) Emerging Bioethical Issues in Health Research: Concerns and Challenges in the African Region (document AFR/RC51/19). Brazzaville: World Health Organization Regional Committee for Africa. Available at: http://www.afro.who.int/index.php?option = com_docman&task = doc_download&gid = 867&Itemid = 2111 (accessed 23 December 2013).

World Health Organization (2001) Putting Women First: Ethical and Safety Recommendations for Research on Domestic Violence against Women. Geneva: World Health Organization. Available at: http://whqlibdoc.who.int/hq/2001/WHO_FCH_GWH_01.1.pdf (accessed 23 December 2013).

World Health Organization (2013) Expert Consultation on Optimization of Health Research Ethics Governance Systems in the Western Pacific Region: Meeting Report. Manila, Philippines: World Health Organization Regional Office for the Western Pacific. Available at: http://www.wpro.who.int/health_research/documents/docs/optimization_health_research_ethics.pdf (accessed 23 December 2013).

World Medical Association (WMA) (1964) Declaration of Helsinki, adopted by the 18th WMA General Assembly, Helsinki, Finland.

World Medical Association (WMA) (1996) Declaration of Helsinki, as amended by the 48th WMA General Assembly, Somerset West, Republic of South Africa.

World Medical Association (WMA) (2000) Declaration of Helsinki, as amended by the 52nd WMA General Assembly, Edinburgh, Scotland.

World Medical Association (WMA) (2013) Declaration of Helsinki: Ethical Principles for Medical Research Involving Human Subjects, as amended by the 64th WMA General Assembly, Fortaleza, Brazil. Available at: http://www.wma.net/en/30publications/10policies/b3/ (accessed 23 December 2013).

Wright R and Decker S (1997) Armed Robbers in Action: Stickups and Street Culture. Boston, MA: Northeastern University Press.

Xinhuanet (2008) CAST issued academic norms: seven kinds of behaviour equals academic misconduct. Xinhuanet, 25 March.

Xueqin J (2002) Chinese academics consider a 'culture of copying'. The Chronicle of Higher Education, 17 May, 48(36): A.45.

Yilmaz I (2007) Plagiarism? No, we're just borrowing better English. Nature 449: 658.

Zarb G (1992) On the road to Damascus: first steps towards changing the relations of disability research production. Disability, Handicap and Society 7: 125–138.

Zeng W and Resnik D (2010) Research integrity in China: problems and prospects. Developing World Bioethics 10(3): 164–171.

Zhai X (2011) Diversified and in harmony, but not identical (和而不同): harmonising international guidelines with cultural values and national traditions. Asian Bioethics Review 3(1): 31–35.

Ziman J (1991) Academic science as a system of markets. Higher Education Quarterly 45: 41–61.

Zimbardo PG (1973) On the ethics of intervention in human psychological research: with special reference to the Stanford prison experiment. Cognition 2: 243–256.

Zimbardo PG, Maslach C and Haney C (1999) Reflections on the Stanford prison experiment: genesis, transformations, consequences. In: Blass T (ed) Obedience to Authority: Current Perspectives on the Milgram Paradigm. Mahwah, NJ: Erlbaum, pp. 193–237. Available at: http://www.prisonexp.org/pdf/blass.pdf (accessed 23 December 2013).

Zimmer M (2008) More on the 'anonymity' of the Facebook dataset – it's Harvard College (Updated). Available at: http://www.michaelzimmer.org/2008/10/03/more-on-the-anonymity-of-the-facebook-dataset-its-harvard-college/.

Zimmer M (2010) 'But the data is already public': on the ethics of research in Facebook. Ethics and Information Technology 12(4): 313–325.

Zinger I (1999) The Psychological Effects of 60 days in Administrative Segregation. Doctoral thesis, Department of Psychology, Carleton University, Canada.

Žižek S (2000) *Enjoy Your Symptom! Jacques Lacan in Hollywood and Out*. New York: Routledge.

Zwanikken, P and Oosterhoff, P (2011) Why a research ethics committee for social science? Reflections on three years of experience at the Royal Tropical Institute, Amsterdam. *Medische Antropologie* 23(1): 165–181.

Zwi AB, Grove NJ, MacKenzie C, Pittaway E, Zion D, Silove D and Tarantola D (2006) Placing ethics in the centre: negotiating new spaces for ethical research in conflict situations. *Global Public Health* 1(3): 264–277.

Author Index

237

Subject Index

Printed in Great Britain
by Amazon